Volume 4A:

GLOUCESTER MIDLAND LINES

Part 2: SOUTH

EASTGATE to STROUD and NAILSWORTH

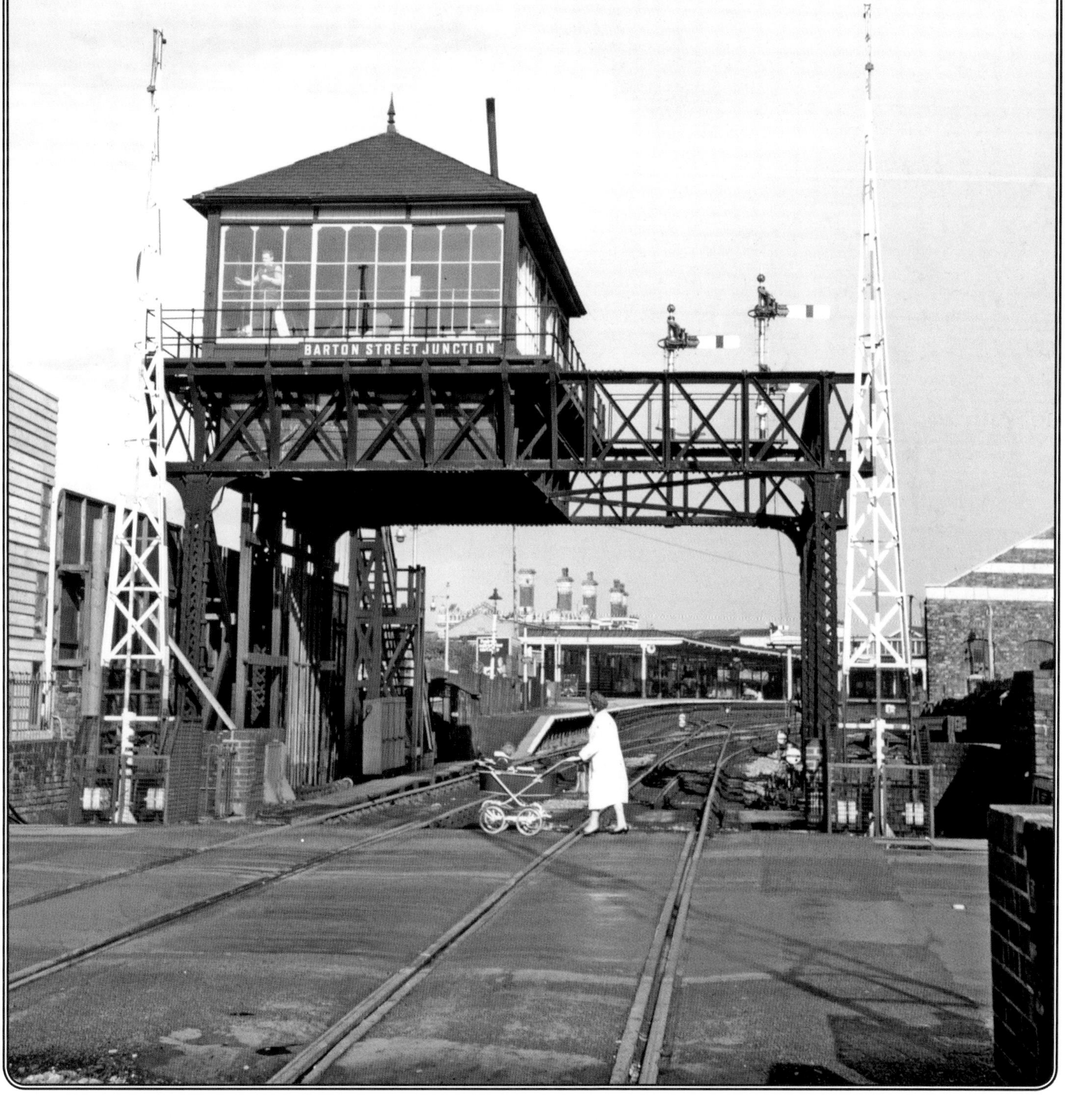

One of those wonderful views that places the railway in context with its surroundings and other modes, rather than just being a picture of a train. On the left, Gloucester Barnwood-based 'Jinty' Class '3F' 0-6-0T No. 47417 has probably come off the Hempsted Branch at Tuffley Junction and is whistling for the gates at California Crossing, which are closed across the railway. The tiny cabin which controlled the crossing can be seen in the centre, just past the cottage built by the Midland Railway for the crossing keeper and his family. On the right, stopped to pick up a passenger on Midland Road, is Bristol Omnibus Company green liveried Bristol Type KSW6B on route No. 3, bound for St. Barnabus Church via Farm Street and Parkend Road. The route of the trackbed here is now a low grass bank but the houses in the background remain, whilst the crossing cabin was rescued and now resides at Toddington. Roy Denison

Previous Page: A quiet moment at Gloucester Eastgate as grandma wheels grandson's pram across Barton Street Crossing in November 1966. Above, the signalman has time between trains to gaze out of the window. The timeless nature of the scene is somewhat spoiled by the Continental style lifting barriers which British Railways had started introducing in the late 1950s. Although visually less satisfying than traditional gates, they were a boon at busy locations such as this but none of the other crossings on the Tuffley Loop were to receive them. NPC

BRITISH RAILWAY HISTORY IN COLOUR

Volume 4A:

GLOUCESTER MIDLAND LINES

Part 2: SOUTH

EASTGATE to STROUD and NAILSWORTH

NEIL PARKHOUSE

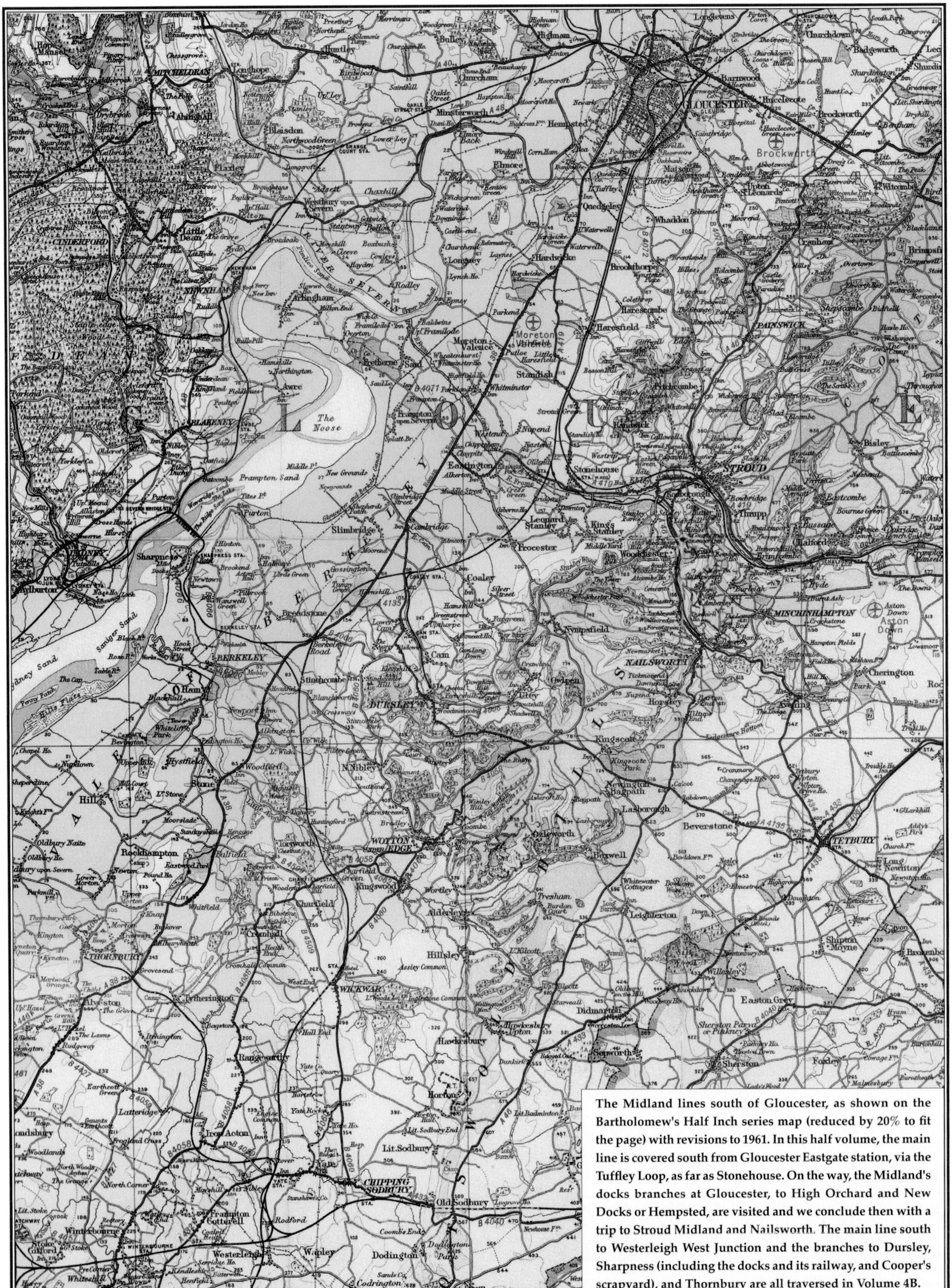

The Midland lines south of Gloucester, as shown on the Bartholomew's Half Inch series map (reduced by 20% to fit the page) with revisions to 1961. In this half volume, the main line is covered south from Gloucester Eastgate station, via the Tuffley Loop, as far as Stonehouse. On the way, the Midland's docks branches at Gloucester, to High Orchard and New Docks or Hempsted, are visited and we conclude then with a trip to Stroud Midland and Nailsworth. The main line south to Westerleigh West Junction and the branches to Dursley, Sharpness (including the docks and its railway, and Cooper's scrapyard), and Thornbury are all traversed in Volume 4B.

CONTENTS

VOLUME 4A: EASTGATE TO STROUD AND NAILSWORTH

Published by LIGHTMOOR PRESS

Designed by Neil Parkhouse

British Library Cataloguing-in-Publication Data. A catalogue record for this book is available from the British Library

ISBN: 9781911038 66 5

LIGHTMOOR PRESS
Unit 144B, Harbour Road Trading Estate,
Lydney, Gloucestershire GL15 4EJ
website: www.lightmoor.co.uk / email: info@lightmoor.co.uk

Lightmoor Press is an imprint of Black Dwarf Lightmoor Publications Ltd

Printed in Poland
www.lfbookservices.co.uk

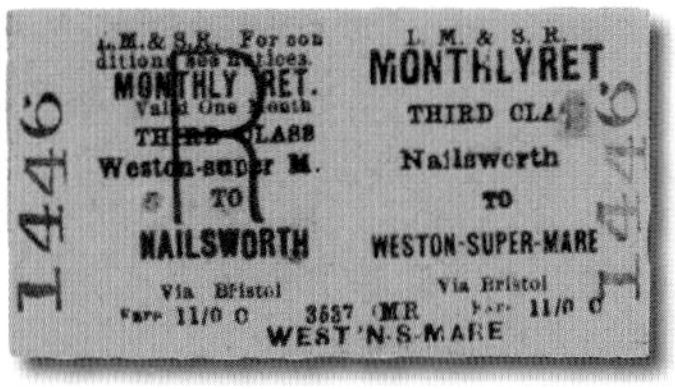

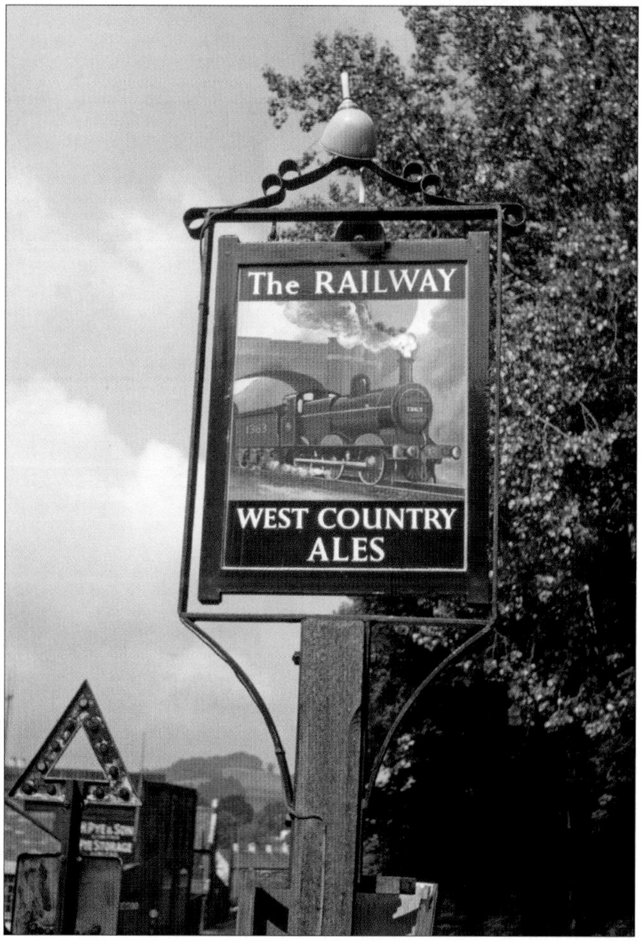

RIGHT: Midland Railway influence on this pub sign, outside The Railway Inn on Dudbridge Hill on 23rd August 1965. The picture is a reasonable representation of Midland No. 1363, a '1357' Class 0-6-0 built in 1878 by Dübs & Co. Under the MR's 1907 renumbering scheme it became No. 3026 but was to be an early withdrawal in LM&SR days, in August 1929, by which date the class had been redesignated as Class '2F'. The Railway Inn later changed its name to The Junction but closed in 2006 and was demolished soon after. B.J. ASHWORTH

More magic from the lens of Ben Ashworth! This delightful study shows his young sons John and Alan sitting on the parapet of the overbridge at Dudbridge Junction on 23rd August 1965, whilst in the background No. 78001 shunts the small yard here. We have met with this engine previously, as it featured in Volume 1 on the Newent Branch. The bicycle was always the photographer's preferred mode of transport and whilst John had his own as well, younger son Alan travelled on the seat fastened on the crossbar, just behind the handlebars. Note the Midland Railway cast iron notice on the wall and the coal men at work in the yard. B.J. Ashworth

INTRODUCTION

There is a phrase that I need to begin this book with, by way of an apology and an explanation: '*No battle plan ever survives first contact with the enemy!*' It is not strictly a quote, being based on the observations of the 19th century Prussian Field Marshall Helmuth von Moltke the Elder, who wrote: '*... no plan of operations extends with any certainty beyond the first contact with the main hostile force.*'. What it means in context here is that my original plan to cover the Midland lines in Gloucestershire in one volume hit the buffers very quickly after paging had started, with a decision being taken to split it in two at Eastgate station and cover the lines south from there separately. This seemed sensible as the line to the north was built by the Birmingham & Gloucester Railway and that to the south partly by the Bristol & Gloucester Railway.

I must now confess that that supplementary plan has also come to grief, the sheer amount of material that has come my way, much of it long after paging had been started, meaning that Part 2 has also now had to be split in to Volumes 4A and 4B in order that readers can actually handle the resultant volumes in comfort. As it stood, we were looking at a single volume in excess of 450 pages! Having both as parts of Volume 4 also keeps the Bristol & Gloucester line and its many branches in one volume. I am therefore hopeful that the many loyal readers and friends who have come to love and enjoy this series, and 'bought in' to the concept behind it, will be pleased that they have such a surfeit of new pictures to study and absorb. Inevitably, the first question I get asked at a show when each new volume comes out is "*When's the next one coming?*", so at least this time I can smile smugly, pick up a copy of 4B and say "*Now!*".

I have tried hard to accelerate the schedule but a new volume every two years is about as good as I am able to manage, largely because of commitments to other authors and their manuscripts but also in part because of the sheer amount of work involved in each book. Whilst most of the pictures to go in each volume are to hand when I begin writing and paging, many more seem to turn up as the work advances, from a variety of sources and for a variety of reasons. Some appear on auction sites and are bought for inclusion very late in the process but often, whilst researching a particular location, an image turns up on a website that I gain permission to use – and sometimes that can turn in to several images. In this volume, David Stowell's pictures are a result of finding one image originally on the Geograph website, whilst in 4B a few of ex-Coaley Junction signalman Gilroy Kerr's slides were first found on Andy Barton's DursleyGlos website but there turned out to be many more.

As I state a little further on, I am well aware of how much enjoyment this series of books has brought to so many people, not just from the numbers sold but from the many of you who have been so kind to pass on comments by letter, email and in person at shows and at the occasional local (to Gloucestershire) illustrated talks that I do. In my mind, there is a point to the way I present these books and the pictures that I include but I realise that there are those who do not wish to tarry too long in one place and see numerous trains passing by or see a station from as many different angles as possible, therefore I would suggest that this series is not for you. If, however, you have ever wondered what it must have been like to spend a day around Tuffley or Standish junctions on a summer Saturday in the early 1960s, then the pictures within these pages will give you a flavour of that and give some idea of the variety of traffic heading past. And whilst the locomotives that are to be seen on the various branch lines over both volumes are generally a little repetitive – the Sharpness Branch perhaps excepted – the main line was without doubt a trainspotter's delight, with little clue even as to what class of engine to expect next let alone which actual class member. Proof of this range is in the fact that only a few of the locomotives pictured appear more than once. At Tuffley Junction, the London Midland and Western regions met, providing even more variety but then south of Standish Junction, where the line split off to head to Swindon, ex-GWR types continued to proliferate on West of England holiday expresses from places like Wolverhampton and on freights bound for Bristol or Avonmouth. As an aside, the main line between Tuffley and Standish will also be covered from a WR perspective in the next volume, *Gloucester to Swindon and Branches*, so within these pages I have illustrated only trains taking the Bristol route at Standish.

There is another reason too for spending as much time as possible at station locations in particular. Many of these books have been bought by railway modellers, looking for inspiration or further detail for a location already chosen. As a keen modeller myself, with a large N gauge model of Grange Court Junction under construction, I can personally vouch for the fact that there are always little areas and bits of any station that you struggle to tie down in detail: What did the open waiting area on the platform side of Grange Court station building look like and, as I'm also including a section of the Hereford line, what was the rear elevation of Longhope station building? I am aware that someone modelling Parkend was able to ascertain the colour of the windown frames on an adjacent house from a picture in Volume 2, so I'm always going to err on the side of putting in as many different views of possible, rather than thinking "*Right, been there, done that, move on!*".

There is one final reason for the picture selection. These books also serve as a tribute to the many photographers who persevered with colour film when it was still really in its infancy but who achieved generally such good results, albeit we can now provide great assistance in improving their slides thanks to the digital age in which we live. Sadly, all too many of them are no longer with us but their pictures remain for us to enjoy, transporting us back to an age now gone and which, despite their very best efforts, preserved lines fail to recreate. You cannot 'preserve' the decay and neglect which many of these pictures show, as the railway network of Great Britain arrived at a defining period of its existence – the peeling paintwork at stations and the work-stained appearance of everyday steam locomotives are not what the paying public want to see when they visit a steam railway. Nor can you recreate the anticpation of what locomotive might be appearing next – the missing 'cop' in your *Ian Allan ABC* perhaps?

A few may also question the level of detail within the captions but I always start from a base of answering questions that I have asked myself. Do we really need a potted history of each and every locomotive depicted? Well yes, in my opinion, we do. Not only does it add to the general interest, it can also help identify a particular train if we know where the engine was based and with most of these pictures being in the last half decade of steam in Gloucestershire, they can often be poignant, with a locomotive in its last few weeks of use. And at least two of the engines seen at work in the pages of this double volume can also later be seen being scrapped at Sharpness. Photographs are but moments in time, a particular event and place frozen for ever but in isolation, so it is only through assembling a number of similar views together that you begin to get 'the bigger picture'.

In addition, most of us only see in a picture what we are told to see or what is pointed out to us, so if you do not mention the interesting building in the background, few will notice it and even fewer probably will wonder what it was. Similarly, those cars waiting at the level crossing – what are they? Most of us know far less about post-war motor cars and other vehicles than we think we do. They look familar but actually are they, so I have also gone in to detail about the road vehicles we see in the pictures. The history of the ships that feature in the dock views at Gloucester and Sharpness, some of which came to interesting if unfortunate ends, are also worth recording. And yes it all takes much longer to write and research but then you can dip in and out of the books time and time again, finding something new or previously missed each time. To emphasise therefore, the intention when setting out to compile and write this series of books was to illustrate, in colour and in as great detail as possible, what we had lost in terms of the stations, goods yards, signals boxes, engine sheds and other railway infratstructure, along with the industrial sites and dock installations that they served. To me, the railway has always been about so much more than just steam locomotives and the trains of a bygone era, wonderful though they were.

In trying to portray all this I set myself no mean task, not least because most railway photographers were working in the much cheaper medium of black & white film, which had the added advantage of lending itself to home development. Colour film in the 1950s and early 1960s was expensive and needed to be sent away to be processed, so many eschewed it. Most photographers were also primarily interested in the locomotives and the trains they hauled, so their pictures tend to have the buildings and other infrastructure either partly or completely hidden. One is then looking for someone who used a different angle to uncover the missing parts. In addition, few photographers ventured in to goods yards, so colour views of that side of the railway are, with a few notable excpetions, usually not to be found. Early colour film was also slow, 10 or 12asa, which meant that stationary trains at platforms were fine but anything moving was likely to blur unless one was standing well back from the line. This meant that many colour pictures of the 1950s and early 1960s were generally more of a panoramic nature than black & white studies, which has given these volumes a much more scenic feel and no doubt has helped contribute to their popularity.

And they have been popular, as I indicated earlier. Without in any way wishing to indulge in any trumpet blowing, it has been heartening to know that so many readers have understood what I set out to achieve and now eagerly await each new volume. The hours spent searching out new images, scanning them, and then cleaning and setting the scans before placing them on the pages prior to researching and writing the accompanying text and captions, all seems eminently worthwhile when emails and letters arrive detailing readers enjoyment, along with their own memories. I have also received a regular stream of kind and enthusiastic comments from readers coming to us at the Lightmoor bookstand at one of the many model railway shows we attend. Such encouragement is much appreciated, as it can be a solitary business putting the books together. I make no claims whatsoever in to having created anything of huge importance in regards to the study of the history of the railways of Great Britain but I do believe that the series is groundbreaking in the use of colour to tell the story of the railways of a particular area in the years before they were changed for ever.

Now it is time for something of a confession – I saw almost nothing of the lines featured within these volumes in their heyday or, indeed, when they were open! Born in ex-L&SWR territory, we lived close to Mortehoe station on the Barnstaple to Ilfracombe line and although very young at the time, I do have some distant memories of that railway when we were there. Moving north to Worcestershire in 1958 at the age of just $3^1/_2$, I have much clearer memories of the two stations at Evesham and, as recounted in *Gloucester Midland Lines Part 1: North*, of Hinton station on the line between Evesham Midland and Ashchurch. However, apart from one brief late night visit to Eastgate a few weeks before it closed, I saw little of the railway in Gloucester before it was all rationalised, nor really of anywhere else in the county.

I had glimpses of the railway at Tewkesbury and at Over Junction but otherwise I missed everything that features in these volumes. I never saw the Gloucester-Hereford line, the Newent Branch or the Severn Railway Bridge. We occasionally went to Bourton but the railway across the Cotswolds to Kingham was never seen and in any case had closed when I was seven. Branch lines to Cirencester, Tetbury, Fairford, Stroud and Nailsworth, Dursley, Sharpness and Thornbury were all unknown to me. Whilst my father had an interest in railways and industrial history – which eventually grew in to something of a passion – the struggle to make a living whilst looking after a growing family and studying to better himself, via evening classes and correspondence courses, left little time for exploring the railway scene. Living in Worcestershire, too, whilst only just over the boundary from Gloucestershire, meant that visits were limited to rare sojourns to Cheltenham for the shops or equally rare trips in the Netherton Farm lorry to Healings Mill at Tewkesbury or to Gloucester Cattle Market. Even the Tuffley Loop managed to escape my attention, despite having moved to the county in 1974, following a movefrom Worcestershire to Buckinghamshire in 1968.

The compilation of these volumes has therefore been – and continues to be – as much a journey of discovery for me as it has been for many of those who have bought and read them. The disappointment of never having seen most of what is featured is tempered by the surge of excitement experienced every time new images are discovered, particularly if they show something that I do not already have a picture of – a goods shed, signal box or halt for instance. I am by nature slightly obsessive about completeness and every volume that goes to print with gaps in it somewhere is an annoyance that I have had to learn to live with. New pictures do turn up of course, many that would have made it in to the original volumes if they had been to hand at the time but that is the nature of things. I will endeavour to make use of such pictures that merit a wider audience in due course but how that is done will vary from book to book. The decision to issue a revised enlarged edition of Volume 1, with the extra forty-eight pages published as a Supplement for those who already had the first edition, seemed a wise way to go about publishing the new material that had turned up since and, indeed, seems to have met with widespread approval. However, not enough new pictures have turned up for the same to be done with the subsequent two volumes, so a final overall Supplement to the series may be the ultimate answer here.

In the meantime, there is much to enjoy and savour within the pages of this volume. I do get asked to present slide shows based on the books as each volume comes out, although I try as much as possible to stay within the county boundaries when doing so; responsibilities with running a busy and growing publishing company and the even bigger responsibilities of bringing up teenage children (Dad taxi duties!) mean that travelling any distance to give talks is not something I can countenance undertaking. However, at those talks I have given up to now, I have maintained that this volume always had the potential to be the best in the series. This is subjective of course, we all have our favourite routes and locations but the mix of main line and branches, with the coverage of some of the latter bordering on the enchanting, makes this a strong contender to outdo previous volumes in the series.

I have also stated in previous volumes and would reiterate here that whilst the books are wonderful excercises in nostalgia, magically brought to life by the fact that they are all in colour, I am in no way suggesting that we should return to that age. Yes we remember those days with great fondness and miss the anticipation of waiting for a train to pass whilst having the time to drink in the sights, sounds and smells when exploring a country branch station somewhere, or the excitement of visiting a large town or city station, with its myriad of train movements, all usually shared with fellow 'spotters'. But – would we really swap the lives we have now to go back to those days permanently, with all the attendant issues that we lived with then without thought, lacking the knowledge and insight we have now? Change is inevitable but should be managed properly so that it is not just for now and that we all benefit. It's just that, to many of us, the railway doesn't look like the railway any more!

Neil Parkhouse, Lydney 2019

THE BRISTOL & GLOUCESTER RAILWAY

The decision to split the coverage of the Midland lines in Gloucestershire in two, with the dividing line at Eastgate station, proved apt in that the main line through the county had originally been promoted and built by two separate companies, the Birmingham & Gloucester Railway (B&GR) and the Bristol & Gloucester Railway (Br&GR), albeit the latter line only reached Standish, near Stonehouse, sharing the metals of the Cheltenham & Great Western Union Railway (C&GWUR) northwards from there to Gloucester.

The C&GWUR was a broad gauge concern running between Swindon and Gloucester, which had been formed in 1836, purchased by the Great Western Railway (GWR) in 1843 and completed the following year. The Br&GR, which had gained its Act of Incorporation in 1839, was formed with the intention of rebuilding the standard gauge Bristol & Gloucestershire Railway, a mineral line connecting collieries to the north of Bristol with the docks in the city, as a main line and then carrying it on north to Gloucester. Realising that it would have to take a similar route at its northern end from Standish to Gloucester to the C&GWUR, Isambard Brunel, engineer of the GWR, persuaded the Br&GR directors to convert their planned line to broad gauge in 1842 and share the tracks over the last few miles. However, the company had to build their own connection in to the city itself, as the C&GWUR was bypassing it and heading for Cheltenham. Whilst the decision to build the line to the broad gauge was to seem an eminently sensible solution at that time, particularly as the GWR had eyes on the new lines linking Birmingham, Gloucester and Bristol, within a year it was to become an anomaly.

A view north through the covered footbridge linking Eastgate with Central station. It has been the lot of railway wives and girlfriends over the years to be dragged around locations such as this and then posed in the picture to make it worth their while coming. Sarah Perriam, the lovely lady seen here on 26th October 1975, had only recently become engaged to the photographer, an event she celebrated by exploring the Tuffley Loop shortly before it closed. Happily, she has long since been Mrs Berry and has been all over the world chasing trains, so the experience cannot have put her off – and now she finds fame too in a railway book! As I've often explained to my wife, "*Well you knew what I was about when you married me!*". PETER BERRY

The Bristol & Gloucester Railway had a ceremonial opening on Saturday 6th July 1844, with regular passenger services starting the following Monday and goods traffic commencing on 2nd September. Following opening of the Br&GR line, Gloucester station was to become notorious as the foremost break of gauge transshipment point between broad and standard gauge railways. The problems were further compounded in 1845, when the GWR were given permission to run their trains into the station following opening of the line from Standish Junction to Kemble on 12th May, pending building of their own station. There were a number of such places on the railway network where transshipment problems occurred but Gloucester seems to have been by far and away the worst and the situation there was immortalised in two engravings – one showing passengers with children being overwhelmed by porters and luggage spilling everywhere as they try to change trains, the other goods being damaged as they are heaved from one wagon to another – which though clearly grossly over-dramaticising things, graphically put the case for the standard gauge lobby. Brunel had in fact accepted as far back as 1838 that his 7ft gauge was likely to be superceded by the narrower standard gauge but the GWR had at that time elected to plough on with their broad gauge empire.

For a brief moment in time, the possibility of the GWR gaining control of the B&GR and Br&GR lines raised the prospect of the wider gauge gaining the upper hand. Any mooted negotiations for these two lines had also been made easier by the fact that the two companies had signed a formal agreement in January 1845, to amalgamate as the Birmingham & Bristol Railway. Thus, at this point in early railway history, with many important lines still to be built, the addition of this route between two of Great Britain's major cities to the expanding broad gauge network would have given it control over the south-west quarter of the country – a West Midlands-West Country axis, with London served directly from both regions and that also covered much of South Wales too. It is possible to conceive that from such a strong base, the 7ft gauge could have prevailed nationwide.

This crucial point in the so called 'Battle of the Gauges' was to be lost by the GWR, however, largely due to a bout of penny-pinching prevarication, although to be fair the finances of that company were also considerably stretched at this time. Entering into negotiations with both companies, the GWR then hesitated over the agreed purchase, probably in the belief that in doing so they could force the price down. They gambled on the fact that no other railway company would be interested in buying the Birmingham & Bristol Railway or, indeed, would have the financial wherewithal to do so.

They reckoned, however, without the Midland Railway and their ambitious chairman, John Ellis. Formed on 10th May 1844 by the amalgamation of the Midland Counties, North Midland and Birmingham & Derby Junction railways, this immediately gave the new company control of the railway map in the East Midlands area, extending north from Birmingham to Leeds. Behind the GWR's back, Ellis swiftly entered into negotiations with the B&BR, seeing the possibilities that a direct connection to Bristol would open up for his new company. He wasted no time in reaching an agreement to

Class '8F' 2-8-0 No. 48474 heads towards California Crossing with a loaded coal train circa 1965. The locomotive, which was a war-time build at Swindon Works in May 1945, carries a Wolverhampton Oxley 2B shedplate on its smokebox door; it was transferred to there from Tyseley in mid-June 1965, so this view is almost certainly in the autumn of that year. The engine, which had previously had a short stint at Bristol Barrow Road in 1962, stayed at Oxley until early March 1967, moving then to Crewe South from where it was withdrawn in September 1967. On the right is a Hillman Minx Series 2, registered FVH 511 in Gloucester in late 1958. Behind it is probably a Triumph Herald of circa 1959, and behind that a Ford Consul, Zephyr or Zodiac Mark 2 of the same period. RICHARD ETHERTON COLLECTION

lease both concerns from July 1845, with the Midland absorbing them completely the following year. The Parliamentary Gauge Commission report of February 1846, which recommended a line of standard gauge rails between Birmingham and Bristol, proved the final nail in the coffin for the GWR's ambitions for their wider gauge. Brunel's 7ft gauge was now doomed, although it took a long time to die, with the final conversion to standard gauge taking place forty-six years later, in 1892.

However, the standard gauge MR was now the owner of a broad gauge railway running between Gloucester and Bristol, with the Act of absorption requiring them to keep the broad gauge rails in place and thus to purchase and operate their own broad gauge locomotives and rolling stock. In 1848, the Midland gained permission to convert their line between Bristol and Standish to mixed gauge and to add a set of standard gauge rails to the line north from there to Gloucester. However, this work was not completed until 1854, at which point the Midland were finally able to dispense with their broad gauge stock, although the additional rails were not to be removed until the wholesale conversion of the remaining broad gauge lines in Gloucestershire to standard gauge in 1872.

Whilst history had decreed that the broad gauge era was finished, these momentous events were to ensure that Gloucestershire's railway network was now going to be developed by two main companies, the Great Western and the Midland. Whilst most of the lines that were still to come were ostensibly promoted and built by small independent companies, most were supported behind the scenes by one or other of the MR or GWR, usually being worked from the outset by the larger company and soon swiftly absorbed by them. The only company in the county to remain independent was the tiny and financially strapped Severn & Wye Railway in the Forest of Dean, which, as we saw in Volume 2, effectively bankrupted itself building the Severn Bridge and ended up being taken over jointly by the MR and GWR.

I have indicated in the previous volumes how little of the railway system in Gloucestershire that existed in 1960 still survives today. Not

including Bristol's northern suburbs, which have moved county at least twice, Gloucestershire once boasted around 110 stations or halts, a total which, under the full implementation of the Beeching cuts, had dropped to just seven by the 1980s: Gloucester, Cheltenham, Stroud, Stonehouse, Kemble, Lydney and Moreton in Marsh. The number has improved slightly since then to ten, with the opening of new stations at Yate, Cam & Dursley and Ashchurch for Tewkesbury, although only the latter occupies the site of an earlier station. There is also a proposal for a new station at Charfield.

As indicated in the previous volume, the Midland lines have suffered closures in comparison with the ex-GWR branches. The Birmingham to Bristol main line remains but now served by the rebuilt (in 1975) ex-GWR Central station in Gloucester, with nothing left of the Midland's new station of 1896, the site of which now lies beneath a supermarket. There is very little also to be found of the Tuffley Loop or the docks lines. None of the original stations remain open between Gloucester and Bristol, Cam & Dursley being a replacement, on a different site, for Coaley Junction. Haresfield has nothing left to show that it ever existed, whilst Stonehouse (Bristol Road) station building has been a very recent loss, demolished without ceremony and seemingly in some secrecy within the last twelve months. The goods shed at Coaley survives, as do the station master's houses at Frocester,

ABOVE: Ex-Midland Railway Deeley 'Dock Tank' 0-4-0T No. 41535 shunts in High Orchard yard in July 1962. Fielding & Platt's works behind were railway served and lines radiated out from here to reach the whole of the eastern side of the Gloucester Docks complex. Nothing remains of this scene today, with a dual carriageway running where the rails once lay and the Gloucester Quays shopping and leisure complex occupying the site of the works but we will study the docks lines in detail within. JOHN STRANGE/NPC

RIGHT: 'Black Five' No. 44888, which we shall see again within these pages, steams briskly away from Haresfield with the 9.15am Bristol Temple Meads to Gloucester Eastgate service on 31st October 1964. Haresfield station, which can just be seen in the distance, only had platforms on the Midland lines. CHRIS BALDWIN

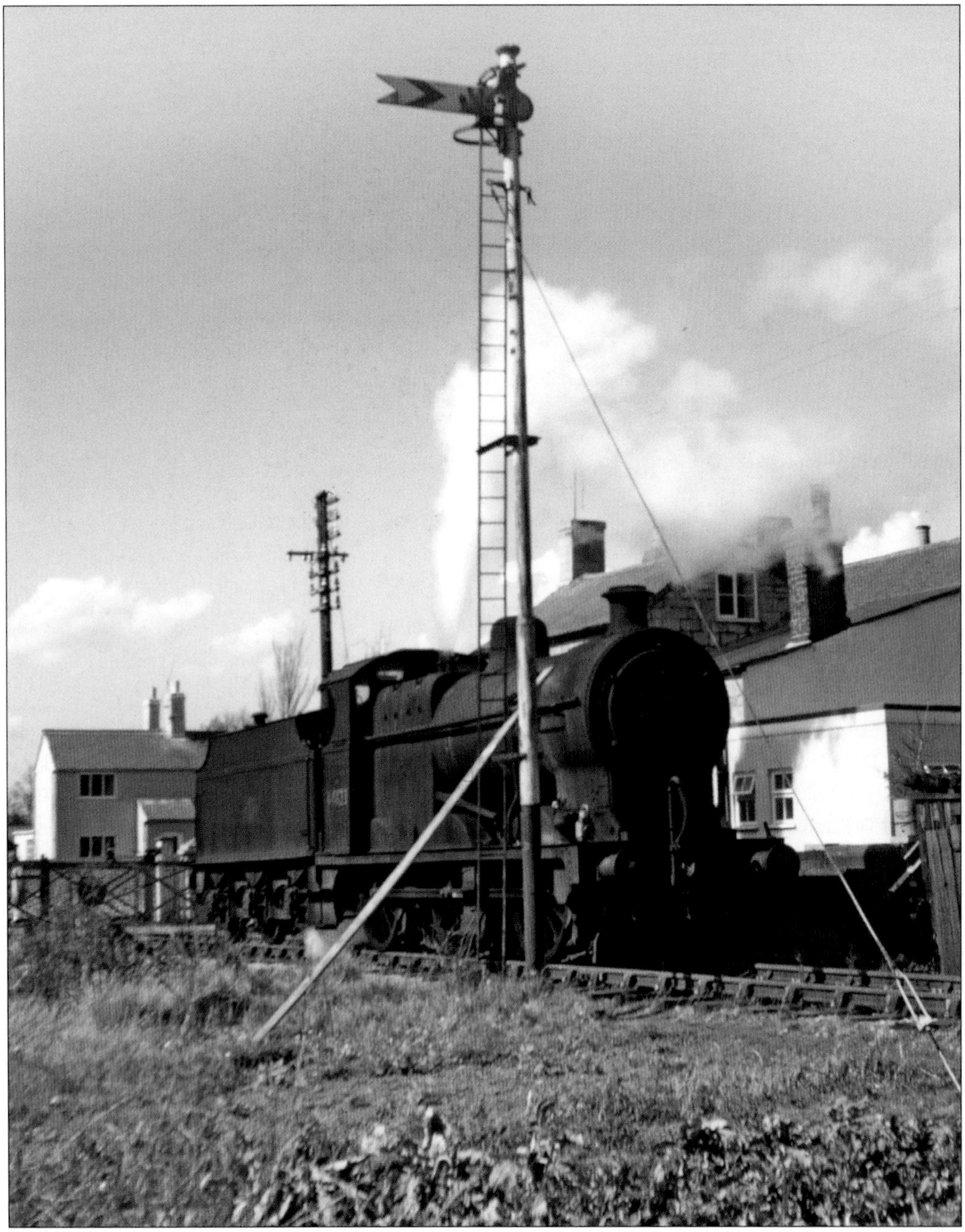

Class '4F' 0-6-0 No. 44123 poses beside the Fixed Distant signal for Stonehouse by the level crossing at Stonehouse Wharf on 27th March 1965. The locomotive was here in connection with a special working, the delivery of a new transformer for Ryeford electricity sub-station, which only involved rail transportation for a very short distance. The operation is shown in some detail later on within these pages. JOHN STRANGE/NPC

Berkeley Road and Wickwar, the latter up on a hillside looking down on the old station site. Charfield is the marvellous exception; although the platforms have long been demolished, as BR inevitably did, the Brunellian station building still stands facing the track, with the station master's house behind and the water tower alongside, complete with its decorative cast iron tank on top. The goods shed also remains, somewhat altered and in commercial use.

The new station at Yate was built largely on the site of the old one but with staggered platforms either side of the road bridge. The goods shed here is also still standing. South from here, the junctions at Westerleigh are much simplified from steam days. The Midland main line no longer runs through to Mangotsfield, continuing for a short distance as a single line to Westerleigh oil terminal but that falls both geographically and in time outside the confines of this volume. There is now a simple trailing junction between the Up line and this short branch. Nothing remains of the single track flyover which carried the connection from the GWR main line over the Midland, before joining it on the Up side, whilst the east chord to Westerleigh East Junction was removed in 1965 although had not been used since 1950.

Of the ex-Midland branches, all have long since lost their passenger services but there is otherwise more positive news on the two which survived in to the 21st century for freight traffic, the Sharpness and Thornbury branches. The former was retained for the nuclear flask and waste traffic to and from Berkeley power station, using the site of Berkeley station goods yard but with trains running round at Oldbury Sidings, Sharpness. An embryonic preservation company, the Vale of Berkeley Railway, is now making good progress with its plans to establish a heritage railway operation on the branch, from a base in an old engine shed at the docks. If all goes well, future plans include rebuilding the stations at both Berkeley and Sharpness to their original form.

Meanwhile, after moth-balling Tytherington Quarry in 2013, residents of Thornbury, which has expanded – and continues to do so – significantly since the town lost its passenger services in 1944, began calling for the branch to be reopened, to alleviate congestion on the A38 into Bristol. Whilst this proposal has made no progress to date, the branch was refurbished in 2018 and re-opened for stone traffic from the quarry. The rails currently end where the branch meets the A38 road but the line could be relatively easily extended through the old tunnel to a new site on the outskirts of the town. However, current plans are to add Thornbury to the new Bristol Metro bus network instead, partly due to the cost of reinstating the line to the town, bringing it up to passenger standards and building a new station (currently costed at £38 million) but also partly because of capacity constraints at Westerleigh Junction.

On the branch lines little of the original infrastructure remains beyond dwellings, bridges, cuttings and embankments. Nailsworth is undoubtedly the finest survival, deservedly Grade II listed and now a private residence. A few survived for many years after closure but have since been demolished to make way for road improvements; Kings Stanley and Dudbridge Junction spring to mind here. The goods sheds and seed stores at Stroud Wallgate also remained up until the 1990s at least, in what was a small industrial yard but all were demolished when the new by-pass, Dr Newton's Way, was built. All that now stands as a reminder of the Midland's presence in Stroud is part of the curved, brick-built viaduct that carried the line in to the terminus.

ACKNOWLEDGEMENTS FOR VOLUMES 4A AND 4B

As regular readers already know, this series of books was inspired by the late Audie Baker, the photograph archivist at Kidderminster Railway Museum, who provided me with scans of Bill Potter's colour transparencies of the Forest of Dean lines over twenty years ago. The concept expanded rapidly from there, although it has taken many years to collect enough pictures to do justice to the lines depicted. Following Audie's untimely demise, KRM curator David Postle has since generously given me full access to the museum's database of colour images, so Bill's work, along with that of others whose pictures now reside in that great archive, can be enjoyed by a wider audience. Consequently, as before, much of the credit for this series must go to them. In addition to Bill's pictures, KRM have supplied important images by Fred Butler, including an extremely rare colour view of a steam hauled freight at Berkeley (Vol. 4B), and John Tarrant.

Bill Potter's colour pictures hopefully serve as a fitting tribute to a talented, unassuming photographer who went out of his way to document both the end of steam and the end of their working lives for many of the lines featured. Ironically, he never particularly rated colour photography himself, much preferring, as so many did, the black and white medium, with film which could be home developed and printed. Nevertheless, some of his pictures within the pages of these two volumes, 4A and 4B, rank amongst the finest railway colour pictures I have seen. After traversing the branches to Dursley, Stroud and Nailsworth, I think that you will agree with that.

As with the earlier volumes, a number of photographers have been most generous and helpful in allowing me access to their collections. I have thanked them fulsomely before and, indeed, do so again but with only a brief mention here: David Bick, Derek Chaplin, John Dagley-Morris, Michael Hale, Alan Jarvis, Trevor Owen, John Ryan and John Strange (most of whose Gloucestershire slides came to me via Alan Sainty, so my thanks again to him too). Sadly, of that list, only John Dagley-Morris and John Ryan are still with us.

A special mention must go Ben Ashworth, whose steam age colour archive numbers less than a hundred pictures but many of which, as we have already seen, are of the very highest quality. Paul Chancellor of Colour-Rail has again been most helpful and continues to turn up some wonderful surprises, such as the close-up of the goods shed at Charfield (4B), and is always prompt in dealing with enquiries and requests. A further special mention should go to Roy Denison, who worked in the railway offices at Gloucester in the early 1960s but who also was blessed with a sense of what was worth pointing his camera at. Some fine views of his grace these pages, such as that of a '4F' shunting the yard at Stroud Midland, but none are more important than his superb study of the slightly obscure station at Frocester, which otherwise appears to have been poorly photographed in colour.

Mentioning Roy, I was originally put in touch with him by that doyen of railway researchers Mike Fenton and it was through Mike that I have subsequently been introduced to Dr Simon Fosbury, who holds the M.E.J. (Maurice) Deane archive. Simon has very kindly allowed me to copy many of the West Country slides in Maurice's collection and I thank him for his generosity, as well as his lovely wife for the delicious snack that she prepared. Such fare is also provided when visiting Roy, so I'm concluding that Mike Fenton must turn up at these places looking hungry and it is then assumed that all railway enthusiasts need feeding!

Internet research can also often turn up gems, which can then lead on to other things. A prime example of this was when I found David Stowell's picture of Painswick Road Crossing signal box on the Geograph website, along with another of California Crossing. You can contact photographers direct from this site but I never like to assume anything so sent off a very formal note, '*Dear David, I am currently compiling a book about ...*' and quickly received the friendly response, '*Hello Neil, that'll be Gloucester Midland Lines Part 2 then*'! Not only was David willing to send me high resolution scans of these two pictures but of a range of others around Eastgate and the Tuffley Loop, which have greatly enhanced the portrait I have been able to paint of this interesting and almost completely lost stretch of line.

In similar vein, Andy Barton, who runs the DursleyGlos website, had made contact some years ago to let me know that he had access to colour images of Coaley Junction but it was only with putting Volume 4B together that I renewed that contact. Having pointed out the pictures on his website that would be of interest, Andy returned to the photographer, Gilroy Kerr, to borrow them again for rescanning. Gilroy it turned out, having been one of the Coaley Junction signalmen in its last years, was taking colour slides from the signal box and had far more than Andy had used. We present a selection here, all full of interest and one of which records a rare visit to the Dursley Branch by a BR 'Standard' Class '3' 2-6-2 tank, as a record of the variety of passing traffic and as a tribute to a railwayman who had the foresight to record some of it. Not many who worked on the railways did – to most it was just a job. My grateful thanks too to Andy for facilitating all of this; I hope he feels that the section on his beloved Dursley Branch makes it all worth while.

Coincidentally, a few pictures taken by a second Coaley Junction signalman, Derek Markey, also feature within, in the section on the Sharpness Docks railway. Derek moved to the box at Berkeley Road in 1963 but it was not until some years afterwards that he began taking colour pictures. Now deceased, he passed his slides to Paul Woollard of Nailsworth prior to his demise and it is thanks to Paul that these rare views of a steel train at the docks in 1983 can be included here.

Another internet find, a view in Gloucester Docks, led to Tony Bowles and the collection of the Restoration & Archiving Trust. Tony has been most helpful in responding to requests for scans and the pictures of photographers Blake Patterson, Paul Riley and Mike Squire, as well as some taken by Tony himself, can be enjoyed within these pages as a result. The trust was formed twenty years ago to archive railway images from around the world with the aim of improving accessibility to them. It is an independent registered charity but also runs the museum facilities for the GWR at Toddington.

David Pollard, a friend who, back in the days when I dealt in old picture postcards, used to chat about all manner of things whilst sat at my stand looking for pictures of Bath Stone mines, left a small collection of hugely interesting colour slides after succumbing too soon to illness. David's wife Nina has passed them on to me for use in these books, whilst David's monumental history *Digging Bath Stone* is in preparation for publication by Lightmoor in 2020.

Gerry Nicholls, of the Stephenson Locomotive Society, has been most helpful in supplying high resolution scans from Mark Warburton's archive and I am likewise grateful to Mark's widow Margaret for permission to publish them. In addition to these, Gerry has also included pictures taken by the late John Grainger.

Tony Dyer, some of whose collection of railway tickets further enhance these pages, also put me in touch with Gerald Peacock, with whom he used to work a long time ago. Gerald, a sprightly octagenarian who worked as a fitter at Bristol Bath Road and Barrow Road sheds before leaving the railway having seen the writing on the wall, took some lovely views around his native city and kindly allowed me to copy all of his colour archive. He also strayed a little way north and the few that are used here add greatly to the coverage of south Gloucestershire and to the Sharpness and Thornbury branches in particular.

Don Mann contacted me after seeing the first volumes and offered his fine collection of mostly Gloucester and Stroud area slides for use. A good number decorate these pages but many more will feature in the next volume. Some would also have been used in earlier volumes, so they will no doubt prove the catalyst for a future supplement at some stage. The appeals within each book have brought further success, with Pete Berry coming forward with some historic views of the very last train at Eastgate, of the interior of the elevated Barton Street Junction signal box and of the crossings on the Tuffley Loop. In addition, Chris Baldwin also made contact and produced some fascinating pictures of diesel workings and junction alterations around Tuffley around 1970. When starting out on this volume I was a little worried about being able to portray the Tuffley Loop properly but thanks to Pete, Chris and David Stowell, their images have helped greatly in covering this important section of the Midland in Gloucestershire.

Finally, I have collected many of the images within these pages myself, spending a small fortune on internet and other auction sites on the way. However, such slides usually come with no provenance, lost somewhere following the taker's demise, so as with previous volumes, these are credited simply 'NPC' for Neil Parkhouse Collection. Where I have received pictures from the collections of people whose names I know, they are given credit first.

As in the previous volumes, the pages that follow are further illustrated with tickets, working and ordinary time table excerpts, labels and other items, collected over a number of years. Much of it is ephemera and tickets that I have collected but some of the latter also come from the collections of Tony Dyer and Roy Denison, so my thanks to them once more. Such items are important in building up a picture of the railway of the period, although I have used more this time from earlier eras, partly because some of these were still being issued right up until the 1960s but also partly because stations such as those on the Nailsworth & Stroud Branch closed to passengers pre-Nationalistaion in any case. Even small tickets can appear large and dominating at actual size, so they have all been reduced by 25%, something that many do not in fact realise, such is the impression the mind gives of how large an Edmondson ticket is in reality. The time table extracts and other ephemera have also all been reduced in size, generally mostly by around 40%.

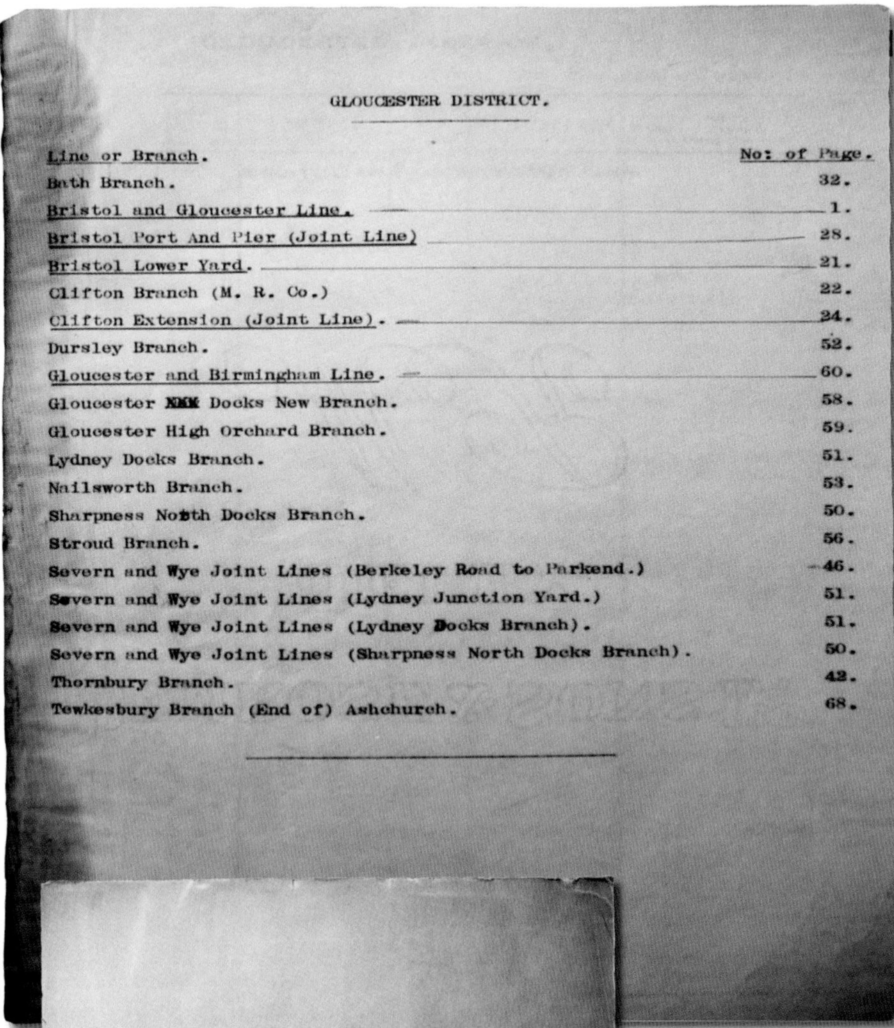

GLOUCESTER DISTRICT.

Line or Branch.	No: of Page.
Bath Branch.	32.
Bristol and Gloucester Line.	1.
Bristol Port And Pier (Joint Line)	28.
Bristol Lower Yard.	21.
Clifton Branch (M. R. Co.)	22.
Clifton Extension (Joint Line).	24.
Dursley Branch.	52.
Gloucester and Birmingham Line.	60.
Gloucester XXX Docks New Branch.	58.
Gloucester High Orchard Branch.	59.
Lydney Docks Branch.	51.
Nailsworth Branch.	53.
Sharpness Nobth Docks Branch.	50.
Stroud Branch.	56.
Severn and Wye Joint Lines (Berkeley Road to Parkend.)	46.
Severn and Wye Joint Lines (Lydney Junction Yard.)	51.
Severn and Wye Joint Lines (Lydney Docks Branch).	51.
Severn and Wye Joint Lines (Sharpness North Docks Branch).	50.
Thornbury Branch.	42.
Tewkesbury Branch (End of) Ashchurch.	68.

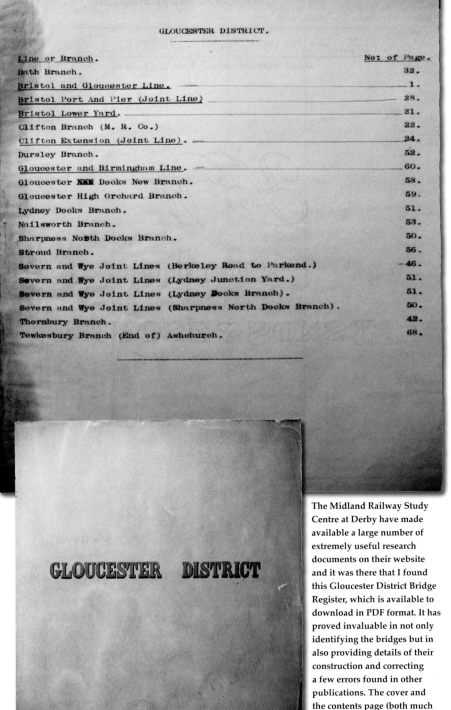

The Midland Railway Study Centre at Derby have made available a large number of extremely useful research documents on their website and it was there that I found this Gloucester District Bridge Register, which is available to download in PDF format. It has proved invaluable in not only identifying the bridges but in also providing details of their construction and correcting a few errors found in other publications. The cover and the contents page (both much reduced in size) are shown here.

I am always on the lookout for further pictures, whether for future volumes or for those already published. Gaps remain to be filled; in this volume I would love to have been able to provide better coverage of the sidings serving RAF Quedgeley, or anything (in colour) of the depot railway itself, whilst Berkeley Road South Junction and Berkeley Loop Junction both resolutely evaded colour film it would appear. Consequently, I would invite anyone who took colour slides in Gloucestershire or who has acquired slides of the area, who would like to contribute to this series to get in touch. I can be contacted direct by email on neil@lightmoor.co.uk or by ordinary mail via the address on the contents page. Whilst mainly interested in the railways, I would also like to see any views taken in the late 1950s/1960s/early 1970s of town scenes, particularly including vehicles, or of local industries, docks or anything else that might be considered of interest.

As the internet continues to grow in size and the amount of research material available on line expands with it, so it becomes easier to do much of your research without moving from your desk. The usual codicils apply with regards to double checking, where possible, any information gleaned but as much of what you find comes from original sources, it can be trusted. The main sites consulted are listed in the bibliography but SixBellsJunction, for rail tours, is always worthy of a special mention. And whilst you cannot beat getting out on the ground when researching long closed routes, Google Earth and Google Street View are powerful research tools at times when deskbound.

When completely stuck, as I sometimes am, I am fortunate that there are a small army of others that I can turn to. Having taken an interest in the series, Nick Freezer kindly offered his considerable experience in regards to diesel multiple units, a subject which throws up all kinds of traps for those like me who have taken them for granted over the years. As ever, Mike Christensen has been more than willing to share his knowledge on signalling matters, a railway subject with more pitfalls than most! Finally, Pete Fidczuk has kindly provided expert details on the tank wagons that feature in a few of the trains depicted within.

Beyond the railway boundaries can also be difficult. Malcolm Bobbitt has always been most helpful on motoring matters and car identification but also put me in touch with another very knowledgeable gentleman, Nigel Stennett-Cox, who has yet to be beaten with a query. We all think that we know a bit about cars and many of the vehicles within these pages look familiar ° but are they? Not only has Nigel kept me on the 'right road', he is a veritable fount of knowledge on virtually all motoring and road transport matters and his detailed replies to my many queries have added hugely to the captions.

I am grateful to everyone who has provided assistance in bringing this double volume to fruition but must emphasise, as ever, that any factual errors which will inevitably remain are entirely my responsibility. I am always happy to receive correspondence from any reader with straightforward corrections or with better or more accurate information on the pictures within these pages. And I am always pleaased to hear from anyone whose memories have been stimulated by the photographs.

Finally, as regular readers will be aware, I have dedicated all of the previous volumes to my family, my late father Dennis, my mum Mary and my lovely and hugely supportive wife Heather. With this volume having had to be split in two, it would seem highly appropriate therefore to dedicate them to our two children, Theo and Freya, currently both at university and thus heading out in to that great adventure called 'Life'! I will leave them to choose as to who is A and who is B but would just like to state, entirely for their benefit, that we are inordinately proud of both of them as young people and that they have given a meaning to our lives without which it would be rather empty – except for the bank account! Kids eh?!

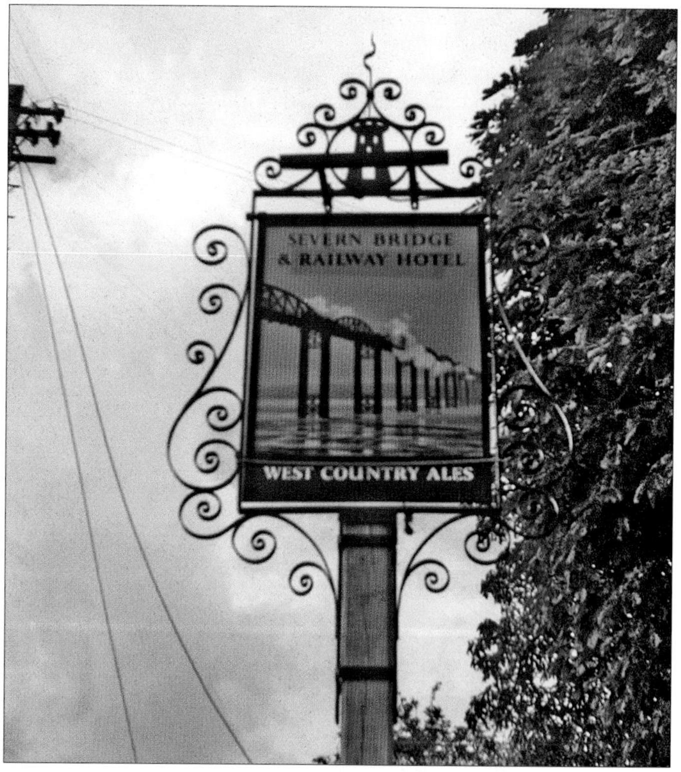

Severn Bridge & Railway Hotel inn sign, August 1966. NPC

SOURCES & BIBLIOGRAPHY FOR VOLUMES 4A AND 4B

Books Consulted

An Historical Survey of the Forest of Dean Railways, Peter Smith, Oxford Publishing Company, 1983

An Historical Survey of the Midland in Gloucestershire, Peter Smith, Oxford Publishing Company, 1985

British Locomotive Catalogue 1825-1923: Vol. 3A Midland Railway and its Constituents, Bertram & David Baxter, Moorland Publishing, 1982

Gloucester Docks, An Historical Guide, Hugh Conway-Jones, Black Dwarf Publications, 2019

Great Western Auto Trailers Part Two: Post Grouping and Absorbed Vehicles, John Lewis, Wild Swan, 1995

Industrial Locomotives of Central Southern England, Roger Hateley, Industrial Railway Society, 1981

Industrial Locomotives of West Glamorgan, M. Potts & G.W. Green, Industrial Railway Society, 1996

Midland Style, George Dow, Historical Model Railway Society, 1975

Peto's Register of GWR Locomotives Vol. 2, Manor 4-6-0s, Irwell Press 1996

Peto's Register of GWR Locomotives Vol. 3, 14XX and 58XX 0-4-2Ts, Irwell Press 1996

Rails to the Forest, Dean Forest Railway Museum Trust, Silver Link Publishing Ltd, 2010

Railway Cranes Vol. 3, Peter Tatlow, Crécy Publishing 2018

Railway Passenger Stations in England, Scotland & Wales, M.E. Quick, Railway & Canal Historical Society, 2003

Sharpness, The Country Dock, Capt. Wilf Rowles, Bailey Litho, 1980

The Bristol and Gloucester Railway, Colin G. Maggs, The Oakwood Press, 1992

The Dursley Branch, Peter Smith, The Oakwood Press, 1981

The Gloucester & Sharpness Canal, An Illustrated History, Hugh Conway-Jones, Tempus, 2003

The Midland Railway – A Chronology, John Gough, Railway & Canal Historical Society, 1989

The Locomotives of the Great Western Railway, Parts 5, 6 & 8, The Railway Correspondence & Travel Society, 1958, 1959 & 1968

The Nailsworth and Stroud Branch, Colin G. Maggs, The Oakwood Press, 2000

The Signal Box, A Pictorial History and Guide to Designs, The Signalling Study Group, Oxford Publishing Co., 1998

The Yate to Thornbury Branch, Colin G. Maggs, The Oakwood Press, 2002

Track Layout Diagrams of the GWR & BR (WR), Sec. 20: Swindon and South Gloucestershire, R.A. Cooke, 1988

Track Layout Diagrams of the GWR & BR (WR), Sec. 37: The Forest of Dean, Lightmoor Press, 2019

Various Public and Working Time Tables (WTT), Appendices and other official railway publications mostly in my own collection

Magazines & Journals Consulted

'Famous Fleets: Birmingham & Midland', Alan Faulkner, *NarrowBoat*, Summer 2008

'Famous Fleets: John Harker', Alan Faulkner, *NarrowBoat*, Summer 2011

'Coaley Junction for Dursley', Roger Carpenter, *Midland Record No. 0*, 1995

'The New Docks Branch, Gloucester', Peter Smith, *Midland Record No. 19*, 2003

'Working the Stonehouse to Nailsworth and Stroud Branch Lines', Bob Essery, *Midland Record No's 27 & 28*, 2008

Websites Consulted

bristolsteam64.co.uk (*train reporting numbers, dates, times but currently off line*)
maps.nls.uk (*National Library of Scotland map database; covers whole of UK*)
shedbashuk.blogspot.co.uk (*loco's on shed at various dates circa 1930s to closure*)
gloucestershirerailwaymemories (*lots of useful detail about train workings*)
www.brdatabase.info (*locomotives database*)
www.coasters-remembered.net (*for coaster histories*)
www.davidheyscollection.com (*for train reporting numbers and much else*)
www.dursleyglos.org.uk (*local history for Coaley, Cam and Dursley*)
www.fieldingandplatthistory.org.uk (*history and recollections of Fielding & Platt*)
www.michaelclemensrailways.co.uk (*useful for WTTs and PTTs in PDF format*)
www.midlandrailwaystudycentre.org.uk (*MR museum site*)
www.ukmotorwayarchive.org.uk (*for motorway opening dates, by section*)
www.oldmaps.co.uk (*huge database of OS maps from 19th century to 1990s*)
www.sixbellsjunction.co.uk (*huge and very useful railtour website*)

CREDIT ABBREVIATIONS
KRM: Kidderminster Railway Museum
NPC: Neil Parkhouse Collection

Carrying a 2E Northampon shedplate on its smokebox door, Class '9F' No. 92138 waits alongside Platform 4 with what is likely to be a southbound iron ore train on Saturday 23rd March 1963. Bound for the steel furnaces of South Wales, these trains normally travelled via the ex-GWR line through Gloucester Central so perhaps it had been diverted for some reason. New in to service on 31st July 1957, No. 92138 had a working life a smidge short of ten years, being withdrawn from Liverpool Speke Junction shed in early July 1967. Don Mann

SECTION 1

GLOUCESTER EASTGATE STATION

From the mid-1920s up until the end of the 1950s, this would have been a typical Gloucester Eastgate scene – a Compound 4-4-0 waiting to depart on a 'stopper' to Bristol. No. 41123 was built by the LM&SR at the ex-Lancashire & Yorkshire Railway works at Horwich in November 1925 and was sent to Gloucester Barnwood shed in May 1957, its final posting. Seen here on 5th May 1959 with the 4.00pm departure from Platform 3 for Bristol Temple Meads via Mangotsfield, it was withdrawn at the end of the year. Platform 1, incidentally, was the bay at the north end of Platform 2. B.J. Ashworth

The history of Gloucester Midland station – Gloucester Eastgate from May 1951 – was detailed in Part 1 of *Gloucester Midland Lines* but is covered here again for those whose interest does not extend to the north of the county. The Bristol & Gloucester Railway (Br&GR), following intervention and pressure applied by Brunel, had been built to the broad gauge (7ft 0$^{1}/_{4}$ins) and thus was able to share the rails of the Cheltenham & Great Western Union Railway (C&GWUR) from Standish to the south-western outskirts of Gloucester. Here, the Br&GR line branched off from the C&GWUR at Millstream Junction, later renamed Chequers Road Junction and finally Gloucester South Junction, by which name it is still known today.

The Br&GR line was bound for the station already established by the Birmingham & Gloucester Railway (B&GR) in St. Catherine's Ward, fronting on to the cattle market (before that was moved in the early years of the 20th century) and opened on 4th November 1840. Although intended as a temporary affair, until the company could afford to extend their line nearer to the city centre, in the event this was never to happen and it was to remain in use for fifty-six years, until finally replaced by the new station which later became Eastgate in 1896. The Br&GR had a ceremonial opening on Saturday 6th July 1844, with regular passenger services starting on the following Monday and goods traffic commencing on 2nd September. The station was also to be shared with the GWR from 12th May 1845, when they finally opened the C&GWUR line from Swindon via Kemble, Stroud and Standish Junction. The problems caused by the break of gauge here in the years between 1844 and 1851, when the GWR opened their own station on the line coming in from South Wales, are well documented and were graphically captured in famous engravings at the time.

On 2nd May 1854, the Midland opened a new loop line, constructed by extending their branch to the eastern side of Gloucester Docks out through the south-eastern suburbs of the city to a new junction at Tuffley. However, the 1844 station remained as a terminus on what was effectively a through route between Birmingham and Bristol, and was thus always something of an operational headache. Trains heading south would reverse back out of the platforms beyond Passenger Junction, the junction with the Tuffley Loop, which they could then follow round to Tuffley Junction. Meanwhile northbound services would travel round the loop, past Passenger Junction, after which they could then reverse in to the platforms. They were then facing the right way for a northbound departure.

Left: Ex-GWR engines commonly appeared at Eastgate but usually 4-6-0s on longer distance workings, so Mogul' 2-6-0 No. 7320, here waiting with a Bristol 'stopper', was an unusual visitor. Having spent much of its BR career bumping around various sheds in South Wales, No. 7320 had a couple of months at Taunton in mid-1964, before transferring to Gloucester Horton Road in the autumn, from where it was withdrawn in November 1964, which provides a small date window for this view. NPC

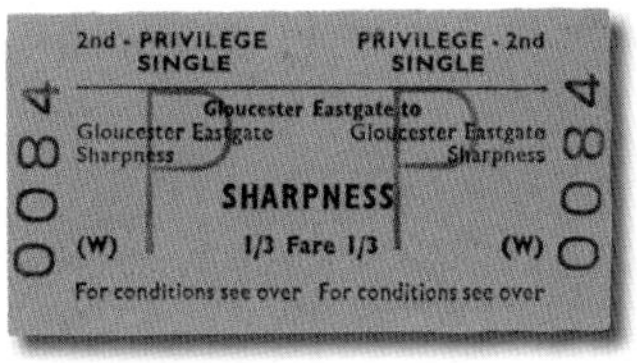

Below: Class '4F' 0-6-0 No. 44165 of Saltley shed stands in Eastgate's Platform 3 with a Birmingham to Bristol 'stopper' on 1st July 1961. This engine was to be withdrawn from the ex-L&NWR shed at Buxton in Derbyshire in August 1964. Note the underslung Up Inner Home signal beneath the canopy in the left foreground. NPC

Not only was this awkward operationally, the station was also coming in for much criticism locally for its poor construction and facilities, a result of its original temprorary nature. However, it was not until the 1890s that the Midland progressed plans to replace it, with a new through station on the Tuffley Loop line. Part of the reason for the prevarication had been the need to find a suitable location for a new engine shed, as the site of the existing roundhouse was required for the new station. The new shed at Barnwood (see *Gloucester Midland Lines Part 1*) was opened in 1895. Gloucester Midland station was opened to passengers on 12th April 1896, whilst the site of the old station, cleared of its buildings and platforms, was used for carriage sidings. Trains heading through Gloucester and the Midland main line could now swing through the city, pausing at the new station before heading straight out again.

The station had two through Down platforms numbered 3 and 4 in the form of an island, with the main station building facing on to the single Up platform, numbered 2, behind which there was also a north facing bay, numbered 1; this bay, certainly in later years, was

RIGHT: 'Jinty' 0-6-0T No. 47308 stands at Gloucester Eastgate on 7th July 1963, prior to setting out with an afternoon Gloucestershire Railway Society (GRS) rail tour along the goods only branches to Nailsworth and Stroud Midland. Departing at 1.25pm, the three-coach special also visited the ex-Midland Gloucester Docks lines, before terminating back at Eastgate at 5.45pm. We shall see much more of this train as we proceed south. NPC

BELOW: 'Royal Scot' Class 4-6-0 No. 46150 *The Life Guardsman* whistles for departure from Platform 4 circa 1962. The much travelled 'Scot' was allocated to Holyhead shed for three years from July 1960 to July 1963 – apart from a short stint at Crewe North in the spring of 1963 – and appears to be carrying a 6J shedplate denoting its North Wales base. New in to service in early June 1930, it was to be withdrawn from Carlisle Kingmoor in late November 1963. NPC

used mainly by the local stopping services to Worcester. The footbridge linking the platforms was also equipped with passenger lifts, the towers for which were a distinctive feature of the station, whilst the bridge then extended northwards across the bay, Midland goods yard and carriage sidings to the GWR station – another highly distinctive and recognisable feature. Originally manned by lift attendants at each end and decorated with an array of enalleled advertising signs and posters, sadly in later years it became rather neglected and unsavoury, rather to be avoided if possible, especially late at night.

With British Rail looking to rationalise the railway at Gloucester, after the run down and wholesale closures of lines in the 1960s, the station fell victim to the problems with the Tuffley Loop and its numerous level crossings. With both BR and the City Council looking to rid themselves of these traffic bottlenecks, Eastgate's fate was sealed and BR took the decision to rebuild and modernise the ex-GWR Gloucester Central station instead. Having been combined for administration purposes as one station from 26th May 1968, Gloucester Eastgate was closed completely on 1st December 1975, by which time it had been reduced to just two lines on either side of the island platform, No's 3 and 4.

Locally based BR 'Standard' Class '5' 4-6-0 No. 73096, clearly in dire need of attention with some oily rags, waits to start away from Eastgate with a southbound 'stopper' for Bristol on 3rd August 1964. The locomotive had arrived at Barnwood in July 1962, transferring over to Horton Road when that shed closed in early May 1964. Its short career ended upon withdrawal from Patricroft shed in November 1965, co-incidentally where it had also begun exactly twelve years earlier. This is an interesting viewpoint, which gives an indication of the expansive nature of the Midland's Gloucester station. The large main station building on Platform 2 is out of sight to the left but there was a another set of buildings further along, just glimpsed in the background through the footbridge, situated on the island formed by Platform 2 and the bay Platform 1. The bay platform can be seen on the left, just behind the wide staircase leading up to the footbridge, with parcels vans beyond that in the parcels bay. The station bookstall was to the right of the staircase but is here hidden by the locomotive. Note the large board in front of the staircase pointing the way to various destinations including Bournemouth; this would have been via Bath and the Somerset & Dorset line but through trains on to the S&D to and from the north had been withdrawn two years earlier. Blake Paterson/Courtesy the Restoration & Archiving Trust/Ref. BPUK0466

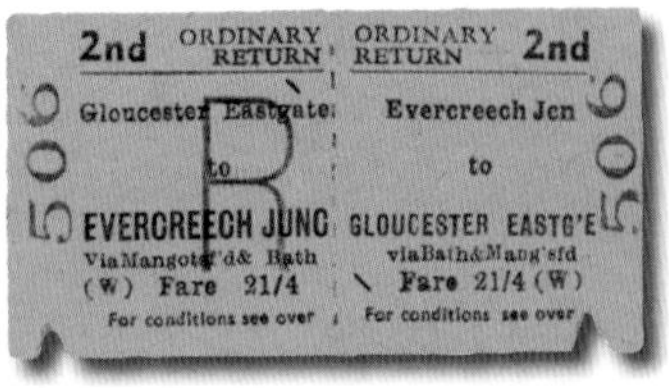

On a filthy wet day circa 1962, 'Black Five' No. 44841 enters Eastgate with an Up express, passing a southbound working the tail of which can just be seen disappearing beneath Barton Street Junction signal box. The reporting number had clearly suffered in the conditions but is 1N32, which in 1962-63 was the 7.35am Bristol to Bradford service. The locomotive was based at Saltley at this date. New from Crewe Works in November 1944, it was withdrawn from Wolverhampton Oxley in November 1966, twenty-two years being a relatively short career for one of these ubiquitous Stanier 4-6-0s.
Paul Riley/Courtesy the Restoration & Archiving Trust/Ref. PR3692

RIGHT: A '9F' on a passenger, with No. 92000 of Bristol Barrow Road shed letting off some steam as it pauses at Eastgate on 8th August 1964 with train No. 1N14. This was a typically busy summer Saturday for West Country holiday expresses returning to the north east, which we can provide detail on courtesy of the Gloucestershire Railway Memories website. In the morning, train No. 1N01, a Bradford relief, had '9F' No. 92160 of Kettering shed at the head, whilst classmate No. 92125 from Saltley was on 1N40, the 10.20am Newton Abbot to Bradford. This was immediately followed by No. 92000, seen here, with what was another Up relief service to Bradford. Whilst the workings were typical, however, three of them being '9F' hauled would have been unusual. No. 92000 became a Gloucester engine when it moved to Horton Road in early March 1965 but only briefly, withdrawal taking place four months later on Friday 2nd July. COLOUR-RAIL

LEFT: Saltley-based 'Black Five' No. 44829 drifts past a group of 'spotters' of all ages as it arrives at platform No. 4 with a Down express circa 1964. The tank in the centre right background was part of the water softening plant installed here by the LM&SR in the 1930s, from which the various water columns – one of can be seen here behind the steel mineral wagon – and Barnwood shed were supplied. In the left distance, a green 'Peak' diesel can just be made out on Horton Road shed. No. 44829 was built at Crewe Works in August 1944 and was to be withdrawn from Bolton shed three months before the end of steam, in early May 1968. KRM

RIGHT: Following on from the bottom picture on the previous page, No. 44841 is now seen starting its train for Bradford out of platform No. 2, not an easy task with a heavy load, on greasy rails on a sharp curve. Gloucester Passenger Station signal box in the right foreground is well illustrated in the previous volume; 'station' on the nameboards mounted just beneath the eaves at either end of the box was shortened to 'ST^{N}' so as to fit.
PAUL RILEY/COURTESY THE RESTORATION & ARCHIVING TRUST/REF. PR3694

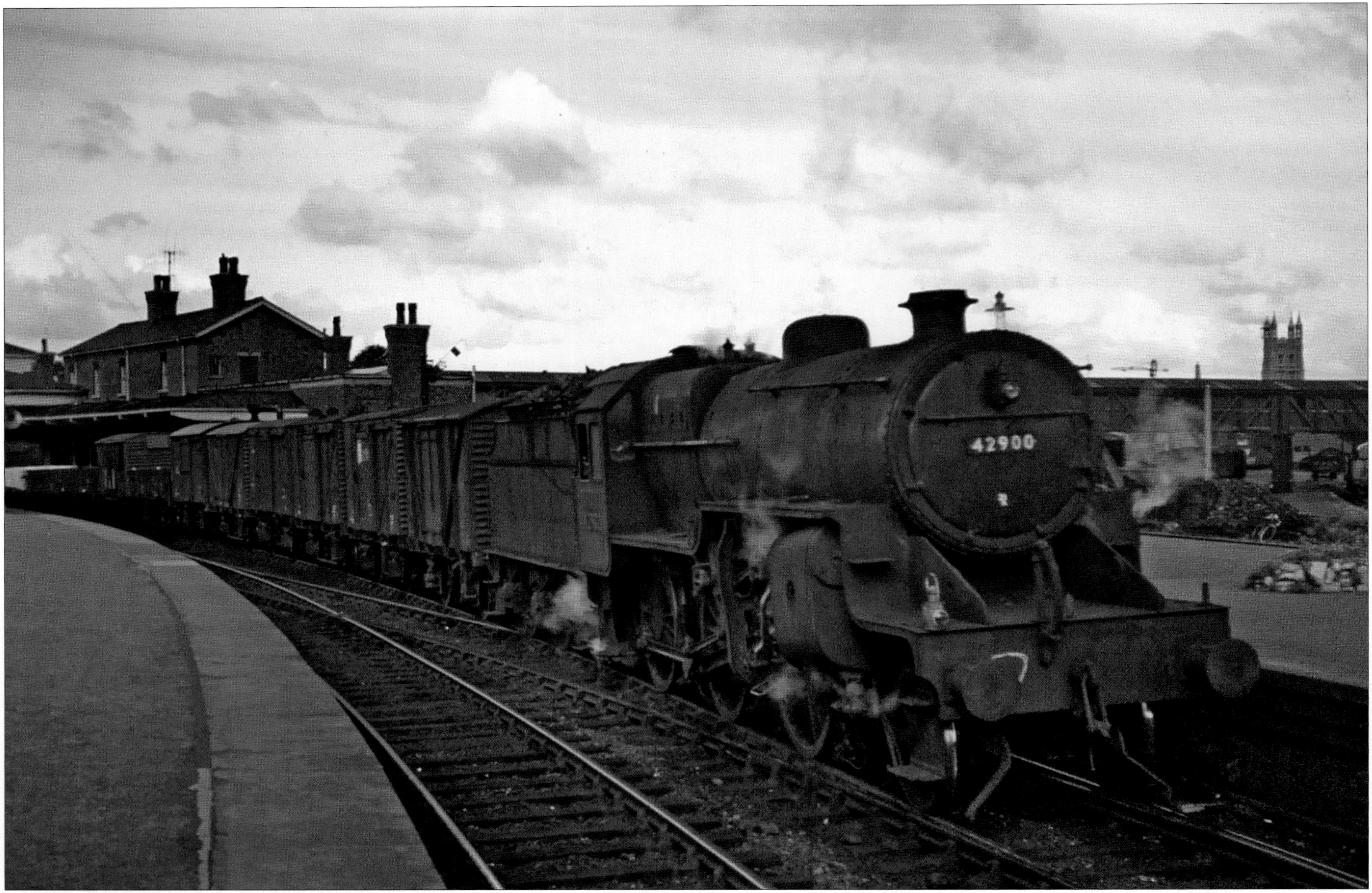

If there was a clear road through platform No. 2, it seems that Up freights would sometimes be routed that way rather than via the goods avoiding lines. Ex-L&MSR Hughes 'Crab' Class 2-6-0 No. 42900 stands at Eastgate at the head of a Bristol to Birmingham freight in December 1963. Built at Crewe Works in August 1930, the engine was transferred in early August 1955 from Kettering shed to Saltley, which then became its home base until mid-June 1964. Moving then to Birkenhead Mollington Street, No. 42900's final posting was to Stockport Edgeley at the beginning of March 1965, withdrawal from there taking place later that year in early October. The large cylinders on these 'Moguls' were positioned at a high angle to remain within the loading gauge whilst keeping the boiler pressure at 180lbs psi but they gave the engines an ungainly look which belied their powerful abilities and they were generally popular with footplate crews. Tony Bowles/Courtesy the Restoration & Archiving Trust/Ref. ARC05624

LEFT: Ex-GWR 'Castle Class 4-6-0 No. 7029 *Clun Castle* stands at Eastgate on 6th October 1964. The engine had already become something of a celebrity by this date, having taken part in three high profile rail tours earlier in the year. No. 7029 had just been allocated to Horton Road, having apparently been withdrawn from Old Oak Common shed a month earlier, where it stayed until the end of WR steam, becoming the last 'Castle' in service when withdrawn officially on 31st December 1965, although it then worked one more BR train from Gloucester to Cheltenham the next day. Bought by Patrick Whitehouse of *Railway Roundabout* fame, it is today preserved at Tyseley and was returned to main line use again in spring 2019. The bay platform No. 1 can be seen on the other side of the signal. DON MANN

RIGHT: Class '8F' 2-8-0 No. 48609 lefts off steam as it waits on the Up Goods road past Eastgate on 8th September 1965. A Leicester Midland engine at this date, it looks in fine fettle here and had more than two years service left, being withdrawn from Patricroft shed in Janaury 1968. R. TIBBITS/COLOUR-RAIL

BELOW: An ex-L&NER presence at Eastgate in 1962, in the shape of 'B1' Class 4-6-0 No. 61227 with a southbound express in platform No. 3. Built by the North British Locomotive Co. in August 1947, the engine carried L&NER No. 1227 for two and a half years, finally being renumbered by BR in February 1950. Based at Colwick shed in Nottinghamshire at the time of this view, it was to be withdrawn from there in September 1963. 'B1's were seen quite regularly at Gloucester on cross-country services between north east England and South Wales. COLOUR-RAIL

44888
44888

44945

LEFT: We met ex-Midland Railway Class '3F' No. 43754 several times in Part 1 of the Midland Lines, as she was a regular performer on both branches from Ashchurch, to Evesham and to Upton-on-Severn. Here, the venerable 1902-built 'old lady' shunts the sidings on the eastern side of Eastgate station in February 1962. There were restrictions as regards the hours which engines were permitted to work in and around Eastgate, as the extract, BELOW, from the *Working Time Table of Passenger Trains Gloucester District, 10th September 1962 to 16th June 1963*, shows. No. 43754 was shortly to celebrate her sixtieth birthday but was then to be withdrawn before the year was out. Being a regular in her latter years on the Upton-on-Severn Branch and spending time at Tewkesbury shed, her smokebox door numberplate was saved by a pair of railway enthusiast brothers from that area, who have also managed to collect much other railwayana from stations and sites on that line. JOHN CHAMPION/COLOUR-RAIL

K158 **SHUNTING ENGINES—continued**

STATIONS	Engine No.	Starting Times	AUTHORISED HOURS Mon.	Tues.	Wed.	Thur.	Fri.	Sat.	Sun.	Total hours per week	PARTICULARS OF WORK AND REMARKS
			H.M.	H.M.	H.M.	H.M.	H.M	H.M.	H.M.	H.M.	
Gloucester Eastgate	1	12. 1 a.m.	—	10 40	10 40	10 40	10 40	11 0	—	53 40	Station Pilot
	—	4.55 a.m.	5 45	—	—	—	—	—	—	5 45	Station Pilot
	—	12.30 p.m.	11 30	11 30	11 30	11 30	11 30	—	—	—	Station Pilot
	—	12.45 p.m.	—	—	—	—	—	11 15	—	68 45	
	2	10.45 a.m.	1 45	1 45	1 45	1 45	1 45	—	—	8 45	Off 9.15 a.m. Bristol.
(Sunday)	1	7.15 a.m.	—	—	—	—	—	—	4 25	4 25	Station Pilot.
	2	4. 5 p.m.	—	—	—	—	—	—	4 30	4 30	Station Pilot.

OPPOSITE PAGE TOP: Birmingham Saltley-based 'Black Five' No. 44888 eases gently through Platform 4 with a van train for Bristol on 5th June 1962. A late war-time build, being new in to service in August 1945, the 4-6-0 spent most of its career in Manchester and Birmingham up until 1963, when it then went 'walk-about' for the last five years or so of its life, with allocations respectively to Leicester Midland, Derby, Burton, Coalville, Patricroft, Trafford Park, Stockport Edgeley, Bolton and Lostock Hall, from where it was to be withdrawn in August 1968, one of the last locomotives to remain in service with BR until the end of steam. Although Saltley's shed staff may have given the engine something of a polish before sending her out, it would seem more likely that she had recently returned from overhaul. Behind, an unidentified '9F' 2-10-0 lets off steam as the crew wait for the road, after No. 44888. ALAN JARVIS

OPPOSITE PAGE BOTTOM: On the same day, another of Saltley shed's 'Black Fives', No. 44945, starts away with a Down semi-fast passenger working bound for Bristol. Note the Saltley 21A oval shedplates clearly visible on the smokebox doors of both 'Fives'. New in to service in January 1946, No. 44945 was withdrawn from Oxley shed in October 1966. ALAN JARVIS

RIGHT: A moody late afternoon view on 6th February 1964, as a weak winter sun sets in the west and locally based Class '4F No. 44045 heads through on the Down goods avoiding line. The locomotive was allocated to Barnwood shed at this date – transferring to Horton Road when Barnwood closed in May 1964 – so this is likely to be a local inter-yard trip working. No. 44045 was to be withdrawn from Horton Road before the year was out. DON MANN

Class '9F' No. 92118 produces a fine display of smoke and steam as it stands on the Down goods avoiding line with a loaded minerals train on 9th October 1963. It would appear, from the engineman just glimpsed up on the tender, if a stop had been made for water to be taken. Saltley was a very large motive power depot, the main base in Birmingham for BR London Midland Region locomotives and in fact the largest shed by allocation on the LMR, with a total of 191 engines based there in 1954. Although regarded primarily as a goods engine depot, it is the reason why so many of its engines feature within these pages and in Part 1. New in to service on the last day of 1956, the 2-10-0 had a short working life. Transferred to Banbury in August 1964 but then back to Tyseley just three months later, No. 92118 was lastly sent up to Carnforth in November 1966, from where it was withdrawn in May 1968. Don Mann

A fine panorama of Eastgate on 8th September 1962, with southbound summer Saturday expresses occupying platforms No's 3 and 4, whilst a healthy crowd of passengers await a northbound service on No. 2. On the right, 'Royal Scot' Class No. 46112 *Sherwood Forester* has just been given the road and is sending up an impressive plume of white steam as it struggles for grip on the rails curving sharply away from the platform. The unidentified 'Black Five' in Platform 3 will have to wait for the 'Scot' and its train to clear the section before it too can depart. No. 46112 was based at Nottingham at the date of this view, so it is possible to speculate that this could be the late running Train No. IV31, the 7.35am from Nottingham, due to depart here at 10.46 but which is only just pulling out ahead of IV33, the 8.10am from Bradford to Penzance, which was due to leave at 11.08. Note that there are several pre-Nationalisation carriages in the consist behind the 'Scot', whilst the railwayman alongside appears to be examining the undercarriages carefully as the train passes. ALAN JARVIS

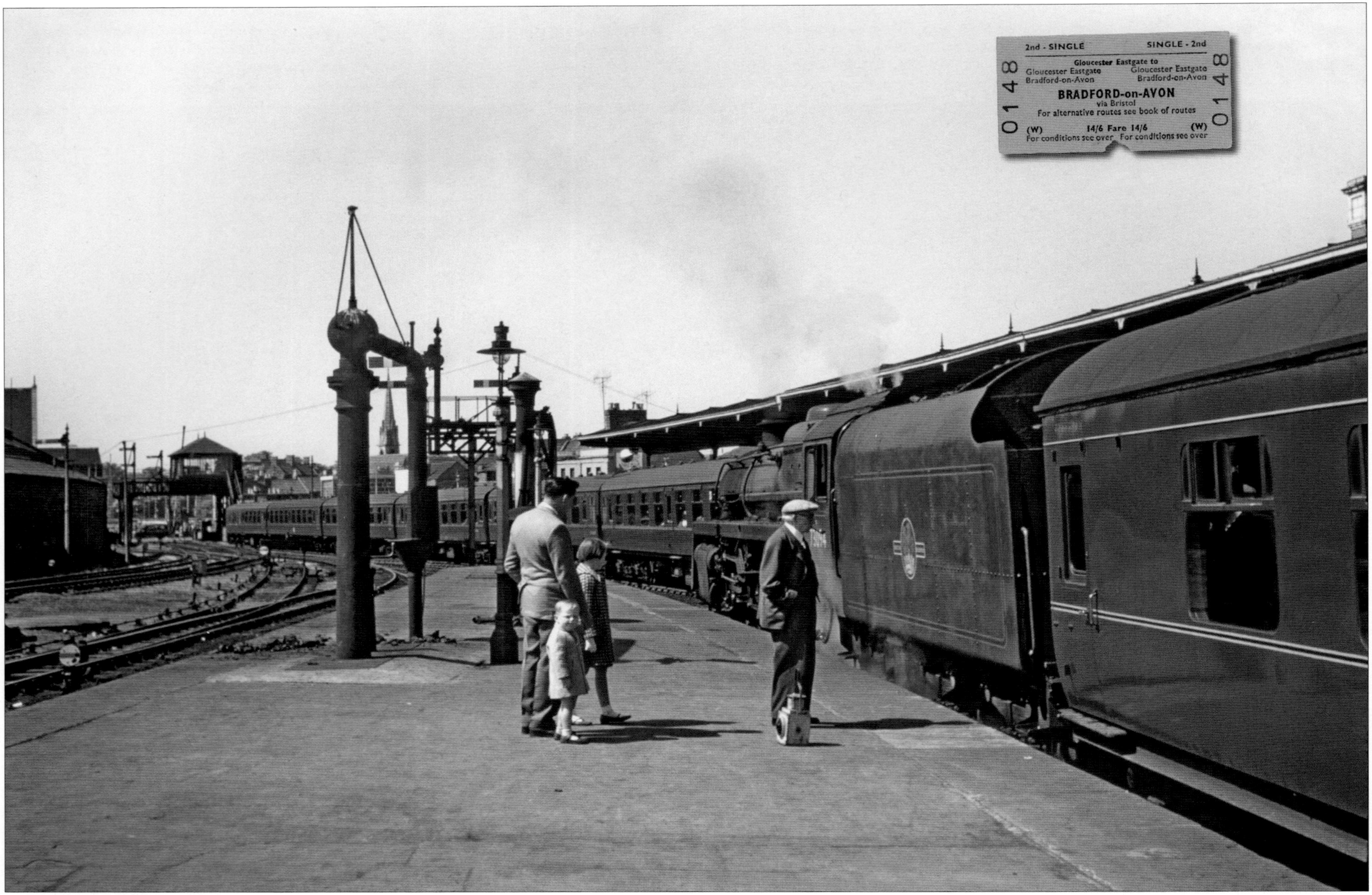

The 'old boy' smoking his pipe appears to be watching the crew of BR Standard Class 5 4-6-0 No. 73094 coupling up to their train, the 11.25am to Bristol Temple Meads (starting from Cheltenham Lansdown), on Wednesday 2nd June 1965. New from Derby Works less than ten years earlier, in November 1955, the locomotive had stints at several sheds, including Bristol Barrow Road and Barnwood, before being withdrawn from the latter in February 1964. Three months later it was reinstated to traffic at Shrewsbury, where it was based at the date of this view. It seems a little odd that such a relatively short run would involve a change of engines here at Gloucester; was this normal for this working I wonder? The lamp would presumably be placed on the front of the engine in due course. Behind, an Up express is arriving at Platform 2 and there is a glimpse of Barton Street signal cabin in the left background. No. 73094, which is wearing BR's attractive lined green passenger livery, was to be withdrawn from Patricroft shed in early May 1967. Roy Denison

LEFT: A poorer quality view but which shows the extent of the sorting sidings to the east of the goods avoiding lines passing Eastgate, circa early 1963. Looking towards Horton Road shed, as noted in the previous volume, the gas holder is also now a memory. NPC

BELOW: Another less than sharp picture, taken from near Barton Street Junction signal box, showing No. 7019 *Fowey Castle* making a spirited getaway southwards on 20th June 1964. The presence of several other photographers on the end of Platform 2 gives an indication that this was no ordinary occasion. They were here for the second run of the Railway Enthusiast Club's (REC) Severn Boar Rail Tour, the first of which, run a fortnight earlier, had been a sell out. Everyone would shortly be packing up therefore and hurrying over to the bay platform at Central to catch the brake van tour of lines in the Forest of Dean. Both trips feature extensively in Volume 2. No. 7019 was based at Wolverhampton Oxley shed at this date. JOHN RYAN

BELOW: By nature of the fact that most of the pictures within these volumes were taken in the last years of steam, we generally do not get to enjoy the locomotives looking their best, so it is a pleasure to see here a 'Jubilee' looking very spruce in BR's attractive lined green passenger livery – although I daresay LM&SR devotees then and now would have objected to their engines being painted in what was essentially GWR/ Western Region colours! No. 45572 *Eire* is seen making its scheduled stop with the Up 'The Devonian'. The view is undated but is likely to be in 1960 or 1961, when the locomotive was based at Bristol Barrow Road. New in to service from North British Locomotive on 1st September 1934, No. 45572 had originally been named *Irish Free State* and it was withdrawn from Willesden shed at the start of 1964. The brick hut on the right and the collection of wooden sheds behind it were demolished circa July 1964. DAVID A. LAWRENCE/COLOUR-RAIL

On 30th June 1967, blue painted diesel-hydraulic No. D1007 *Western Talisman* waits at Eastgate with train No. 1A70, crossing with a northbound service in the hands of a green liveried Class '120' Swindon Cross-Country unit, which is just departing for Cheltenham and possibly beyond from Platform 2. Coming new out

A similar panorama to that on page 27 but now in the diesel era, with green liveried Sulzer Type '4' No. D13 waiting to leave Platform 4 with train No. 3V20, a parcels service for Bristol, photographed from a northbound express entering Platform 2 on 19th January 1967. With steam around Gloucester on the Midland line having carried on until late summer 1966, accoutrements of the steam age still remained, such as the water crane on the right. Later designated Class '45' under the 1973 TOPS (Total Operations Processing System) renumbering scheme but known as 'Peaks' by enthusiasts after the initial ten which bore the names of British mountains, No. D13 became No. 45001 and lasted in service until January 1986. The photographer would leave his train at Cheltenham Lansdown, to make it back home to Bishops Cleeve. Bill Potter/KRM

RIGHT: Railcar No. M55004 stands alongside Platform 3 on 2nd August 1967, in a view which again gives a clue to how busy the station still was at this period. The decline to closure in 1975 was to be rapid. The railcar, one of twenty later designated Class '122' and intended as replacements for the old GWR railcars, was built in the city by the Gloucester Railway Carriage & Wagon Works in May 1958 and was originally allocated to Tyseley. Nicknamed 'Bubble Cars', all have now been withdrawn but several have been preserved, although not No. M55004. With all of the intermediate stations south from Gloucester having been closed by the date of this view, it is likely that this single railcar now sufficed for a Cheltenham to Bristol via Eastgate working. NPC

ABOVE: 'Peak' No. D42 rattles past on the goods avoiding lines with a train of bogie bolster wagons carrying steel bar on 30th June 1967. The 'Z' in the train reporting number was for '*excursion, military and special trains running within the Western Region*', so may not relate to this working at all. New in to service on 19th July 1961, at the date of this view the 'Peak' was allocated to Bristol Bath Road, which had been shut as a steam shed in September 1960 and rebuilt as a diesel depot. Later renumbered No. 45034 under TOPS, the locomotive was first withdrawn in July 1987 but then reinstated in the September, finally being taken out of service in July 1988. BILL POTTER/KRM

K48

TIME ALLOWANCES FOR FREIGHT TRAINS—continued.

BARNT GREEN AND CHARFIELD

DOWN	Point-to-Point Allowances		
	Class 7	Class 8	Class 9
	Mins.	Mins.	Mins.
Barnt Green	—	—	—
Blackwell	5	6	6
Bromsgrove Station	12	12	12
Bromsgrove South*	3*	3*	3*
Stoke Works Junction	5	5	5
Stoke Works Junction	—	—	—
Droitwich	8	9	14
Worcester	12	13	20
Abbotswood Junction	9	10	12
Dunhampstead	8	9	12
Abbotswood Junction	12	13	15
Ashchurch	19	21	27
Cheltenham (High Street)	14	16	16
Cheltenham Lansdown	2	2	3
Gloucester Eastgate	15	16	16
Gloucester E.S. Junction	—	—	—
Gloucester South Junction	3	3	3
Standish Junction	14	16	23
Standish Junction	19	21	25
Berkelety Road	14	15	20
Charfield	9	—	13

UP	Point-to-Point Allowances		
	Class 7	Class 8	Class 9
	Mins.	Mins.	Mins.
Charfield	—	—	—
Berkeley Road	8	9	13
Stonehouse	12	13	19
Standish Junction	5	5	5
Standish Junction	—	—	—
Gloucester South Junction	13	15	16
Gloucester E.S. Junction	3	3	3
Gloucester Eastgate	14	16	22
Churchdown	8	9	12
Cheltenham (High Street)	9	10	12
Ashchurch	13	16	16
Abbotswood Junction	20	23	32
Abbotswood Junction	—	—	—
Worcester	9	10	12
Droitwich	12	13	19
Stoke Works Junction	9	10	15
Dunhampstead	13	14	20
Stoke Works Junction	9	10	14
Bromsgrove	5	5	7
Blackwell	10	12	12
Barnt Green	4	4	5

*—These times are for pass or stop.

LEFT: This extract from the from the *Working Time Table of Freight Trains, Gloucester District, 17th June to 8th September 1963*, gives the time allowances for freight trains in both the Up and Down directions between Barnt Green (south of Birmingham, at the top of the Lickey Incline) and Charfield.

RIGHT: A view north through the severely rationalised station circa 1973, looking from beneath the canopy on the now disused Platform 2, across to the island platform which now served the two remaining Up and Down lines. Whilst operationally by this date the arrangement made sense, it would not have added to the convenience for passengers, despite the availability of the lifts. The closure of platforms No's 1 and 2, and the lifting of all superfluous trackwork was carried out in 1968, leaving just the two lines either side of the island platform and a scissors crossover at the Horton Road Junction end, with a corresponding single crossover at the other end just south of Barton Street Crossing. SEAN BOLAN

BELOW RIGHT: A similar view from the island platform just two days before final closure, on Saturday 29th November 1975. Note that the white painted platform edges of the previous picture had disappeared but the wooden superstruture of the footbridge and lifts, and the canopy valancings had all been given what looks to be a fairly recent fresh coat of white paint, despite the fact that closure had been planned for some time. Perhaps, in this instance, rather than simply wasting money to justify closure it was in recognition of the fact that with Central closed for some months, it was as well to give passengers as good an impression of the railway at Gloucester as possible. The proliferation of parcels trolleys was also due to Central being closed. J.L. LEAN/COLOUR-RAIL

BELOW: A panorama of Eastgate, with an Up Class '50' hauled train leaving, taken from the site of Horton Road yard in February 1975. In the foreground, the yard had been cleared of all locomotive sidings, along with the turntable, water tower and coaling stage. Central station is largely hidden in the right background behind the GWR goods shed, also now long demolished. NPC

The footbridge linking the ex-GWR Central station with Eastgate was long a feature of the railway scene at Gloucester. Some 250 yards in length, as we saw in Midland Lines Part 1, it could also be a vantage point for an enterprising photographer wishing to capture views of the general railway layout. There was an extension at the Eastgate end serving the island platform, with lifts down to platform level, which in an earlier era had merited a lift attendant. Over the years the footbridge had been well maintained and lit, and its walls covered with enamelled advertising signs and posters. By the end, as these two views show, the first circa 1973 and the second on 29th November 1975, it had become as negelected as the rest of the station, with peeling paint and not a poster in sight. Sean Bolan; J.L. Lean/Colour-Rail

Whilst the change from the bustling station of the previous pages to the final closure in late 1975 seemed to happen all too quickly, the run down of Eastgate following the closure of Platforms 1 and 2 in 1968 was akin to a death by strangulation. As such, few witnessed the last rites as the station finally slipped in to posterity in the early hours of Monday 1st December 1975. The Swindon-built 'Western' Class diesel-hydraulics were also on their last legs by this date, so it was perhaps fitting that the last arrival, at 4.00am, was hauled by No. D1048 *Western Lady*, train No. 1C91 from London Paddington. There were a few parcels waiting to be loaded but otherwise Pete Berry and a small band of other keen photographers, realising the importance of the occasion and having made a special effort to be there at this ungodly hour, pretty much had the platform to themselves. The train terminated here as the track between Eastgate and Tramway Junction was now severed. Peter Berry

Right: Prior to the previous picture, an unidentified Class '47' was photographed awaiting the train's arrival alongside platform No. 4, to take it on to Cardiff. Peter Berry

Below: With train reporting No. 1C77 showing on its front destination panel, the Class '47' prepares to leave with the final departure from Eastgate station. The photographer recalled not bothering to make a note of the locomotive's number, as '47s' were boring in comparison to the Western Region 'Westerns', 'Hymeks' and 'Warships'. With the latter two classes already extinct by this date and the 'Westerns' on the way out, photographing them was much more important. However, the locomotive might be No. 47124, which Bill Potter photographed arriving earlier that day (page 50). Peter Berry

Left: Each night this passenger and, more importantly, parcels train left London Paddington around 1.00am. After many stops *en route*, it arrived at Gloucester at around 4.00am but because Central was being rebuilt at this date, the train had to use Eastgate. In addition, the tracks between Eastgate and Tramway Junction had been severed so the only access was over the Tuffley Loop. Thus the the Class '47' had to head for Cardiff via Tuffley Junction, Westerleigh and through the Severn Tunnel. The next day, the lines west of the station were also severed and Eastgate station was history. After the last train had left, the final movement at the station was the departure of No. D1048 *Western Lady*. As she drifted along platform No. 3, the crew stopped and posed at the request of the small band of photographers who wanted to properly document this historic occasion. Moments later, Eastgate fell silent for the final time. New in to service on 15th December 1962, No. D1048's fate was much happier. Withdrawn fifteen months after these pictures were taken, on 22nd February 1977, she was saved for preservation and now resides at the Midland Railway Centre at Butterley in Derbyshire. However, the locomotive is currently still under long term restoration and although cosmetically restored in 2009, *Western Lady* has not been operational since being saved. Peter Berry

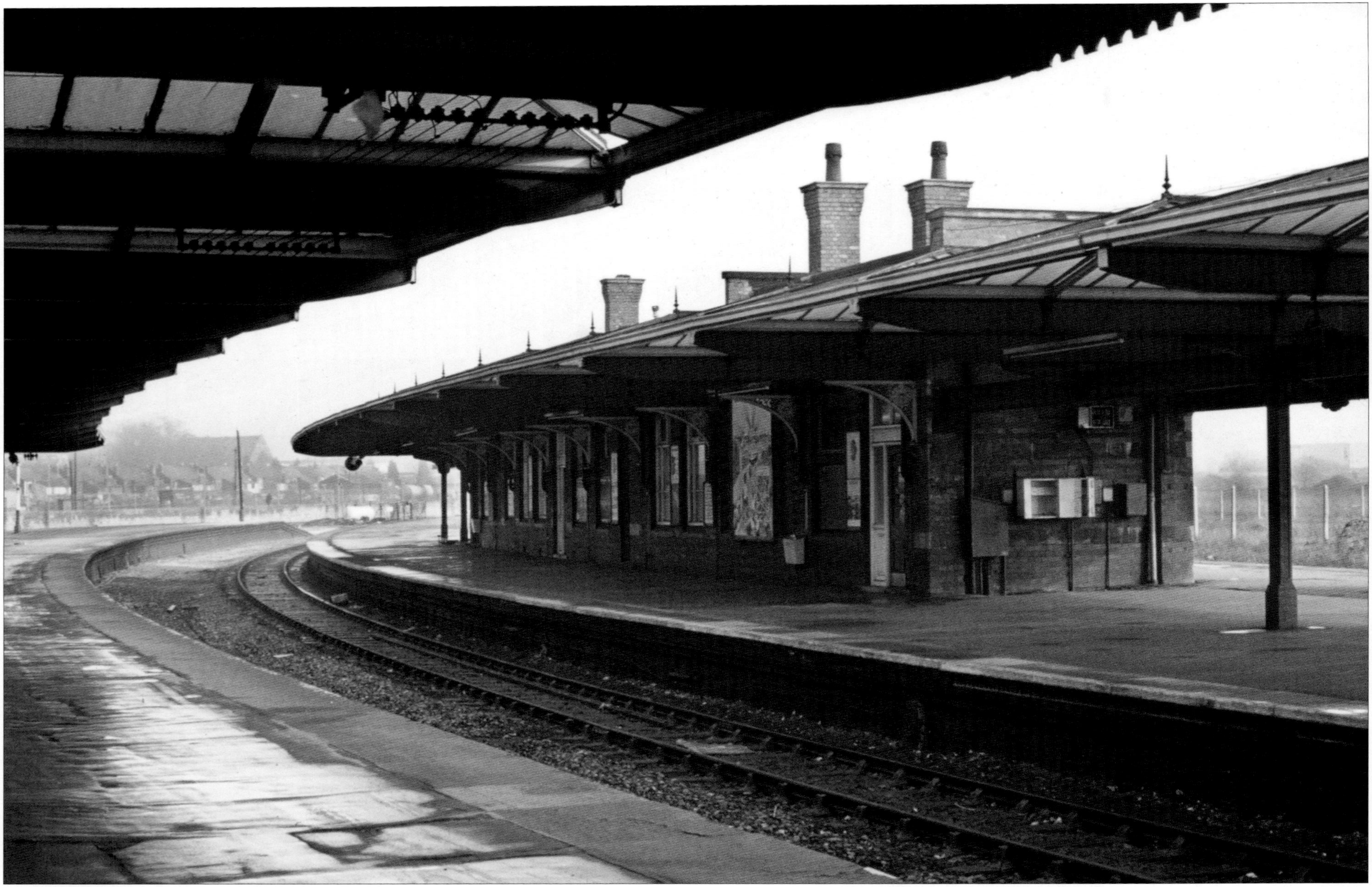

Three months later, in February 1976, the photographer returned to take a few more pictures before demolition work commenced. This fine study from platform No. 2 of the building serving the island platforms No's 3 and 4 contains much useful detail. There was still an array of posters on display but the rails now have a coating of rust. To save passengers having to cross back over to Platform 2 via the footbridge, this building also contained a refreshment room, as well as lavatories for both sexes and waiting rooms. Beneath the canopy in the background on the far right, the site of the goods avoiding lines and High Orchard Branch sorting sidings had been cleared completely, whilst in the left background, the Horton Road coaling stage and water tower had gone along with some of the sheds. Peter Berry

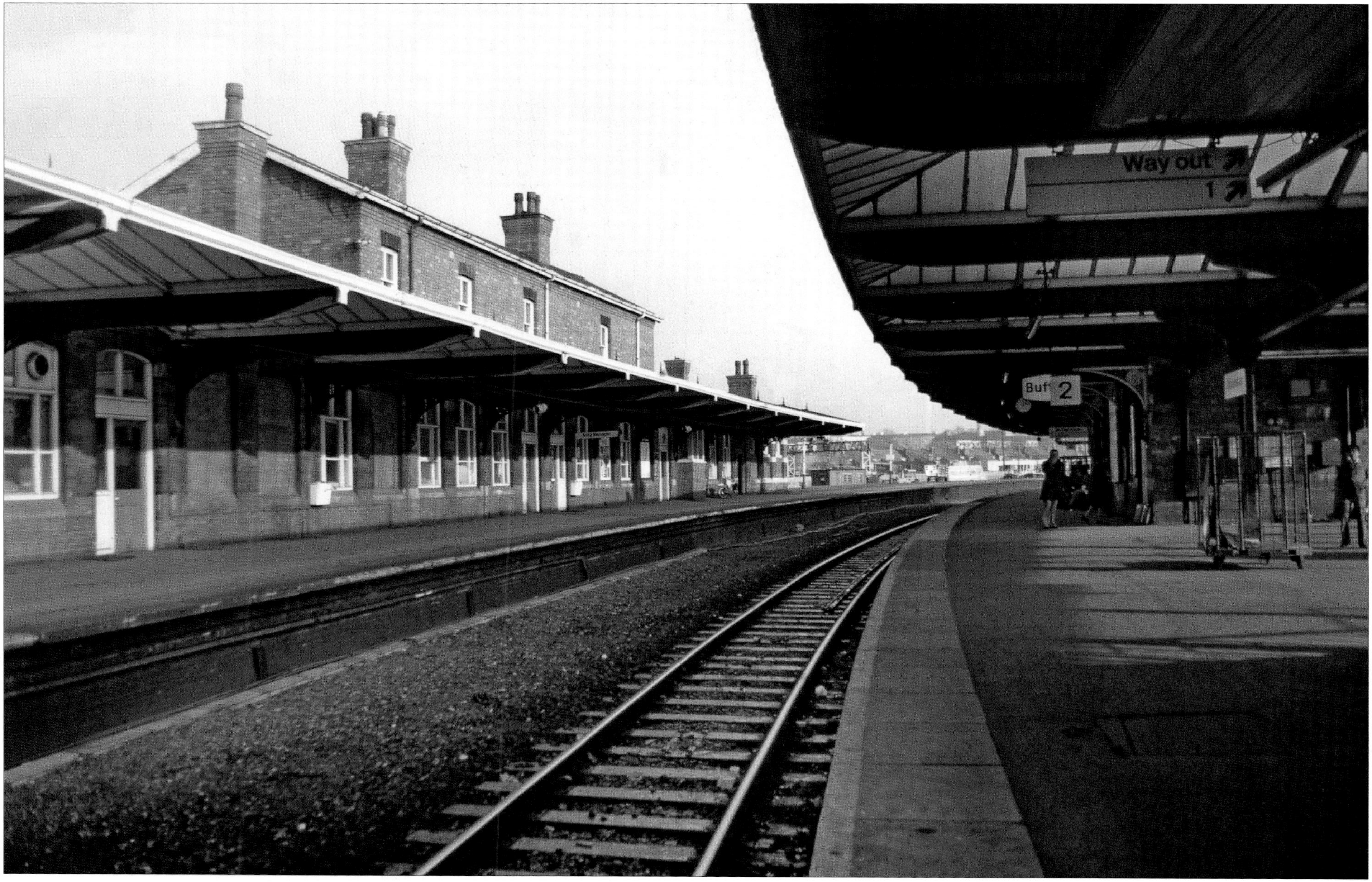

Switching platforms and looking back the other way, the buildings provided on the island formed by the bay platform No. 1 and platform No. 2 were mentioned a little earlier. Seen here on 29th November 1975, they comprised a two-storey centre section with single storey extensions at either end, and housed a refreshment room and kitchen, along with ladies and gents waiting rooms and lavatories. The booking office and hall, and the stationmaster's, guards, porters, parcels and other offices were all within the main building, back the other side of the footbridge on Platform 2. With the signage still in place in this view, it can be seen that the buffet room on the right remained open right up until closure, whilst the area manager had an office in the building on platform No. 2. Bill Potter/KRM

Another photographer to record the dying days of Eastgate and, as we shall see in due course, the signal boxes and crossings on the Tuffley Loop was David Stowell. This is his view from the forecourt through the entrance to the goods yard on 16th November 1975 and shows the rarely seen side of the station building that faced on to the bay Platform 1. The parcels platform, which had lines either side, is in the centre of the picture, behind the Gloucester-registered (7787 FH) Austin A40 'Farina' model of circa 1964. On the left is the rear end of an ermine white Ford Cortina Mark 1 four-door, probably with the bigger than standard 1500cc engine judging by the 5/60 section rear tyre showing. The author's first car was a red one of these, bought in 1972, registration No. 250 VWL, which remains his favourite ever set of wheels! The lack of extraction vents on the rear pillar indicate that the model seen here dates from the September 1962 to autumn 1964 production period. Behind the railings sits a Hillman Avenger and on the extreme right is a Ford Escort Mark 1, the numberplate GWE 831J indicating that it was first registered in Sheffield, whilst the J suffix dates it as an August 1970 to July 1971 model. David Stowell

Left: More detail of the buildings on the deserted Platforms 2 and 3 in this view looking southwards through the station on Saturday 16th November 1974, a damp and miserable day. The lamp glowing in the distance is on the side of the station bookstall. David Stowell

British Railways Board (W)
2662
PARKING TICKET FOR MOTOR CAR OR THREE-WHEELED VEHICLE AT
GLOUCESTER EASTGATE
Registration No.
Fee
Available on day of issue only
For conditions see over
2662

Right: Exactly a year later, on 16th November 1975, the photographer captured this view under the canopy on Platform 2, showing the metal bracket still in place which had held one of the Starter semaphores up until 1968. The scooter, which just happened to be parked there, is a 1960 Gloucester-registered Lambretta TV175. This model replaced the LI series for that year and set Lambrettas off to great popularity in the 1960s, not least in the hands of the 'Mods'! David Stowell

Below: With demolition underway, this was the view from the station entrance on 11th April 1976. Note the 'Station' sign now in use by the entrance to the goods yard to point the way for unknowing members of the public back towards Central station. Again the selection of vehicles on view is interesting. The furthermost green car is a Vauxhall Viva HB Series of circa 1969. The HB ran from late 1966 to late 1970 but the colour and trim options, such as the vinyl roof on this one, mark it out as a late example. The white rarity, even then, is a Jensen 541 model of circa 1962. The corner of another Ford Escort Mark 1 appears on the extreme right, it being the regular and very popular 'L' model regarding its trim level and probably with the base 1100cc engine. David Stowell

Above and Below Left: Two more detail studies, showing the rarely photographed, typically decorative Midland Railway glass and cast iron canopy that covered the station entrance. There were hopes that the canopy could be saved but it was not to be, such was the indifferent attitude then to architectural gems such as this. Note the bulbous bottoms to the columns, designed to protect them from being struck by the wheels of horse-drawn carts, vans and drays. The stone setts were another common feature not often seen today. Beyond, the substantial nature of the long footbridge linking Gloucester's two stations is emphasised by the massive stone piers on which it was supported, whilst in the background there is another glimpse of the long ex-GWR goods shed. The white car on the right is a circa 1973 Datsun Cherry 100A. In the picture on the left, demolition of one end of the station building had opened up a view through to the skeletal ironwork of one of the lifts. Both Peter Berry

Below: The station slumbers in winter sunshine a few weeks after closure, with the line to the right of the island platform having already been lifted and the one remaining track severed at the Barton Street Crossing end. The black smoke in the background is drifting from the boiler chimney at Gloucester Royal Hospital. Peter Berry

Left: An unidentified Swindon-built Class '120' DMU in green livery runs over the crossing and under Barton Street Junction signal box on 25th March 1968, during the period of great change here, as indicated by the redundant track panels piled up on the left. By the end of May, all that would be left of the track layout at Eastgate would be the two lines running either side of the island platform No's 3 & 4. The old lamps and BR totems would also be replaced, and the semaphores on the gantry dismantled, with the box reduced to ground frane status. J.L. Lean/Colour-Rail

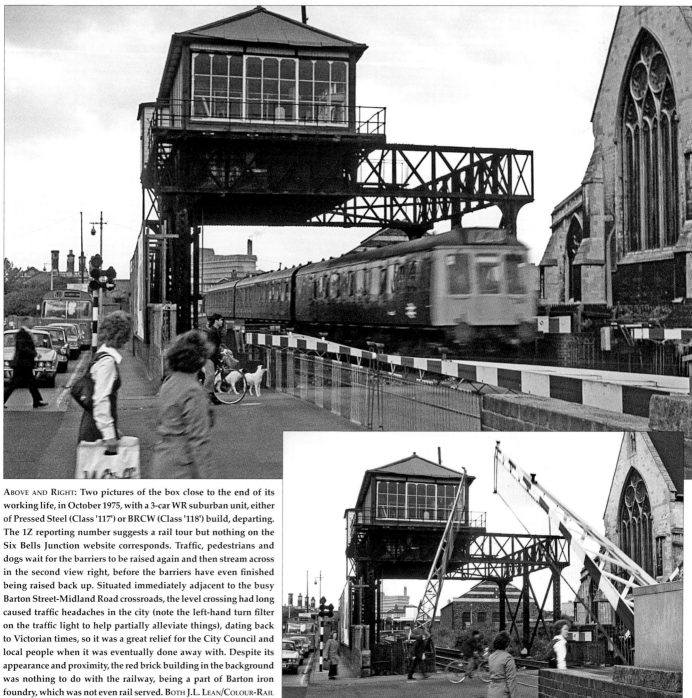

Above and Right: Two pictures of the box close to the end of its working life, in October 1975, with a 3-car WR suburban unit, either of Pressed Steel (Class '117') or BRCW (Class '118') build, departing. The 1Z reporting number suggests a rail tour but nothing on the Six Bells Junction website corresponds. Traffic, pedestrians and dogs wait for the barriers to be raised again and then stream across in the second view right, before the barriers have even finished being raised back up. Situated immediately adjacent to the busy Barton Street-Midland Road crossroads, the level crossing had long caused traffic headaches in the city (note the left-hand turn filter on the traffic light to help partially alleviate things), dating back to Victorian times, so it was a great relief for the City Council and local people when it was eventually done away with. Despite its appearance and proximity, the red brick building in the background was nothing to do with the railway, being a part of Barton iron foundry, which was not even rail served. Both J.L. Lean/Colour-Rail

ABOVE: Barton Street crossing and signal box in October 1972, from an angle that also provides a glimpse of the rear of the structure. The Gloucester Area resignalling project of the late 1960s saw the box 'closed' on 25th May 1968 and 'opened' the next day reduced to ground frame status, operating the lifting barriers, the crossovers at either end of the station and a handful of colour light signals. On the left is the new swimming pool, prior to the leisure centre being added. NPC

BELOW: A view from a similar date, with cars passing over the crossing. The brick hut on the left was probably a war-time addition, purpose unknown. On the crossing are a blue Austin A55 Mk. 2 'Farina' Traveller, which were made between 1959 and 1962, and an Austin or Morris 1100 'ADO 16' model. These were Britain's best selling car in almost every year of their 1962-73 production life, apart from three years when they were just pipped by the Ford Cortina. NPC

ABOVE: Rekindling more memories for older Glostonians, this is the road aspect of the crossing looking east from the end of Eastgate Street and along Barton Street on 16th November 1975, and providing a clear view of the rear of the box. Front right is a Triumph Toledo of circa 1972, with a circa 1969 Ford Cortina Mk 2 behind and then a similar vintage Vauxhall Viva HB. Heading up Barton Street are two further Ford Cortina Mk 2s, the one in distal red being a 'Super' version. DAVID STOWELL

BELOW: Under the watchful eye of the signalman, an Up service heads over the crossing in to Eastgate in May 1975. The unit is a Class '119' Gloucester Cross-Country three-car set with the DMS and TSLRB in view, so there would be another power car on the rear end. The front unit is either a Class '118' BRCW three-car set or a '121' (Pressed Steel single unit), most likely the former. The traffic lights were interlinked with the level crossing controls and incorporated an extra phase that was only used when the crossing was closed, to allow traffic to continue straight ahead or turn left in to Eastgate Street. The cars are a circa 1964 Gloucester-registered Austin 1100 Mk. 1 in snowberry white, a green Vauxhall VX1800 and another 1100. A Morris Minor 1000 faces them, followed by a Hillman or later 'badge-engineered' Chrysler Avenger estate car. DAVID STOWELL

A Bristol Omnibus Company single-decker waits to turn left at the traffic lights on Midland Road during a quiet period between trains on Wednesday 20th September 1972. Bristol Commercial Vehicles Ltd was established in 1943 and was part-owned by Leyland Motors by the date of this view. The bus is a Bristol 'RE' model of 1967 vintage. Service 508 was bound for York Road in Barnwood, via Barton Street and Eastern Avenue, whilst the HW denotes its first registration as being – unsurprisingly – Bristol. Bill Potter/KRM

Above: The view of the station from inside the cabin on 29th November 1975, the last full day of operation. Look at the polished floor and full coal buckets! Peter Berry

Opposite Page Right: All that remained of the Barton Street Junction lever frame on 29th November 1975 – it had once extended to 48 levers. Photographer Pete Berry recalls being desperate to take views inside the box and began climbing the steps up. However, part way up it suddenly dawned on him that if he knocked and asked permission to enter he might be refused and the chance would be lost forever. So, plucking up courage, he just opened the door and walked right in and started taking pictures, much to the amazement of the signalmen who simply stood and watched. Politely thanking them on leaving, these two views now stand as a rare and valuable colour record of the interior of the box and the view from it. Peter Berry

RIGHT: Leaving Eastgate station, passing beneath the signal box and heading out on to the Tuffley Loop, we shall first deviate to the west (right) to traverse the High Orchard Branch to Gloucester Docks. Taken from the end of the island platform, again on the last day, Class '47' No. 47124 arrives with train No. 1E30. BILL POTTER/KRM

BELOW: An unidentified 'Hall' Class 4-6-0 storms away from Eastgate on the Tuffley Loop with a lengthy mixed freight in November 1964. The line in the foreground is the High Orchard Branch, which had deviated off from the main line on the near side of the level crossing in the left background, at Barton Street Junction. NPC

BELOW: With the disused stub of the docks line in the foreground, a DMU heads towards Barton Street crossing and Eastgate in April 1975. With the allotments on the left already showing signs of neglect, this would be the last crop of vegetables for the local railwaymen to whom they belonged. Halls & Keck Ltd, the building contractors who owned the yard behind the wall on the right, had been founded in 1903 as W.B Halls Ltd, the name change occurring in 1963. Halls & Keck later moved to new premises elsewhere in Gloucester and traded latterly as a leasing company, which was dissolved in 2017. The site here is now occupied by a large modern store. DAVID STOWELL

SECTION 2

THE HIGH ORCHARD DOCKS BRANCH

Deeley 'Goods Tank' 0-4-0T No. 41535, one of the regular docks branch shunters at Gloucester, poses with her driver at the entrance to Barnwood shed circa 1962. Built at Derby Works in February 1922, shortly before the Midland became a part of the LM&SR in the 1923 Grouping, the engine was allocated here in May 1957 and remained until September 1963, when it was sent to Swansea East Dock. Its final posting was to Neath Court Sart shed in June 1964, from where it was then withdrawn just over two months later. John Tarrant/KRM

Now largely completely redeveloped as an upmarket shopping, eating out and residential centre, Gloucester Docks were central to the railway coming to the city in the first place. Occupying a strategic place close to the upper limit of the tidal reaches of the River Severn, Gloucester was first granted the formal status of being a customs port by Queen Elizabeth I in 1580 and a new customs house was built adjoining the river quay. The existing Customs House, now the home of the Gloucester Regiment HQ and museum, dates from 1843. This was built following the growth in trade at the port through the 18th century, which led to the construction of the Gloucester & Berkeley Canal and that in turn led to an even greater amount of trade and the expansion of the docks themselves.

The Act for construction of the canal was granted in 1793 but financial problems caused work to be stopped in 1799 with only about five miles of the canal south from Gloucester having been dug. Money was found to open the lock at Gloucester in 1812 to allow river craft direct access to the new dock basin, which had also attracted the attention of the Gloucester & Cheltenham Tramroad by 1809, the year in which this concern gained its Act, opening for traffic in 1811 (a potted history of the G&CT is given in the Introduction to the previous volume). Work on the canal was able to begin again in 1817, with its line now shortened by making Sharpness the destination for its river entry rather than a point south-west of Berkeley. The experienced and talented Thomas Telford was also brought in as consultant engineer, although even he could not prevent further financial and management difficulties causing the project to drag on for another decade. The junction with the Stroudwater Canal was made in 1820 but it was not until 1827 that the rest of the canal was completed. The docks were also expanded at this time with the construction of the Barge Arm, to keep the main basin free for larger sea-going vessels.

With the further expansion of dock facilities during the 1840s, culminating with the opening of the Victoria Dock in 1849, coupled with the repeal of the Corn Laws and a reduction in import duties, the port now became an important destination for the country's rapidly growing railway network. First to be enticed were the promoters of the B&GR, whose original intention, as related in the previous volume, had been to build a line directly from Birmingham to Gloucester missing out all other large centres of population en route. Following the opening of the B&GR's line and the company's subsequent absorption by the Midland Railway, the latter gained parliamentary approval for

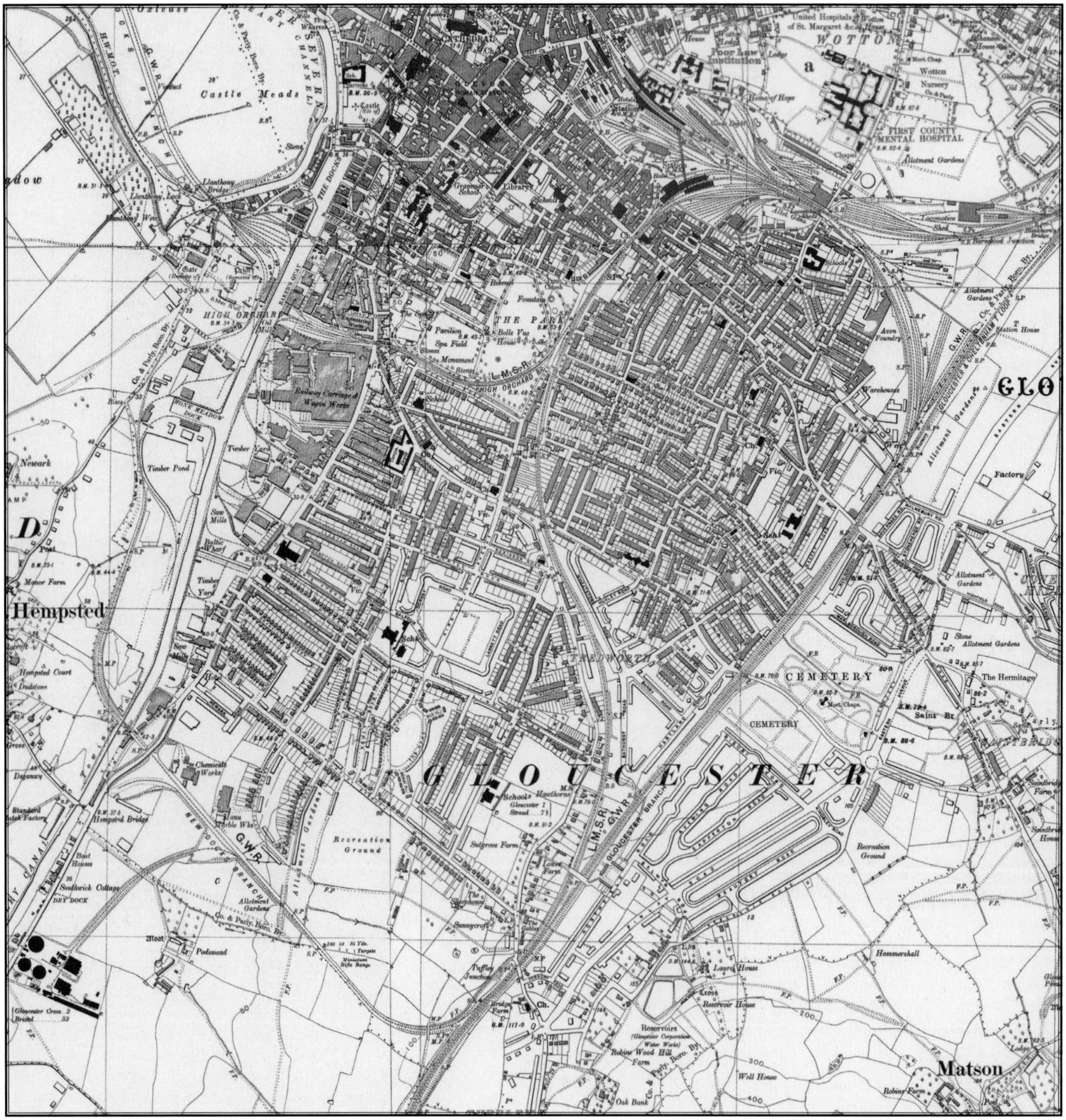

Gloucester, its docks and associated railways from the 1938 edition 6 inch Ordnance Survey. Top right are the two stations, with Barnwood shed, which supplied the locomotives for working the LM&SR dock branches, shown near the right-hand edge of the map. The High Orchard Branch can be seen leaving the Tuffley Loop south of the LM&SR station – not yet named Eastgate – and skirting The Park, before crossing Bristol Road to reach High Orchard. Opposite is the GWR's Llanthony Yard and note that Castle Meads is still just a meadow; the power station was a war-time build, begun in 1940. At the bottom of the map, the Hempsted or New Docks Branch turns away west off the main line at Tuffley Junction; the section running across the canal to the GWR side was closed around the date of this survey.

a branch to High Orchard and the east side of the docks, which was opened in 1848, six years before the GWR completed their Llanthony Branch serving the west side of the docks. There was a direct connection between the two companies' lines running across Llanthony Bridge. In 1875, the GWR gained running powers over the MR's lines.

The railway system serving the docks expanded rapidly into the second half of the 19th century, with lines and sidings radiating out in all directions, serving the various docks, quays, warehouses and factories. Initially, many of these lines, sidings and connections were built and owned by the Gloucester & Berkeley Canal Company, which became the Sharpness Docks & Gloucester & Birmingham Navigation Company in 174 and who were the owners of the canal and the docks at either end. The operation of the lines was leased jointly to the GWR and MR until 1875, when the licence was revoked and both then had to pay a rent for their use. This was far from a satisfactory or simple arrangement and, as a result, an agreement was reached in 1880 for the GWR to work the west side and the MR the east side of the docks. One important rail related business sited near the docks was the Gloucester Railway Carriage & Wagon Company, which opened its first factory here in 1875.

Barnwood shed was covered in some detail in the previous volume but this fascinating study of Deeley 'Dock Tank' No. 41535 heading back on shed circa 1960 has turned up since that was published. Note that these diminutive engines had no bunkers, so coal was piled on the tops of the tanks and firebox just forward of the cab and then thrown by hand in to the grate. This view is from near the coaling stage, with the old workshops forming a backdrop. Note the open wagons loaded with sand and clinker in the left background, standing in front of the sand drying house with its attendant furnace chimney. David Pollard/NPC

A new line opened to serve the docks in 1898 was a Midland construction, built in the teeth of fierce opposition from the GWR, as it breached the 1880 agreement but it nevertheless gained Parliamentary approval. The New Docks Branch left the Midland main line at Tuffley Junction, running to Hempsted Sidings before crossing the canal via a swing bridge to serve the western side of the docks. It did link to the GWR but the western section cannot have produced much traffic and the line was closed beyond Hempsted Sidings in 1938.

The principal trades handled at the docks were timber, wheat and flour, salt, barley, building materials, and wine and spirits, whilst several large engineering and other works were sited in and around the area served by the dock lines. The commercial aspect of the docks lasted well in to the 1960s, before then going in to a steep decline that saw almost all traffic lost by 1980, certainly to the docks

On 21st November 1970, the RCTS's Cotswold Edge Rail Tour heads on to the High Orchard Branch from Eastgate at 12.10pm. Starting out from Birmingham New Street at 9.35am, the Metropolitan-Cammell Class '101' 3-car set had travelled via Stoke Works Junction and Droitwich to Worcester, before then heading back to the Midland main line and south to Gloucester. The ex-GWR Llanthony Yard was visited first, followed by this trip to High Orchard Sidings. The return to Birmingham was via the Honeybourne line, Leamington and Coventry, with the actual arrival noted as 15.53pm. The DMU comprised Driving Motor Brake Second No. 50304 and Driving Motor Composite Lavatory No. 50338, sandwiching Trailer Composite Lavatory No. 59115. Bill Potter/KRM

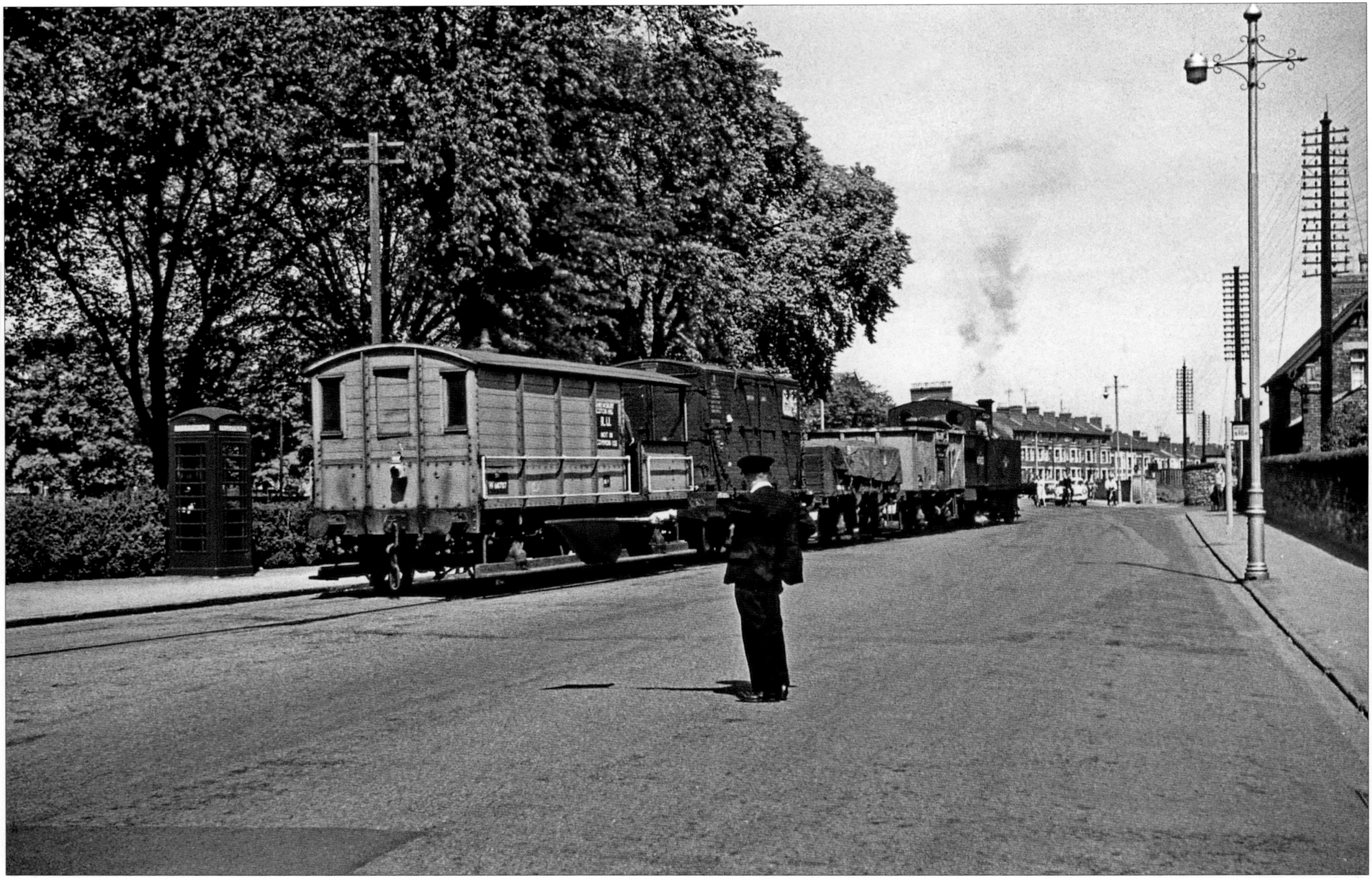

The High Orchard Branch's crossing of Parkend Road was gated at both ends but only over the railway. Rail traffic was never of a level to justify the expense of providing road gates for a crossing which was at such an oblique angle and neither did road traffic, although drivers using this section of highway today might find that difficult to believe. On 13th May 1961, the flagman holds back the few vehicles waiting for Fowler Class '3F' 0-6-0T No. 47623 to cross with a short freight from High Orchard yard. The ex-GWR 'Toad' brake van is labelled 'RU' for Restricted Use and 'NOT IN COMMON USE' but the lettering at the top is sadly not quite decipherable. The 'Jinty' was built for the LM&SR by William Beardmore & Co. of Glasgow in November 1928, one of a batch of sixty the firm completed in the latter part of that year. They had already constructed a batch of fifty-one earlier in 1928 and went on to build another sixty in 1929. Transferred from Sheffield Millhouses to Barnwood shed in May 1955, No. 47623 remained Gloucester-based until November 1963, when it moved down to Bath Green Park for a short stint as a banker prior to being withdrawn in early April 1964. MARK B. WARBURTON

ABOVE AND ABOVE RIGHT: **Two shots from the Gloucestershire Railway Society's afternoon tour of 7th July 1963, which had already visited the Stroud Midland and Nailsworth branches by the time we see it here leaving the High Orchard Branch. The picture above shows the footbridge which gave access over the line from The Park to Weston Road, whilst the second view was taken as the tour was about to cross back over Parkend Road.** BOTH JOHN RYAN

RIGHT: **Meanwhile, photographer Mark Warburton had positioned himself on Parkend Road to capture this view of the tour trundling across under the watchful eye of the flagman and passing behind California Crossing signal box.** MARK B. WARBURTON

BELOW: **The cast iron footbridge in August 1976, after the track had been lifted. A standard product built from a kit and with a span of 42ft 3ins, it did not belong to the MR, being erected by Gloucester Corporation in 1894-95.** BILL POTTER/KRM

themselves, although coasters still occasionally sailed up the canal to serve a petroleum depot below Llanthony Bridge. Now, apart from the repair of historic ships in the old dry dock, all trade to and from the docks has finished and they are a leisure and residential amenity, with the surviving warehouses converted to various uses and nearly all traces of industry long gone.

Rail traffic to and from the Midland's side of docks also dropped markedly after 1963, the year in which the two iconic MR Deeley 0-4-0 Dock tanks, which had proved quite an attraction for photographers during the six years they had spent allocated to Barnwood engine shed, were withdrawn. Hempsted Sidings were officially closed in 1969 but the Hempsted Branch remained open for another eighteen months or so to service the gas works siding, until this too was shut on 14th January 1971. The High Orchard Branch, meanwhile, despite losing most of its connections in 1966-67, also remained open to serve the GRC&W Company's sidings but eventually was also closed completely four days before the Hempsted Branch, on 10th January 1971. The massive redevelopment of the area that has occurred since has wiped out almost all sign of the existence of both branches and the myriad of lines that served the docks. This includes the site of the GWR's Llanthony Yard, which remained in use until 1985 and then lay derelict for many years but now lies beneath the new Gloucester College. Of the extensive network of lines that served the docks, the only visible remaining piece of infrastructure is the three arch brick-built bridge (there is another, well hidden, near the site of Tuffley Junction) that carries Bristol Road over the route of the Hempsted Branch, just before it crossed over the Gloucester & Sharpness Canal.

K178 **Engine Restrictions**—continued

Diesel Engines—continued

350 h.p. Diesel Electric Shunting Locomotives Nos. 15101–15106.

Engine route classification—Uncoloured.*

Maximum Permissible Speed—20 m.p.h.

Average Speed for Timing Purposes—15 m.p.h.

*—These engines are "Yellow" when used for any duty other than shunting.

300 h.p. Diesel Hydraulic Shunting Locomotives, North British Locomotive Company. D.2900.

The above type of Locomotive has been classified "Blue" for route availability purposes over the Western Region subject to the following stipulations:—

Prohibitions:—

All "Uncoloured" and "Yellow" routes.

Stroud Branch.

Nailsworth Branch.

Ashchurch to Upton-on-Severn.

Severn & Wye Line—Sharpness to Speech House Road, including all Branches.

Restrictions:—

Gloucester Docks (Llanthony) Branch ...	To work Main Line only. NOT to work beyond 1 m.p. in Llanthony Yard.
Bullo Docks Branch	To work Main Line only.
Gloucester Docks (High Orchard)	To work Main Line only. NOT to work beyond Level Crossing at Canal End of High Orchard Yard. Not to work from High Orchard Yard in the direction of Merchant's Road or Albion (Goat) Crossing pending tests.
Hempstead (Tuffley) Branch...	To work Main Line only.

204 h.p. Diesel Mechanical Locomotive—D.2XXX.

Engine Route Classification ... ... **Uncoloured**

Subject to the following restrictions over Gloucester High Orchard Branch:—

Merchant's Road Siding	Not to pass the face of Thompson's building. Shunting to be carried out with a minimum of 2 empty wagons.
Fielding and Platt's Siding	Not to pass Drop Shutter Doors, and any shunting to be carried out with one empty wagon.
The Basin	PROHIBITED, with the exception of two long sidings running alongside the Inner Basin Dock.

Left and Below: Details of diesel engine restrictions for the docks branches, from the *Working Time Table of Freight Trains, Gloucester District, 12th June to 10th September 1961.*

Engine Restrictions—continued **K179**

Diesel Engines—continued

B.R. DIESEL LOCOMOTIVES

B.R. Type	Power, etc.	Wheel Arrangements	Route Colour	Class No.
1	800 h.p. diesel electric ... ... (B.T.H. and N.B. Loco.)	B.B. ...	Blue* ...	D.8200 and D.8400.
2	1,000 h.p. diesel electric ... (N.B. Loco.) Also permitted as Single or Double Unit over Yellow routes specially authorised for 53XX class engines.	B.B. ...	Blue ...	D.6100.
†2	1,000 h.p. diesel hydraulic ... (N.B. Loco.)	B.B. ...	Blue ...	D.6300–D.6305.
†2	1,100 h.p. diesel hydraulic ... (N.B. Loco.)	B.B. ...	Yellow ...	D.6306–D.6357.
2	1,100 h.p. diesel electric ... (E.E.C.)	B.B. ...	Red ...	D.5900
2	1,160 h.p. diesel electric ... (B.C. & W.)	B.B. ...	Red ... Blue ...	D.5300–D.5319. D.5320–D.5346.
*2	1,160 h.p. diesel electric ... (B.R. Sulzer.)	B.B. ...	Red ... Blue ...	D.5000–D.5049. D.5050–D.5150.

†—May travel over Yellow routes not exceeding 40 m.p.h. with the following exception:—

Gloucester Docks (High Orchard) ... Not to work past level crossing at Canal end of High Orchard.

***—Restrictions:—**

Gloucester (Docks Branch)...	Care to be taken when working into Branch at Docks Branch Junction. Not to work past 1 m.p.h. in Llanthony Yard, and to work on Main Lines only.
Gloucester (High Orchard)...	To work on Main Line only. Not to work past level crossing at Canal end of High Orchard Branch, or towards Merchants Road or Albion Crossing.
Hempstead (Tuffley Branch)...	To work on Main Line only.
Bullo Docks Branch	To work on Main Line only and speed not to exceed 25 m.p.h.

Working into Sidings will be investigated as the need arises.

General Instructions:—

(*a*) These Locomotives are prohibited over Sidings and connections having a minimum radius of less than 4½ chains.

(*b*) The lateral and horizontal dimensions given for under-clearances as shewn on B.R.L.I. Locomotive gauge must be strictly adhered to, including allowance for maximum drop due to wear on tyres, etc.

Left: Watched by the California Crossing signalman and with a flagman in attendance, an unidentified BR 0-6-0 diesel shunter (later Class '08') rumbles slowly over Parkend Road with just a single brake van in tow. The slide is undated but the Hillman Imp on the left gives us a clue. First manufactured by the Rootes Group in 1963, as a direct competitor to the British Motor Corporation's iconic Mini, this example carries the registration No. HOO 490C, marking it out as a 1965 model; it looks quite new so the picture could well date from that year. In May 1965, Horton Road shed had an allocation of ten of these 0-6-0 diesels. The rails crossed the road at quite an acute angle, such that cyclists had to take care not to let their wheels slip between the rails and flip them off their bikes. David Pollard/NPC

Viewed from across Weston Road, Type '1' 0-6-0 diesel shunter No. D3992 rumbles slowly through the sylvan surroundings of The Park with a trip freight for High Orchard Sidings circa 1970. Built by BR at Derby Works in September 1960, the locomotive became Class '08' No. 08824 under the TOPS scheme in September 1974. Sent new to Tyseley, it transferred to Gloucester Horton Road in December 1961 and stayed there until early February 1973, when it was reallocated to Bristol Bath Road, as Gloucester's requirement for trip shunters had declined dramatically following closure of the docks branches and most of the goods yards. Further allocations to Plymouth Laira and St. Blazey preceeded transfer then to the Eastern Region in 1976. It became part of the English, Welsh & Scottish Railway fleet following the privitisation of BR in 1996, which in turn was acquired by the German national rail operator Deutsche Bahn in 2007, which rebranded the company as part of their logistics arm, DB Schenker, in early 2009; it now trades as DB Cargo UK. No. 08824, meanwhile, was sent to Crewe electric traction depot in 2005, painted in L&NWR black and renumbered as No. IEMD01. In October 2015 it was bought by the Harry Needle Railroad Company and was subsequently stored at the Barrow Hill roundhouse site, where it was photographed apparently stored out of use in December 2018. MIKE SQUIRE/COURTESY THE RESTORATION & ARCHIVING TRUST/REF. MSZZ4291

On 4th June 1962, Class '4F' No. 43924 of Barnwood shed makes its leisurely way through the Park with a short freight from High Orchard Sidings. It is perhaps a little surprising that so few photographs were taken on this attractive section of line but by this date workings were infrequent. The factory buildings visible in the background beyond the chimney was part of Fielding & Platt's extensive engineering works. None of this infrastructure remains today, with the route of the railway here now hidden beneath the A430 Trier Way, which links Parkend Road to Hempsted Lane via a new bridge over the canal. However, the statue in The Park on the right still stands, facing the new road. Bill Potter/KRM

K170 **Engine Restrictions**—continued

ENGINES AUTHORISED Western Region	B.R. Standard	Diesel	L.M. Region	Remarks
GLOUCESTER DOCKS	**BRANCH (HIG**	**H ORCHARD) (including**	**High Orchard Goods Line)**	—Route colour, **Red.**
None...	**All except:—** 4-6-2 71XXX	**All except:—** 10000–10001, 10201, 10202, 10203 } As single & double Units **The following are not to work beyond the level crossing at Canal end of High Orchard Yard:—** 5000–5050, 5300–5319, 5500–5699, 5700–5719, 5900–5909, 6100–6157, 8000–8034, 8200–8236, 8400–8409.	**All except:—** 4-6-2 46200–46212, 46220–46257 2-8-0 53800–53810 4-6-0 No. 46170 0-6-0 57232–57691 0-4-4T 55237–55269 0-6-0T 56151–56376	

Above: Engine restrictions for the High Orchard Branch, from the *Working Time Table of Freight Trains, Gloucester District, 12th June to 10th September 1961*. The route availability was based on the GWR system of No Disc, through Yellow, Blue and Red up to Double Red, so the route availability was high, in theory at least! As can be seen, there was little in the way of locomotive types of the period that were not permitted to work on the line, apart from 'Britannia' and 'Princess Royal' Class 'Pacifics', the ex-S&DJR Class '7F' 2-8-0s, 'Royal Scot' No. 46170 *British Legion* and various smaller ex-MR/LM&SR classes, whilst most ex-GWR classes were barred from going beyond High Orchard Sidings – I think that the level crossing referred to is that where the lines passed over Baker Street/Merchants Road.

LOCAL SERVICES AND TRIPS **K129**

INTER-YARD TRIPS—GLOUCESTER

("K" HEADCODES)

Maximum Load of trips (Weekdays and Sundays) 50 wagons, except those from "T" Sidings to Upper Yard which must not exceed 35 wagons unless agreed by Control.

It should be definitely understood by the whole of the staff concerned that these trips must be given special attention.

Trips from Upper Yard to "T" Sidings to run via the Goods or Main Lines as convenient, and arrangements must be made for a Siding to be available for the reception of the trips at their booked time. The trips must have preference over all other trains except Passenger, Parcels and "C," "D" and "E" Headcode Freight Trains.

WEEKDAYS

		9F53		0B37	9F54		9F54	9F55	0F55 SO		9F55 SX	0F55 SX		0F55 SO		0F56 SX
		a.m.		a.m.	a.m.		a.m.	a.m.	p.m.		p.m.	p.m.		p.m.		p.m.
Barnwood Sidings	dep	....	....	8‖ 0	....	....	....	11 20	....	....	....	....	....	....	....	7‖40
Upper Yard	arr	...	...	...	...	...	...	11 43	...	...	...	...	...	...	...	...
	dep	6 40	....	....	9 50	....	11 0	....	1‖55	....	2 17	5‖35	....	6† 0	....	....
High Orchard	arr	...	...	8‖20	10 0	...	...	...	2‖ 5	...	2 25	5‖45	...	...	...	7‖55
Hempstead Sidings	arr	7 5	....	....	....	....	....	....	....	....	....	....	....	....	....	....
Quedgeley	arr	...	...	...	...	...	11 20	...	...	...	...	...	...	6†20	...	...

		9F56 MX	0F54 SO	0F54	9F53	9F54 SO	9F54 SX	9F55 SO	9F55 SX	0Z55 SO		9F55 SX	9F55 SO	9F56 SX	0B37 SX	9F56 SX Q
		a.m.	a.m.	a.m.	a.m.	p.m.	p.m.	p.m.	p.m.	p.m.		p.m.	p.m.	p.m.	p.m.	p.m.
Quedgeley	dep	....	SUS-	....	....	12 20	12 15	....	....	....	....	....	6 50	....	....	....
Hempstead Sidings	dep	...	PEN-	...	10 30	...	...	...	...	...	...	...	...	...	...	...
High Orchard	dep	....	DED 10‖10	10‖25	....	....	....	2 40	3 15	3‖30	....	6 23	....	8 45	9‖35	....
Upper Yard	arr	...	...	10‖35	10 55	12 43	12 38	2 50	3 25	...	...	Z	7 10	9 5	...	...
	dep	12N40	....	....	12 0	2 0	2 0	....	....	....	....	Z	7 50	....	....	11 25
Barnwood Sidings	arr	12 45	10 22	...	12 5	2 5	2 5	...	...	3‖45	...	6 35	7 55	...	9‖52	11 30

N—Goods Shed.
Z—On Tuesdays and Thursdays, Upper Yard arr. 6.33, dep. 6*52, Barnwood arr. 6.57 p.m.

Right: The local services and inter-yard trip workings serving High Orchard, Hempsted Sidings and RAF Quedgeley, from the *Working Time Table of Freight Trains, Gloucester District, 12th June to 10th September 1961.*

A rare view of two locomotives on the High Orchard Branch on 4th June 1962, with Deeley 0-4-0T No. 41535 at rest whilst No. 43924 alongside gently starts reversing towards the level crossing of Bristol Road, accompanied by a shunter holding his coupling pole. The '4F' was presumably about to couple on to the train of vans which Bill then photographed it hauling past The Park in the previous picture; the trees in the background form the western corner of The Park. The works with the metal chimney on the left was a laundry and there had also been a footbridge over the branch in the foreground, which had been removed a year or two before the picture was taken. No. 43924 was to be transferred away to Bristol Barrow Road shed around ten weeks after this picture was taken and was withdrawn in June 1965, after a working life just shy of forty-five years. Note the crossover points just in front of the '4F'. Bill Potter/KRM

ABOVE: No. 41535 stands on the east side of Southgate Street level crossing circa 1962. I have yet to locate a full view of the crossing, either in black and white or in colour; unfortunately, whilst many came here to photograph the little 0-4-0 dock shunters at work, it seems no one bothered to record the level crossing. This does surprise me, as I would have thought the opportunity to capture a train running across the street would have been too good to resist – but perhaps that's just me! There is a partial view here of it and of Southgate Street Crossing signal box, which had been downgraded to ground frame status since 1954. John Gough's *Midland Chronology* notes '*replacement box 5.7.1904*' but what can be seen of the structure here looks to be an LM&SR design, suggesting it had been replaced again at some stage. The double line was worked Reception inwards and Departure outwards from California Crossing, without block or bell along the 704 yard long section. Onwards from Southgate Street Crossing there was a single line section, worked by train staff, 506 yards to Albion Crossing. Passing in front of the box is a stylish road coach of circa 1951 vintage, probably an A.E.C. 'Regal' chassis with coachwork by Harrington of Hove whose trademark was the dorsal fin at the rear, designed to act as an air extractor as well as for streamlined good looks. Note the ropes hanging from the handrail on No. 41535's smokebox door. NPC

GLOUCESTER HIGH ORCHARD BRANCH

BETWEEN CALIFORNIA STREET CROSSING AND HIGH ORCHARD GOODS YARD

Southgate Street Crossing

Referring to Rule 99, the normal position of the level crossing gates at Southgate Street Crossing is across the railway.

When the Shunter at High Orchard Yard becomes aware that a train proceeding from California Crossing requires to pass over Southgate Street Crossing, or a train requires to proceed from High Orchard Yard over Southgate Street Crossing, he must proceed to Southgate Street Crossing and place the crossing gates across the roadway for the passage of the train.

The crossing gates must be replaced across the railway after the train has passed over the crossing.

The key to the hut at Southgate Street Crossing is kept in the Shunters' cabin at High Orchard Yard.

SINGLE LINE BETWEEN HIGH ORCHARD GOODS YARD AND GLOUCESTER DOCKS

A Shunter must walk in front of propelled wagons on this line, the propelling to be limited to 25 vehicles.

GLOUCESTER DOCKS LINES AND THE LINE IN LLANTHONY ROAD

When wagons are being moved by an engine on any of the Docks lines, or on the line in Llanthony Road leading to and from the Llanthony Yard a Shunter must walk in front to see that the line is clear, that the points are in the proper position, and to warn persons as may be necessary.

Before a train passes in either direction over the curve between the Gloucester Docks line and the line in Llanthony Road, a Shunter must be at the footpath crossing over the curve to warn persons as may be necessary.

BETWEEN HIGH ORCHARD GOODS YARD AND LINES ALONGSIDE GLOUCESTER AND BERKELEY CANAL, AND ON THE MERCHANTS ROAD LINES

A Shunter must walk in front of wagons taken from High Orchard Goods Yard to the lines alongside the canal, and see the line is clear, and that all the points over which the wagons have to pass are in the proper position. Another Shunter must be at the Merchants Road Crossing near to High Orchard Goods Yard, to warn persons approaching on the Merchants Road until the vehicles reach the crossing. He must then place himself in the best position to enable him to repeat to the Driver any signal that may be given by the Shunter who has gone forward to see that the line is clear.

A Shunter must walk in front of each train proceeding towards High Orchard Goods Yard on the lines alongside the canal to see that the line is clear and the points are in the proper position, and each train must be brought to a stand at Messrs. Price and Walker's timber wharf near to the Wagon Works until the Shunter in front has reached the Oil Mills and satisfied himself that all is right for the train to enter the goods yard. He must then signal to the Driver to start, and after doing so must proceed to the Merchants Road Crossing to warn persons approaching on the Merchants Road, and remain there until the engine has passed.

Before the crossing at the junction of Baker Street and Merchants Road is fouled by a train or engine, one of the Shunters must be at the crossing to warn persons approaching the crossing in any direction.

When wagons are being moved by an engine on the lines in the Merchants Road, a Shunter must proceed in front of the wagons to see the line is clear and the points are in the proper position, and to warn persons as may be necessary.

LEFT: Instructions for working the High Orchard Branch, including Southgate Street level crossing and the various lines around the docks and the roads that they ran along or crossed, from the *Sectional Appendix to the Working Time Table, October 1960.*

Taken on 13th May 1961, this picture precedes the view on page 54, with 'Jinty' No. 47623 seen here preparing to leave High Orchard with the short trip freight that was bound for one of the other Gloucester yards. Watched by one of the yard staff, the driver climbs back in to his cab at the same time as the driver of No. 41535, which was engaged on shunting duties around the various dock sidings. Perhaps the men had enjoyed a spot of lunch together in the yard office. Mark B. Warburton

ABOVE: No. 41537 shunts a pair of box vans in High Orchard yard in March 1963. On the right is part of the Atlas Engineering Works of Fielding & Platt Ltd, with Baker Street running unseen between the black corrugated iron clad building and the wagon on the right. Most of the sidings in the yard terminated where the wagons can be seen in the left background, but one continued to turn southwards (left) to then run north and south along Baker's Quay, parallel to the canal; this line served various maltings and mills which fronted the canal, the Gloucester Railway Carriage & Wagon Company's works and timber merchants at Baltic Wharf, further south along the canal. Another line turned right (north) out of the yard to run along Merchants Road. Meanwhile,as we shall see over the page, a further pair of lines curved away to the right behind the box vans, bisecting Fielding & Platt's works, to head to Victoria Dock. PHILIP RILEY/COURTESY THE RESTORATION & ARCHIVING TRUST/REF. ARC12

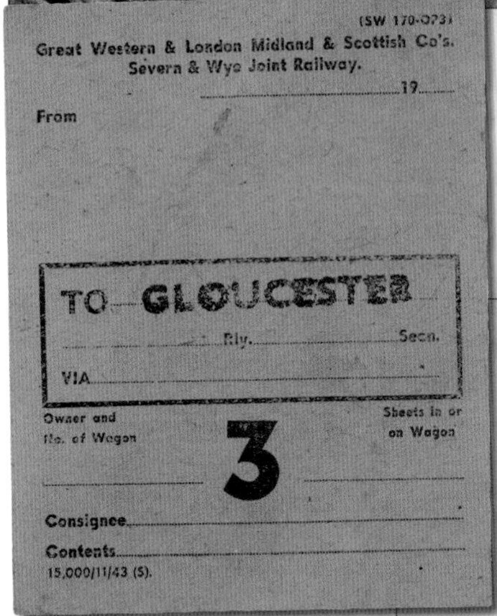
(SW 170-073)
Great Western & London Midland & Scottish Co's.
Severn & Wye Joint Railway.
19
From
TO GLOUCESTER
Rly. Secn.
VIA
Owner and No. of Wagon
3
Sheets in or on Wagon
Consignee
Contents
15,000/11/43 (S).

RIGHT: With a shunters pole perched on its buffer beam, No. 41537 poses for a portrait between duties at High Orchard Sidings on 25th April 1963. The engine is standing a little further to the west of the previous picture, with the part of Fielding & Platt's factory seen behind equating to the roofline visible above the box vans in that view. As an aside, Lightmoor Press co-director Ian Pope's father Alec spent his working life at Fielding & Platt, where he became great friends with Tony Dyer, some of his collection of railway tickets being used to further grace the pages of this series. NPC

LEFT: Gloucester's port had long been important to the local economy, contributing greatly to its growth as a city and industrial centre. This is the cover of a booklet published in 1932, in English, French and German, promoting its facilities. NPC

BELOW: Conversation piece at High Orchard Sidings, as yard staff and the crew of No. 41537 take a brief break between shunting manoeuvres, in a view taken from Southgate Street level crossing in 1961. Almost the full extent of the sidings can be seen behind, overseen by the bulk of Foster Bros oil and cake mill in the left background. Of particular note here is the rail entrance on the right in to the Fielding & Platt factory, via a kick-back off a short stub siding, which meant that anything accidentally running out of the building would not foul one of the shunting lines. Of even greater interest, on the left there is a very rare glimpse of the rear of the Gloucester Railway Carriage & Wagon Company's shunting engine, a Bagnall fireless 0-4-0, Works No. 2871 of 1947 and named *Badgeworth Hall*, which had been here from new. It was shortly to be retired, with dumper trucks then used subsequently, as and when required, for shunting rail vehicles around but was not immediately disposed of, finally going to Hayes Metals of Gloucester in March 1963; it was scrapped in December that year. COLOUR-RAIL

On 12th August 1958, around fifteen months after first being allocated to Barnwood shed, No. 41535 was photographed whilst at rest between duties in High Orchard yard. Baker Street, which ran west from the bottom end of Southgate Street to join Merchants Road, can be seen behind the fence on the right, in front of which a pair of tracks curve away, over the road and through a gap between the buildings of Fielding & Platt's works. In the left background, some box vans can be seen standing on one of these lines beneath the overhead walkway which joined the two portions of the works. Running northwards through this narrow alleyway – which F&P workers nicknamed 'Goat Alley' – and with sidings serving a cabinet works on the west side and Matthews Works on the east side (both removed in 1954), a single track carried all the way out the other end to cross Llanthony Road and reach Victoria Dock, as we shall shortly see. This is the earliest colour view we have taken in the Midland dock system, which suffered some rationalisation in 1961 and post which year most of the pictures that follow were taken. Nevertheless we can present a pretty good picture of what the area looked like and the lines that still remained in the early to mid 1960s over the next few pages. Bill Potter/KRM

No. 41535 at rest in High Orchard yard with Fielding & Platt's works again forming the backdrop, in August 1962. Derek Chaplin

The number of photographs, both in black & white and colour, taken of the two Deeley shunters No's 41535 and 41537 in and around the various railway locations at Gloucester are testament to their popularity – being something a bit different from the norm even in steam days – and the numerous cameramen who tracked them down. Here, in July 1962, No. 41535 reverses past part of Fielding & Platt's premises, whilst carrying out shunting operations in High Orchard yard. Fielding & Platt was founded in October 1866 by Samuel Fielding and James Platt (James Platt also became a director of the Gloucester Railway Carriage & Wagon Company, whose factory was on the opposite side of High Orchard yard), both engineers from Lancashire, to manufacture small machines and engineering components at their Atlas Ironworks in Gloucester. From the early 1870s, the company specialised in hydraulic machinery, after being approached by Ralph Hart Tweddell, who was looking for someone to build the portable hydraulic riveter he had designed, which saw Fielding & Platt rapidly expanding in to world markets subsequently. The wide range of items the company made included marine, stationary, portable and traction engines, and boilers, furnaces, hydraulic presses, travelling cranes and machinary for making girders, with examples of their products being used in the construction of the Forth Bridge and Blackpool Tower. The company finally closed in 2003. Nothing remains of this industrial scene today, whilst the photographer would be standing in the middle of a section of dual carriageway. JOHN STRANGE/NPC

RIGHT: The first of a selection of views of the GRS rail tour of 7th July 1963 that we saw a few pages ago crossing Parkend Road and skirting The Park, in High Orchard yard. Again it is well worth erring on the side of too many as they show various aspects of the infrastructure and works here, all now gone. 'Jinty' No. 47308 stands with its train of three maroon liveried carriages as enthusiasts swarm around the sidings. The two lines in the foreground are those curving away from the yard northwards between the premises of Fielding & Platt to Victoria Dock. Behind the train is part of the vast works of the Gloucester Railway Carriage & Wagon Company. Some of their buildings, a little further to the south and fronting on to Bristol Road, do still remain in other commercial use today. JOHN RYAN

ABOVE: Looking eastwards, with the level crossing over Bristol Road in the right background and No. 47308 having run round its train ready for departure, as enthusiasts climb back on board. The crossing was situated at the point where Southgate Street met Bristol Road and the railway company named it Southgate Street Crossing. BILL POTTER/KRM

LEFT: As proof of the fact that each of these pictures shows something a little different, there is a glimpse here in the left background (and the rather cruel inset enlargement) of the rarely pictured Southgate Street Crossing signal box, which had been closed as a block post and downgraded to ground frame status in 1954. There is also a closer partial view of the brick-built yard office on the right. BILL POTTER/KRM

RIGHT: A side-on study of the 'Jinty' that hauled the tour. Class '3F' No. 47308 was an early LM&SR era build, coming new from the Hunslet Engine Company of Leeds on 31st March 1925. It was not a Gloucester-based engine and was to be withdrawn just over a year after these pictures were taken, from Bath Green Park shed in August 1964. Incidetally, the High Orchard name, after which the immediate area and subsequently the yard became known, dates to Medieval times. In 1135, the monks of Llanthony Priory in the Black Mountains of Wales were driven out and founded a daughter cell in Gloucester, Llanthony Secunda Priory; the 'High Orchard' of fruit trees was on land which was owned by the priory. BILL POTTER/KRM

LEFT: A little more detail in this three-quarter view of the locomotive as it runs round its train, showing the door in the western end of the yard office. This was the last enthusiast tour to visit the yard in all its glory; severe rationalisation of the High Orchard Branch saw the sidings here cut back to just four in 1966-67, plus two short stubs presumably for crippled wagons, with the line to Victoria Dock lifted completely; the Merchants Road siding remained and there was also still a connection in to the GRC&W Co. works. BILL POTTER/KRM

RIGHT: High Orchard Sidings on 10th October 1970, with the DMU forming the Dean Forest Railway Preservation Society's Severnside rail tour visiting. It was not immediately apparent in which direction we were looking here, until a website was found with a couple of aerial views of Fielding & Platt's works taken in the late 1960s and early 1970s respectively. These showed the large new building to the right of the DMU under construction; it was a new Assembly Hall for F&P and was built on the site of the sidings seen to the left of the 'Jinty' above. It too has not survived closure of F&P's engineering works. The factory buildings to the left are part of the GRC&W Co. works, which also feature in the left background of the picture at the top of the previous page. Another view of this rail tour, arriving at Llanthony Yard on the ex-GWR side of the docks, can be found on page 42 of the first volume in this series, *West Gloucester & Wye Valley Lines* (2nd edition 2018), along with a ticket for the tour. The light was seemingly starting to fade by the time the DMU reached High Orchard, as indicated by the glowing electric lamp on the wall on the left, although the tour still had to visit Sharpness after leaving here, before returning to Newport via the Severn Tunnel. BILL POTTER/KRM

No. 41535 shunting wagons on Merchants Road alongside the premises of the AEI Lamp & Lighting Co. Ltd on 4th June 1962. Associated Electrical Industries was formed in 1928 through the merger of British Thomson-Houston Company Ltd and Metropolitan-Vickers Ltd, and was a well known name at this time, with premises all over the country. In 1967, AEI was acquired by the General Electric Co. (GEC), creating the UK's largest electrical group. The whole industrial area surrounding the docks was once served by a complicated network of interlacing lines, established at a time when the railways nationally were the main carrier for all manner of goods. With the gradual erosion of this dominance by road transport over the decades following the two world wars, by the date of this view the battle for goods traffic had largely been lost, with road transport not bound by BR's common carrier status, which meant that any and all loads had to be accepted, able to siphon off virtually all of the profitable aspects of the business. This siding originally ran the length of Merchants Road but had been shortened in 1961, with the section beyond the train beneath the grey lorry having been lifted. Merchants Road is today an upmarket, stone-paved, pedestrian thoroughfare, bordered on one side by the Gloucester Quays outlet village but, perhaps surprisingly, the AEI buildings seen here still remain, now occupied by a company manufacturing concrete moulds. Bill Potter/KRM

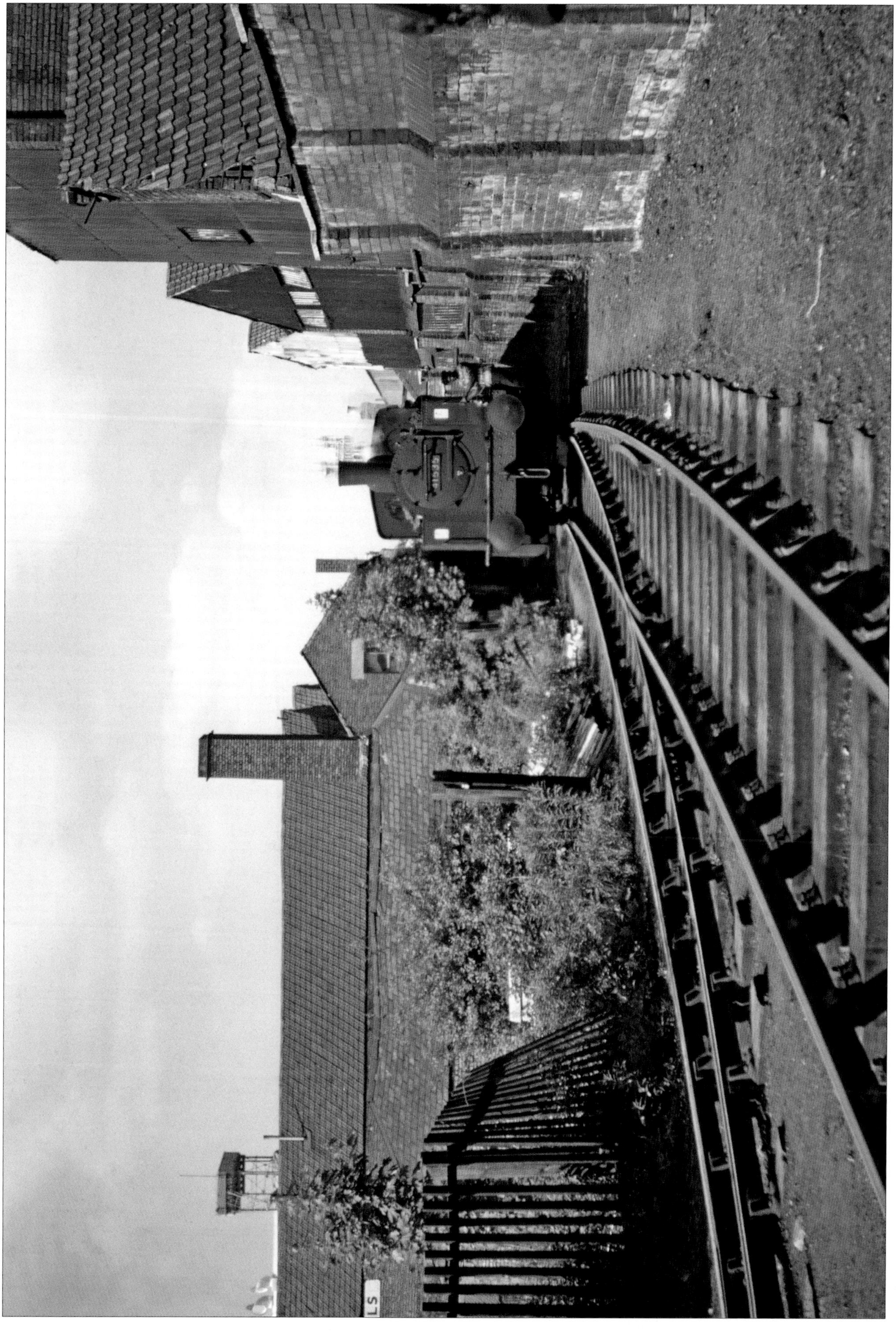

A scene so completely lost today that the tower of Gloucester Cathedral in the background is the only thing in sight that still remains. Taken on the same day as the previous picture, No. 41535 approaches Llanthony Road crossing as it leaves Victoria Dock. Note the West Indian fireman perched on the front footplate, who will guide the engine safely across the road. Quite a number of the so-called 'Windrush Generation' of migrants found employment on BR and with London Underground. The line to the left made its way along Llanthony Road and over the swing bridge to the ex-GWR side. BILL POTTER/KRM

ABOVE: Taken shortly after the previous picture, the driver of No. 41535 waits for the fireman to signal it is safe to procced over Llanthony Road crossing with a short train of vans from Victoria Docks. Views in and around the docks system are scarce, particularly in colour, so despite the similarity of the two pictures they both merit inclusion. The route of the railway here is now a private car park and walkway, bounded on both sides by new buildings. BILL POTTER/KRM

K41

LOCAL SERVICES AND TRIPS—continued

INTER-YARD TRIPS—GLOUCESTER

It should be definitely understood by the whole of the staff concerned that these trips must be given special attention.

Trips from Upper Yard to New Yard must not exceed 50 wagons and trips from "T" Sidings to Upper Yard which must not exceed 35 wagons unless agreed by Control.

Trips from New Yard to Docks Branch Sidings must not exceed 60 wagons.

Trips from New Yard to Old Yard must not exceed 30 wagons.

Trips from Over Sidings to Barnwood must not exceed 50 wagons.

Trips from Docks Branch Sidings to Vew Yerd must not exceed 54 wagons.

Trips from Upper Yard to New Yard to run via the Goods or Main Lines as convenient, and arrangements must be made for a Siding to be available for the reception of the trips at their booked time. The trips must have preference over all other trains except Passenger, Parcels and "C," "D" and "E" Head Code Freight Trains.

	9F60	9F60	9F53	9F53	9B48	9F60	9F53	9F60							
	MX														
	am	am	am	am	am	am	am	am							
Barnwood Sidings .. dep	..	..	..	..	..	..	..	..	..	..	..	..	..	..	..
New Yard	5 18	6 30	6 55	7 30	8 22	8 33	8 52								
Upper Yard	..	..	7* 0	7*50	..	8 38	..	9 30	..	..	..	..	..	..	..
Eastgate Goods Yard															
Old Yard	5 25	6 38	..	..	..	..	9 0	..	..	..	..	..	..	..	..
High Orchard								9 45							
D.B.S. Sidings	..	..	..	..	8 38	..	..	..	..	..	..	..	..	..	..
Hempsted				8 5											
Quedgeley .. arr	..	..	..	..	..	..	..	..	..	..	..	..	..	..	..

	9F52 SX 9F60 SO	9F60	9F57	9F60	9F60	9F60	9B48								
		SX	SX	SO	SX	SX		SX							
	am	am	PM	PM	PM	PM	PM	PM							
Barnwood Sidings .. dep	11 40	..	11 50	..	..	..	..	..	..	..	..	..	..	..	..
New Yard		11 10	12 0	2 30	3 30	6 0	11 45	1 35							
Upper Yard	12 10	..	..	2 35	3 35	6 5	..	..	..	..	..	..	..	..	..
Eastgate Goods Yard															
Old Yard	..	..	..	..	..	..	..	1 43	..	..	..	..	..	..	..
High Orchard															
D.B.S. Sidings	..	..	..	..	..	..	12 0	..	..	..	..	..	..	..	..
Hempsted							m'nt.								
Quedgeley .. arr	..	11 30	..	..	..	..	..	..	..	..	..	..	..	..	..

LEFT: The local services and inter-yard trip workings serving High Orchard, Hempsted Sidings and RAF Quedgeley, from the *Working Time Table of Freight Trains, Gloucester District, 17th June to 8th September 1963*. Note that the five daily weekdays trips to High Orchard shown in the 1961 WTT extract on page 58 had now dwindled to just one daily working, from the Upper Yard at 9.30am, arriving at 9.45am. Departure times are shown in the extract on the next page.

Right: The return trips, from the *Working Time Table of Freight Trains, Gloucester District, 17th June to 8th September 1963*. The single return working from High Orchard is shown as departing at 1.00pm on Saturdays and 4.50pm on weekdays, with just 10 minutes allowed in this direction for the journey to Upper Yard. The latter is the ex-Midland goods yard which was situated between the two stations and pictures of it can be found in the previous volume.

K42

LOCAL SERVICES AND TRIPS—continued

Inter-Yard Trips—Gloucester—continued

	9B08	9F57	9F60	9F60	9F52	9F57	9F57	9F60	9F60	9F59
	MX			SX			Q	SX	SO	SX
	am	am	am	am	am	am	am	PM	PM	PM
Quedgeley dep	..	..	..	..	..	..	..	12 50	..	..
Hempsted	..	..	..	..	10 30	..	..	..	..	..
Over Sidings	..	..	..	..	..	10 50	..	..	..	..
D.B.S. Sidings	1 35	..	..	..	..	..	..	..	..	..
High Orchard	..	..	..	..	..	..	..	..	1 0	..
Old Yard	..	..	..	..	..	..	11 35	..	..	1 5
Eastgate Goods Yard	..	..	..	..	..	..	..	..	..	..
Upper Yard arr	..	..	..	..	..	..	..	1 13	1 10	..
Upper Yard dep	..	6 40	9 5	10 15	..	..	..	2 0	..	..
New Yard	..	6 45	..	10E 20	..	..	..	..	..	1 10
Barnwood Sidings arr	1 51	..	9 10	..	10 55	11 5	11 40	2 5	..	..

	9F60		9F57	9F60		9F60	9F60	9F52
	SO	SX	SO	SX	SO	SX	SO	SX
	PM	PM	PM	PM	PM	PM	PM	PM
Quedgeley dep	..	..	..	..	..	..	..	..
Hempsted	..	..	..	..	..	..	..	..
Over Sidings	..	..	..	..	..	..	..	..
D.B.S. Sidings	..	2 57	..	..	..	..	..	..
High Orchard	..	..	..	4 50	..	..	..	..
Old Yard	..	..	3 15	..	..	..	..	5 35
Eastgate Goods Yard	..	..	..	..	..	..	..	..
Upper Yard arr	..	..	..	5 0	..	..	..	..
Upper Yard dep	2 15	..	..	..	5 5	5 20	..	..
New Yard	2 20	..	3 20	..	5 10	5 25	5 30	5 40
Barnwood Sidings arr	..	3 10	..	..	..	..	5 45	..

	9F59	9F60	9F52	9F52	9F52	9F57		9B08
								SUN
	Q	SX	SX	SX	SX Q	SX		
	PM	PM	PM	PM	PM	PM		am
Quedgeley dep	..	..	..	..	..	..	..	..
Hempsted	..	..	..	..	..	..	..	..
Over Sidings	..	..	..	..	..	..	..	..
D.B.S. Sidings	..	..	..	..	..	..	..	..
High Orchard	..	..	..	..	..	..	..	1 55
Old Yard	6 20	..	6 35	7 15	..	..	..	..
Eastgate Goods Yard	..	..	..	..	9S15	11 0	..	..
Upper Yard arr	..	6 15	..	..	..	..	..	..
Upper Yard dep	..	..	..	..	..	..	..	..
New Yard	..	..	6 40	..	9 30	..	..	..
Barnwood Sidings arr	6 25	6 20	..	7 20	..	11 15	..	2 8

E—Engineers Sidings.

S—Shed.

Below: No. 41537 rounds the north-east corner of Victoria Dock with a short train of box vans in March 1963. Prominent in the left background is Priday, Metford & Company's flour mill, which they had taken over in 1886; they were originally built in the 1850s as the City Flour Mills. The suction plant seen here was installed in the 1920s, with an overhead conveyer taking grain to the mill. Wheat deliveries switched from barge to road transport in the 1970s and the mill closed in 1994 but the building survives, minus the unloading equipment, along with all of the other properties partly in view behind the train. A pedestrian walkway now follows the route of the rails.
Philip Riley/Courtesy the Restoration & Archiving Trust/Ref. arc11

Left: A second view of No. 41537 alongside Victoria Dock in March 1963, on its way back towards Llanthony Road crossing. The dock was opened in 1849 and is entered by a narrow cut in the east side of the main basin. Its excavation in the late 1840s provided soil for the lengthy railway embankment between the River Severn and Over Junction, constructed by the Gloucester & Dean Forest Railway. In the left background are the Victoria Warehouse of 1849, furthest, which still remains but minus its wooden extension, and the Britannia Warehouse of 1861, which was completely rebuilt in a similar style following a major fire in 1989, is now apartments. The smaller buildings have all gone. LM&SR No. 1537 was at Gloucester by March 1930, staying here until withdrawal as No. 41537 in October 1963.
Philip Riley/Courtesy the Restoration & Archiving Trust/Ref. arc10

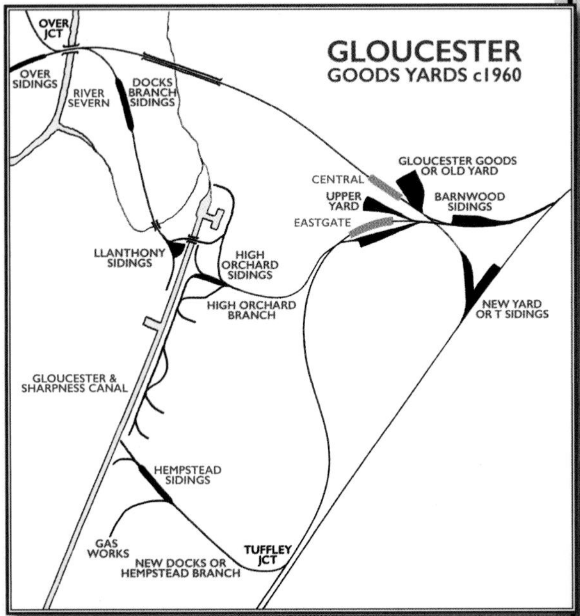

Above: Map showing the the various sidings, goods yards and locations around Gloucester referred to in the trip working and shunting engines WTT extracts.

K181

Shunting Engines—continued

STATION	Engine No.	Starting Time	AUTHORISED HOURS Mon.	Tues.	Wed.	Thur.	Fri.	Sat.	Sun.	Total Hours per Week	PARTICULARS OF WORK
Gloucester (Barnwood Sidings) (Diesel)	7	7.15 a.m.	$16\frac{3}{4}$	$18\frac{7}{12}$	$18\frac{7}{12}$	$18\frac{7}{12}$	$18\frac{7}{12}$	$14\frac{7}{12}$	$3\frac{1}{2}$	h. m. 109 10	Shunts Barnwood Sidings until 1.50 a.m. **MX** 3.30 a.m. (**Suns.**). On Saturdays finish at 2.0 p.m. (or as ordered), re-start 6.0 p.m.
Gloucester (Upper Yard) (F.52) (Diesel)	8	6 .0 a.m.	$16\frac{1}{4}$	$21\frac{1}{4}$	$21\frac{1}{4}$	$21\frac{1}{4}$	$21\frac{1}{4}$	$21\frac{1}{4}$	—	122 30	Shunts Upper Yard, and works 2.50 a.m. **MX** Upper Yard to "T" Sidings. Stables in Wagon Repairs Sidings from 10.15 p.m. **SX**, until 1.0 a.m. **MX**. Proceeds to Central Shed 10.15 p.m. **SO**.
Gloucester (Goods Yard) (Target 14) (F.54)	10	6.10 a.m.	$7\frac{11}{12}$	$7\frac{11}{12}$	$7\frac{11}{12}$	$7\frac{11}{12}$	$7\frac{11}{12}$	$12\frac{3}{4}$	—	52 20	5‖55 a.m. ex Shed shunts Goods Yard, then works 8.0 a.m. Upper Uard to "T" Sidings, 8.35 a.m. "T" Sidings to Upper Yard, 9.50 a.m. Upper Yard to High Orchard, 10‖25 a.m. **SX** L.E. High Orchard to Upper Yard, 11.0 a.m. **SX** Upper Yard to Quedgeley, 12.15 p.m. **SX** Quedgeley to Upper Yard and Barnwood, 10‖10 a.m. **SO** L.E. High Orchard to Barnwood, 11.20 a.m. **SO** Barnwood to Upper Yard, 11.55 a.m. **SO Q** Upper Yard to "T" Sidings, 12.30 p.m. **SO Q** "T" Sidings to Upper Yard, 12‖45 p.m. **SO** L.E. Upper Yard to High Orchard, 1.15 p.m. **SO** High Orchard to Upper Yard and Barnwood, 2‖20 p.m. **SO** L.E. Barnwood to Upper Yard, 4.35 p.m. **SO** Upper Yard to "T" Sidings, 5.10 p.m. **SO** "T" Sidings to Upper Yard, 6.0 p.m. E.B.V. **SO** Upper Yard to Quedgeley, 6.50 p.m. **SO** Quedgeley to Upper Yard and Barnwood.
Gloucester (Goods Yard) (F.58)	11	6. 0 p.m. **SX**	4	4	4	4	4	—	—	20 0	5‖45 p.m. ex Shed. Shunts Goods Yard and Upper Yard as required. Also works 7.30 p.m. Goods Yard to Upper Yard, 7.55 p.m. Upper Yard to Goods Yard.
Gloucester (High Orchard and Docks)	12	8.20 a.m.	$13\frac{1}{4}$	$13\frac{1}{4}$	$13\frac{1}{4}$	$13\frac{1}{4}$	$13\frac{1}{4}$	5	—	71 15	Shunts High Orchard–Docks. On Saturdays leaves High Orchard L.E. for Shed at 1.35 p.m. During the period whilst livestock is dealt with temporarily at Eastgate the engine will shunt at the Pens until 7.0 p.m. or finish.
Gloucester (Hempstead) (F.53)	13	5.40 a.m.	$6\frac{5}{12}$	$6\frac{5}{12}$	$6\frac{5}{12}$	$6\frac{5}{12}$	$6\frac{5}{12}$	$6\frac{5}{12}$	—	38 30	Works 5.40 a.m. Upper Yard to "T" Sidings. Light Engine ex "T" Sidings. 6.40 a.m. Upper Yard to Hempstead. 10.30 a.m. ex Hempstead and 12.0 noon Upper Yard to Barnwood Sidings.
Gloucester ... ... (F.55)	14	11.20 a.m.	$7\frac{1}{12}$	$7\frac{1}{12}$	$7\frac{1}{12}$	$7\frac{1}{12}$	$7\frac{1}{12}$	—	—	35 25	Works 11.20 a.m. Barnwood Sidings to Upper Yard. 12.30 p.m. Upper Yard to "T" Sidings, 1.10 p.m. "T" Sidings to Upper Yard, 2.17 p.m. Upper Yard to High Orchard, 3.15 p.m. High Orchard to Upper Yard, 4.35 p.m. Upper Yard to "T" Sidings, 5.10 p.m. "T" Sidings to Upper Yard. 5‖35 p.m. Light Engine Upper Yard to High Orchard, 6.23 p.m. High Orchard to Barnwood.

A—Works 5.45 a.m. Freight ex Gloucester (daily); shunts Stroud Yard. (Assists 8.0 a.m. Passenger ex Cheltenham from Stroud to Kemble, when required), then proceeds to Brimscombe for assisting Up Trains or Shunting. Shunts at Stroud from 3.25 p.m. **SX** and, upon completion, assists 8.40 p.m. Gloucester to Old Oak Common from Stroud to Sapperton Sidings, when required, unless by arrangement it is more advantageous to do so from Brimscombe. Thence take up Banking requirements. Proceed to Gloucester Shed 8.10 a.m. (Tuesday to Saturdays) for re-servicing, but on the occasions the 8.0 a.m. Passenger ex Cheltenham is assisted, this engine to be intercepted at Stroud to berth Tail traffic off 7.35 a.m. rail car ex Gloucester and 7.58 a.m. Passenger ex Swindon on advice.

On Saturdays shunts at Stroud from approximately 1.0 p.m. To work 1.50 p.m. **SO** Passenger, Stroud to Gloucester when required, in which case engine to be returned to Stroud immediately. Assist 8.55 a.m. Parcels ex Fishguard from Stroud to Sapperton Sidings, afterwards proceeding to Gloucester Shed unless otherwise ordered by Control.

C—Off Shed 5.5 a.m. **MX**, 7.35 a.m. **MO**. Works 5.18 a.m. **MX** "T" Sidings to Old Yard. 6.35 a.m. **MX** "T" Sidings to Old Yard. 9.10 a.m. and 11.45 a.m. Over Sidings to Barnwood, thence to Shed. (Additional trip 10.30 a.m. ex Over Sidings or Dock Branch Sidings by Control arrangements.)

Right: Details of the shunting engines for the various Gloucester yards and the docks lines, including the hours to be worked and where they were time-tabled to be, from the *Working Time Table of Freight Trains, Gloucester District, 12th June to 10th September 1963.*

A superb evocation of dock-side shunting, as No. 41535 comes off the line that ran the length of Baker's Quay, to head back to High Orchard Sidings on 4th June 1962. The view is looking south along the Gloucester & Sharpness Canal and the short train has just passed by the Foster Bros oil and cake mill built in 1862, which had a wooden frontal extension that was again carried over the quay on pillars. Also known as Llanthony Provender Mill, it was Grade II listed but empty and derelict when it was almost completely destroyed by a pair of teenage arsonists on 3rd October 2015, who were subsequently jailed for their crime. A block of new apartments built on the site since were constructed to a similar and sympathetic design. The new High Orchard lift bridge now carries St. Ann's Way across the canal just beyond the barge moored to the quay, linking Southgate Street/Bristol Road with Llanthony Road. Bill Potter/KRM

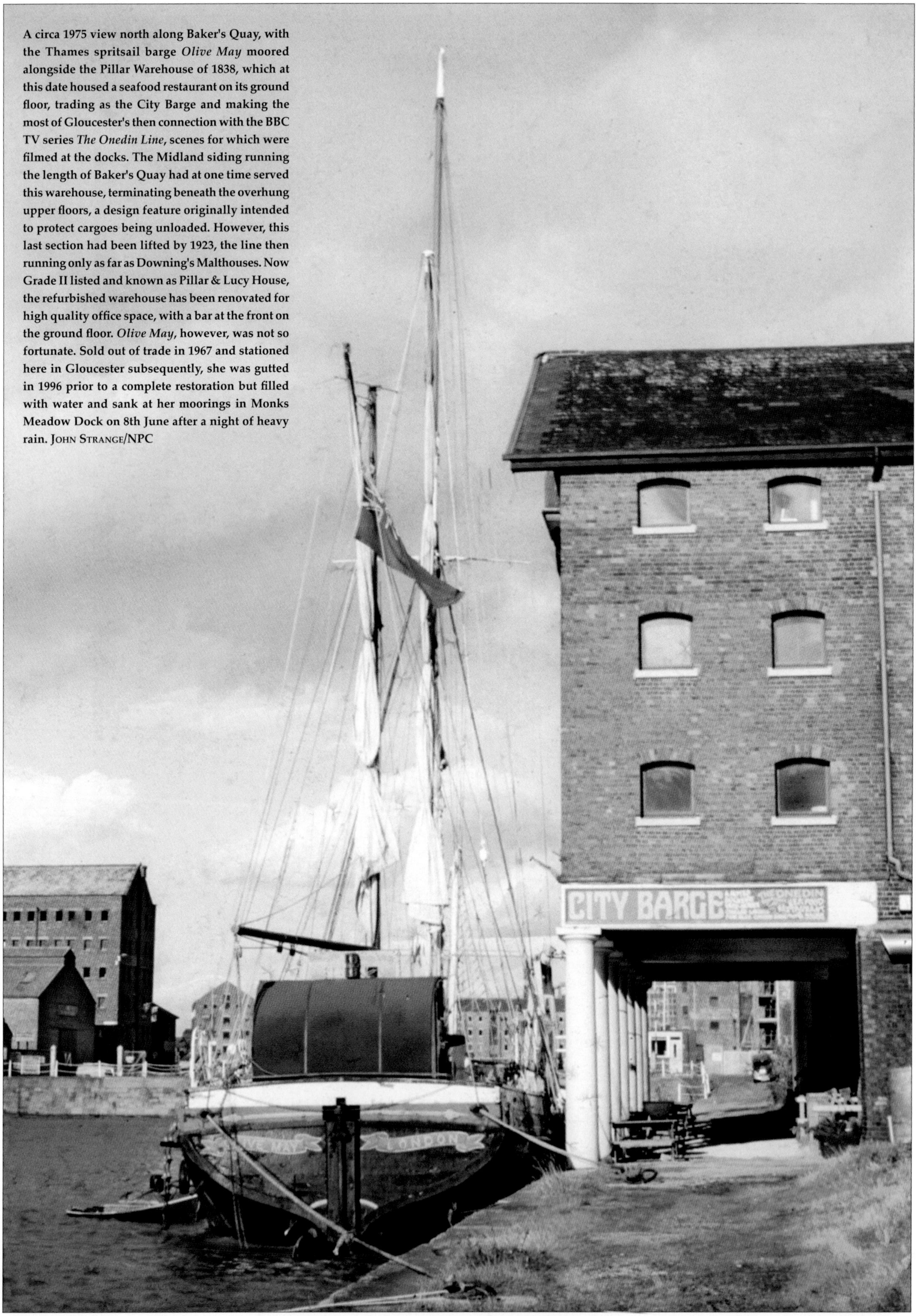

A circa 1975 view north along Baker's Quay, with the Thames spritsail barge *Olive May* moored alongside the Pillar Warehouse of 1838, which at this date housed a seafood restaurant on its ground floor, trading as the City Barge and making the most of Gloucester's then connection with the BBC TV series *The Onedin Line*, scenes for which were filmed at the docks. The Midland siding running the length of Baker's Quay had at one time served this warehouse, terminating beneath the overhung upper floors, a design feature originally intended to protect cargoes being unloaded. However, this last section had been lifted by 1923, the line then running only as far as Downing's Malthouses. Now Grade II listed and known as Pillar & Lucy House, the refurbished warehouse has been renovated for high quality office space, with a bar at the front on the ground floor. *Olive May*, however, was not so fortunate. Sold out of trade in 1967 and stationed here in Gloucester subsequently, she was gutted in 1996 prior to a complete restoration but filled with water and sank at her moorings in Monks Meadow Dock on 8th June after a night of heavy rain. JOHN STRANGE/NPC

RIGHT: The German coaster *Marianne-C* of Rendsburg discharging a cargo of grain for West Midlands Farmers at Bakers Quay in August 1975. Built at Hamburg in 1958, she was originally named Nordkyn, becoming *Marianne-C* under the ownership of Max Claussen in 1966. The year after this picture was taken she changed ownership and was renamed *Moana-M*, then becoming *Moana-B* in 1986. Sold to Argentine owners in 1989, her name changed again to *Nordic*, then *Antilles Star* in 1992, *Cayacoa* in 1995 and *Progreso I* in 2000. Records of her disappear after 2012. The roofless Downing's Malthouses can be seen just in front of the vessel, with the Pillar Warehouse beyond. DENNIS PARKHOUSE

LEFT: Looking south down the Gloucester & Sharpness Canal from a vessel passing through Llanthony swing bridge in June 1966, with the Pillar Warehouse on the left and Downing's Malthouses behind the coaster *Anthony M*. On the right, railway wagons can be seen in front of the British Waterways warehouse on Llanthony Quay. NPC

RIGHT: The view back up the canal towards Llanthony swing bridge, showing the stern of *Anthony M*, which was moored between the Pillar Warehouse and Downings Maltings. Built in 1944 for the German Navy as *Gohren* (which is a small resort on the Baltic coast of northern Germany), she was captured in 1945 and operated by the Ministry of War Transport as *Empire Tigity*. London-based Metcalf Motor Coasters Ltd took ownership of the vessel in 1947, renaming her *Anthony M* and she was sold to Effluent Services Ltd of Macclesfield in 1970, who changed her name again to *Kinder*. She was scrapped at Garston Dock in 1983. NPC

LEFT: Looking back again but from a little further south, showing the full canalside frontage of the then roofless Downing's Malthouses on the right. These were rail served from the quayside/front and from a siding on the south side, whilst further large malthouse buildings at the rear had their own siding on Merchants Road, with the upper floors of them all being connected by covered walkways. They remain derelict and undeveloped at the time of writing. The structure in the right foreground, a corrugated iron transit shed built by the Midland Railway in 1867, also still (just) stands today and hopefully will be refurbished and retained. The coaster *Con-Brio* on the left is moored alongside British Waterways Llanthony Depot. The vessel was Dutch-built in 1958 and is recorded as still in existence under the flag of Curaçao in the Dutch Antilles but little else could be gleaned about her. NPC

RIGHT: The trip boat *Belle* at the entrance to the lock connecting the main basin and the River Severn in June 1966. Many of these pictures of the docks were taken from on board the vessel as it made its way south down the canal to Sharpness, the trip having started out some way north of here at Stourport on Severn; it was on the return journey when seen here. Vinings Warehouse (lettered Reynolds Flour Mills) still stands (now with Reynolds Warehouse painted on it in a similar style), along with the actual Reynolds Warehouse beyond it, as does the lower Biddle Warehouse beyond. Llanthony Warehouse at the far end now houses the British Waterways Museum. However, an infill construction now blocks the view from here of the Britannia and Albert warehouses facing on to Victoria Dock behind. NPC

LEFT: A view much earlier in the day from the bow of *Belle* as it nosed out of the lock and in to the main basin. A line of rails had been carried over the lock at about the point where the boat is here. An extension of one of a pair of sidings in front of the North Warehouse, it ran to a wagon turntable in front of the Lock Warehouse, out of sight on the photographer's right, from which a single siding then ran the length of the West Quay in front of the West Quay Warehouses. It remained in place in to the 1960s but was latterly little used. There had been a second line, which ran out on to Commercial Road and then swung west to cross the bridge at the north or river end of the lock and run along Severn Road to Llanthony Yard but this was removed circa 1930. NPC

A March 1963 view over the Main Basin to the North Warehouse, with a rare glimpse of a rake of box vans on the North Quay. In the right near foreground, behind the British Waterways tug *Stanegarth*, can be seen the entrance to the Barge Arm, which was built in 1824-25 as a place where smaller craft could be unloaded without blocking up quay space around the Main Basin, which could therefore be kept clear for the larger sea-going sailing ships arriving here. Llanthony Warehouse just features on the right and facing it across the Barge Arm are, respectively, Biddle Warehouse, built in 1830, and Shipton Warehouse, completed three years later. Many of the warehouses were named after the men who financed their construction, in these cases Stroud-based miller John Biddle and the merchant J.M. Shipton. They remain today, converted as residential apartments, whilst the North Warehouse was refurbished and is now the main offices for Gloucester City Council. The rails of the two sidings remain in front of it, with a steam crane standing on one as a static display. The large modern block in the background was the then recently constructed new Bearland police station, which looked down on to Gloucester prison. NPC

Looking north across the Main Basin in April 1966, towards the entrance lock from the River Severn, with the North Warehouse on the right, with two cranes, one on tyres and one rail-mounted, in front and the Lock Warehouse in the centre. The bridge that carried the railway track on to West Quay and which was for wagons only, had crossed the lock just behind the gates. On the left can be seen five of the nine West Quay Warehouses, built between 1830 and 1834 but out of use and derelict by the date of this picture; they were all demolished a year or two later. DAVID BICK/NPC

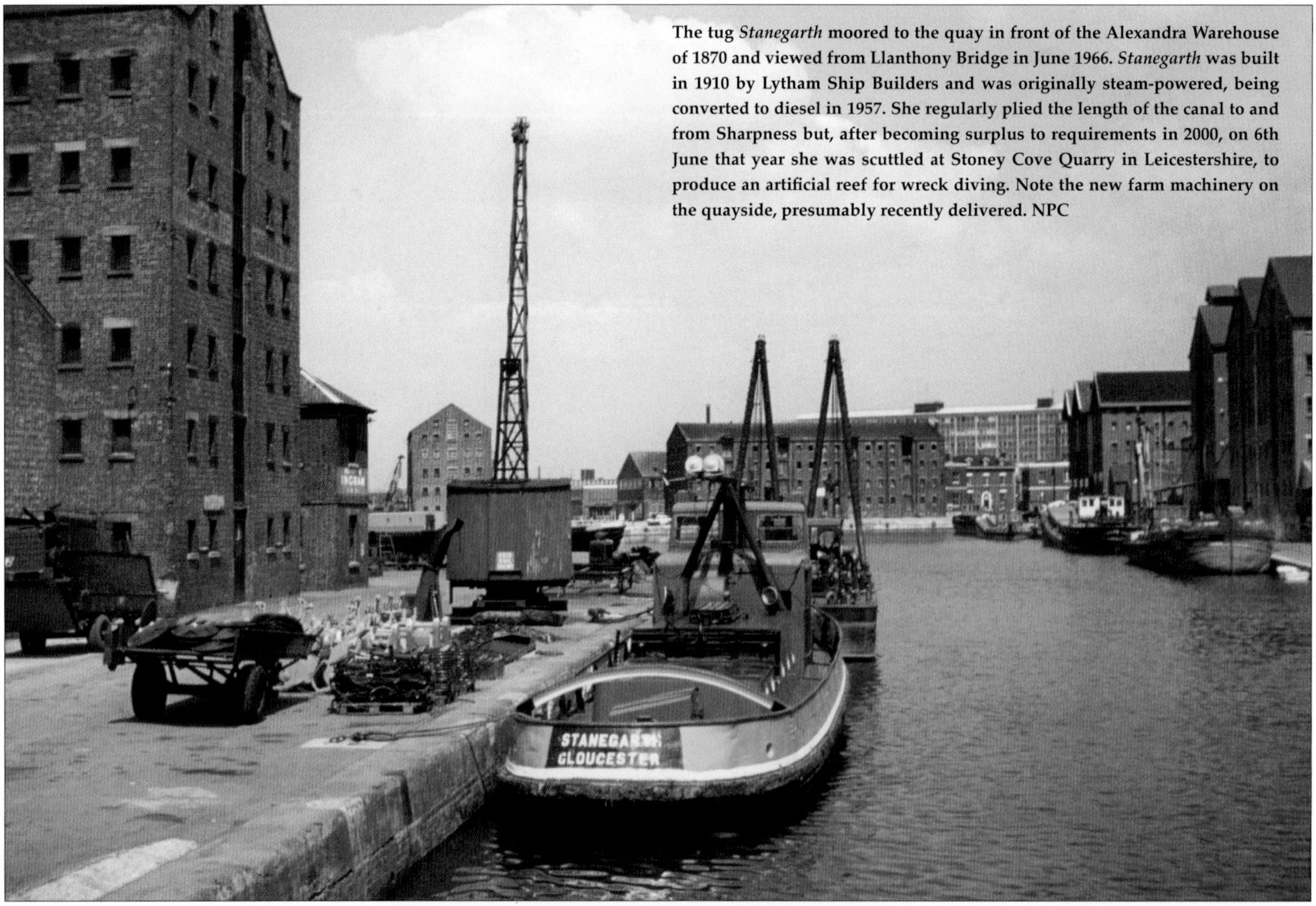

The tug *Stanegarth* moored to the quay in front of the Alexandra Warehouse of 1870 and viewed from Llanthony Bridge in June 1966. *Stanegarth* was built in 1910 by Lytham Ship Builders and was originally steam-powered, being converted to diesel in 1957. She regularly plied the length of the canal to and from Sharpness but, after becoming surplus to requirements in 2000, on 6th June that year she was scuttled at Stoney Cove Quarry in Leicestershire, to produce an artificial reef for wreck diving. Note the new farm machinery on the quayside, presumably recently delivered. NPC

Above Left and Right: Two studies of the semaphore crossbar signal which protected Llanthony swing bridge, taken circa 1965 and on 3rd May 1964 respectively. When the red crossbar faced the canal, as here, it informed vessels that the bridge was closed, turning through ninety degrees to face road traffic when it was opened. The lamp above performed a similar role with red and white lights alternating in the aspects. The full height of the Alexandra Warehouse can be seen behind; it has been converted for use by the University of the West of England in recent years, as their Gloucester campus and library. Note the rails embedded in the road; this line linked the GWR and Midland systems on either side of the canal. David Pollard/NPC; John Ryan

Right: Llanthony swing bridge as seen from the trip boat Belle heading through in June 1966. This bridge was a replacement for an earlier wooden bridge of 1794, built in 1862 and laid with lines of mixed broad and standard gauge rails in order that the GWR and the Midland could both make use of it and share trade to an extent on both sides of the canal. Seen here near the end of its life, it was replaced in 1972 by the present bascule lift bridge, road use of which is now restricted to buses, taxis and bicycles only. NPC

After another day's trip working and shunting at the docks, No. 41535 makes its way light engine back to Barnwood shed, through Eastgate and past Gloucester Goods Junction, on 4th June 1962. The Horton Road coaling stage ramp can be seen in the left background, with a glimpse of locomotives on shed on the right, through the gap between No. 41535 and the carriage. The MR '1528' Class 0-4-0Ts were designed by Richard Deeley as 'Yard Shunting Engines', the first batch of five being built in 1907, with five more then following in 1921-22 under the reign of Henry Fowler. No. 1530 of the first batch went new to Gloucester in 1907 and the long association of the class with the area was what led to them also being referred to as 'Dock Tanks'. Note the miniature shunt signal in the foreground. Bill Potter/KRM

SECTION 3

THE BRISTOL & GLOUCESTER LINE
THE TUFFLEY LOOP

'Jubilee' No. 45739 *Ulster* blasts away from Barton Street Junction bound for Bristol Temple Meads in March 1962. The locomotive was based at Leeds Holbeck shed at this date, so this is likely to be a service from Bradford. New in December 1936, it was to be withdrawn at the start of 1967. Roy Denison/Colour-Rail

When the Bristol & Gloucester Railway (Br&GR) first opened in July 1844, it shared the route of the GWR-sponsored Cheltenham & Great Western Union Railway (C&GWUR) north from Standish Junction as far as the site of Gloucester South Junction, which was originally known as Chequers Road Junction and overseen by Gloucester No. 1 Signal Box. Here it branched off north-westwards to meet the Birmingham & Gloucester Railway (B&GR) line coming in from Cheltenham at what became Tramway Junction and to share their terminus station. The Br&GR and the B&GR became a part of the Midland Railway in 1845, whilst the GWR opened their own station on the line to South Wales in 1851 but the rapid expansion of the railway system in Gloucester meant the arrangement of the MR's station was awkward to work, with trains coming in and locomotives having to change ends to head out again.

The problem was only partially solved by the

Western Region influence, in the form of Wolverhampton Oxley shed's work-stained No. 6870 *Bodicote Grange*, heading through Eastgate with a mixed freight in August 1964. John Strange/NPC

opening of the Tuffley Loop on 22nd May 1854, although this was built to the standard gauge and thus allowed the Midland to dispense with the operation of broad gauge trains. The line was effectively an extension of the High Orchard Branch to the docks, with the twin tracks of the loop curving away from the docks branch between Barton Street Junction and what was to be the site of California Crossing. The line then swept around a gentle, elongated, S-shaped curve, running through what was then mostly farmland and open countryside, to rejoin the line to Bristol at Tuffley Junction.

The High Orchard Branch already crossed Barton Street and Parkend Road on the level but the new line also required a level crossing of Tredworth Road, near its junction with Stroud Road. In addition, the rapid development of new housing to the south-east of the city, stimulated by the coming of the railways and the consequent growth in industry, led to the requirement for two further level crossings, probably opened a few years after the loop line, at Farm Street and California. Midland Road, which no doubt took its name from the railway, ran parallel to the loop line on its east side, linking the roads of the new Barton Lane Estate started in 1853, to the south of Falkner Street. Construction was slow and a touch haphazard, bringing villas and semi-detached residences to a part of Gloucester that was previously mostly terraces of workers housing; becoming known as California, it was described in 1871 as '*a strange mixture of neat villas, fragrant pigsties, and Newtown shanties*'. The two new crossings at California and Farm Street joined Midland Road and Parkend Road at two points around half a mile apart, effectively forming a loop. However, Farm Street was later reduced to foot crossing status, although it retained a cabin right up until closure.

The Tuffley Loop proved useful for the Midland but train operation was still severely hampered by its terminus station, as recounted previously, so the only other major event in what was otherwise a largely uneventful life, was the relocation of Gloucester station in 1896. Thereafter, with trains now able to call directly without having to reverse, the line served a useful role allowing north-south services to swing through the city. The loop performed this function for 121 years and may well have continued to do so in to the 21st century if it had not been cursed by so many level crossings. It was this factor above all others which precluded any new Gloucester station being sited at a place whereby the loop could still be used. With the City Council keen to be rid of the crossings if the line could be closed, the decision for BR was easy – close Eastgate and retain Central. Accordingly, the line was closed with the station on 1st December 1975.

Little remains to show its existence today, although its route can be traced quite easily on GoogleEarth as little of it has actually been built on. This was because it had largely become surrounded by housing along its entire length over the years of its existence, so encroachement in most places is in the form of garden extensions rather than new build. The Painswick Road crossing keeper's cottage survives, in somewhat altered form, at the junction of Stroud Road and Tredworth Road; the crossing was actually of the latter and was nowhere near Painswick Road, although Tredworth Road does eventually join it some half a mile to the west. One of the signal boxes, from California Crossing, was also saved for further use by the now defunct Dowty Railway Preservation Society and can today be found on the narrow gauge system at Toddington station, whilst the name Midland Road remains as a reminder of the MR's once extensive presence in Gloucester.

Another 'Jubilee', No. 45562 *Alberta*, coasts over California Crossing towards Eastgate station with train No. 1N17 on 10th August 1963. This was a summer Saturday holiday express from the West Country to Newcastle, which the Leeds Holbeck-based 'Jubilee' would have taken over at Bristol Temple Meads. New from the North British Locomotive Co. in August 1934, No. 45562 spent most of its BR career allocated to Holbeck, apart from a two and a half year sojourn at Farnley Junction from April 1964 to December 1966. It then went back to Holbeck, from where it was withdrawn in early November 1967. Note the fair in The Park on the right. NPC

Still wearing BR green livery with a light grey bodystripe, 'Peak' No. D24 growls away from Barton Street Junction wth train No. 1V31 for Bristol Temple Meads on 4th June 1972. Built at Derby Works and new in to service on 15th April 1961, No. D24 was redesignated as Class '45' No. 45027 under TOPS in February 1975. It was withdrawn in May 1981 and scrapped at Swindon two years later. It was based at Leeds Holbeck depot when photographed here. The terraces on the left face on to Park Road. Bill Potter/KRM

Looking the opposite way from the other side of the line, with the houses on the left at the north end of Midland Road, just before it turns through ninety degrees and becomes Pembroke Street. Class '47' No. 47250 has just rumbled over California Crossing with an Up mixed freight on 31st May 1975. Note the High Orchard Branch still in place in the foreground, as far as the crossing but beyond that it had been lifted. Bill Potter/KRM

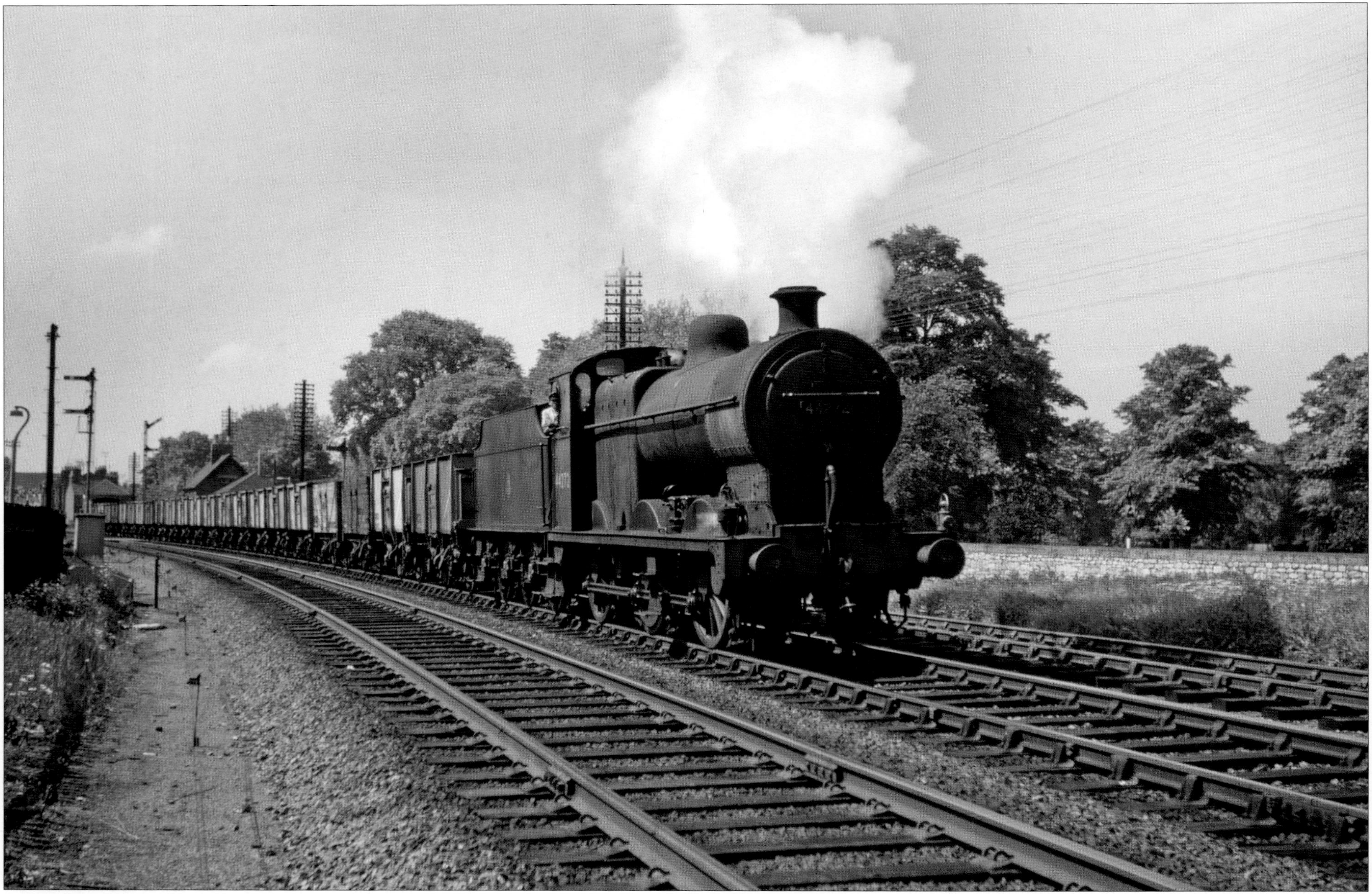

The Tuffley Loop was an interesting and attractive stretch of railway, which is remembered with much fondness by those Old Glostonians who had a penchant for watching trains pass by. This highly evocative shot – another gem from the camera of that prolific and talented master of the art Bill Potter – captures ex-LM&SR Class '4F' No. 44272 heading north over California Crossing with a train of coal empties on what was clearly a very warm day – 4th June 1962. The locomotive was based at Barnwood shed at this date – although shortly to transfer away to Templecombe to spend its final months working on the Somerset & Dorset Joint line – whilst the train is fairly short, so this may well be empties returning from the gas works served by the Hempsted Branch. Mostly comprised of steel mineral wagons, there are a couple of older wooden-bodied examples near the head of the train. Park End Road begins its run parallel with the railway just the other side of the stone wall on the right, with trees in the north-east corner of The Park beyond that. Bill Potter/KRM

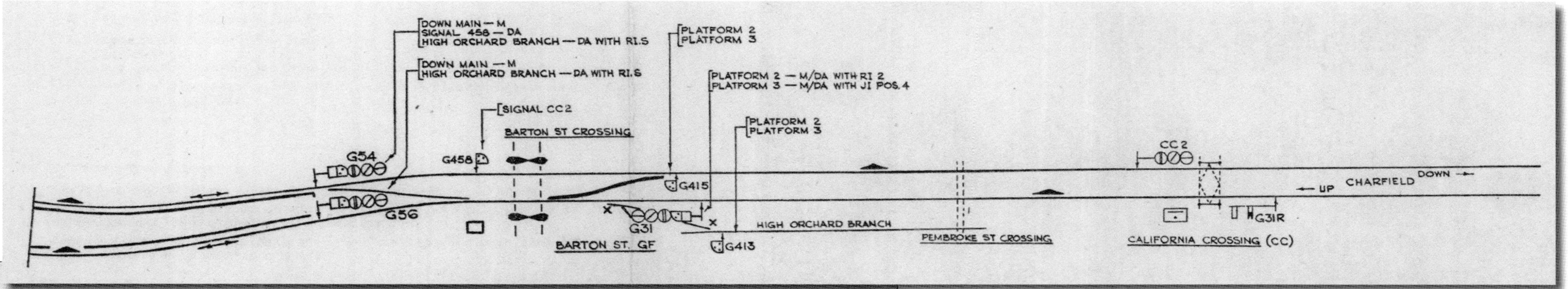

Above: This diagram, which shows the new arrangements at Eastgate and along the loop as far as Painswick Road, is taken from one of the many notices published to cover the Gloucester area resignalling that was carried out between 1966 and 1969. The cover for this notice is also shown below. NPC

Left: California Crossing and its diminutive box on 19th July 1968, with the gatekeeper posing in the doorway, shortly after the Tuffley Loop had been resignalled with colour light signals over the weekend of 25th-26th May. The semaphore visible in the background was the docks branch Home signal protecting Midland Road crossing.
David Stowell

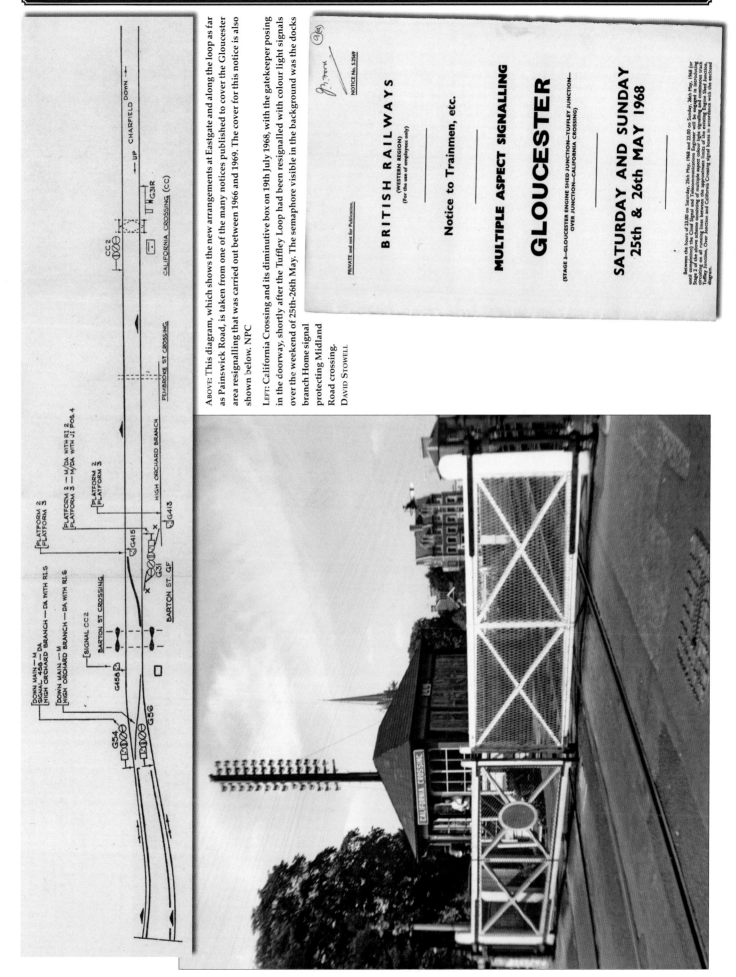

PRIVATE and not for Publication.

NOTICE No. S.2569

BRITISH RAILWAYS
(WESTERN REGION)
(For the use of employees only)

Notice to Trainmen, etc.

MULTIPLE ASPECT SIGNALLING

GLOUCESTER

(STAGE 2—GLOUCESTER ENGINE SHED JUNCTION—TUFFLEY JUNCTION—OVER JUNCTION—CALIFORNIA CROSSING)

SATURDAY AND SUNDAY
25th & 26th MAY 1968

Between the hours of 23.00 on Saturday, 25th May, 1968 and 22.00 on Sunday, 26th May, 1968 (or until completion) the Chief Signal and Telecommunications Engineer will be engaged in introducing Stage 2 of the above scheme consisting of multiple aspect colour light signalling and continuous track circuiting on all running lines between the approximate limits of the existing Engine Shed Junction, Tuffley Junction, Over Junction and California Crossing signal boxes in accordance with the enclosed diagram.

Right: California Crossing signal cabin in October 1975, with a colour light signal, Gloucester panel No. G58, now protecting the approach. Resignalling of the Gloucester area was carried out in stages in 1968-69, with colour light signals replacing all of the semaphores and most of the manual boxes – apart from those controlling crossing gates – being taken out of commission. Although the box here survived until the end, note that the crossing keeper's cottage had already been demolished, probably circa 1970. J.L. Lean/Colour-Rail

Above: With Central closed for rebuilding in 1975, Eastgate's final role was as Gloucester's main station for a few months. Near the end, on 29th November 1975, a BRCW three-car unit of Class '118' – which looks to be Bristol-based unit No. B478 – heads to Swindon passing the crossing box which to the end remained in virtually original condition apart from the loss of most of its levers. A replacement for an earlier box, this cabin was opened on 26th September 1920. Peter Berry

Left: Some seven months earlier, in April 1975, the same Class '118', No. B478, was photographed heading over the crossing towards Eastgate, past the pw huts and allotments bordering Parkend Road. David Stowell

ABOVE AND BELOW: Contrasting studies of California Crossing. With the gates closed to trains, an Austin Mini heads over the railway in February 1975, above, whilst a 1965 Ermine white Ford Cortina four-door deluxe can be seen on the left. Behind is a Series 2 Land Rover of the early sixties. The second view, below, shows the crossing and rear of the cabin from Midland Road in late afternoon sunshine on 16th November 1975. BOTH DAVID STOWELL

ABOVE: The last use of the Tuffley Loop was by the demolition train, seen here at California Crossing in January 1976. The railwaymen's allotments in the foreground would also disappear in due course. DAVID STOWELL

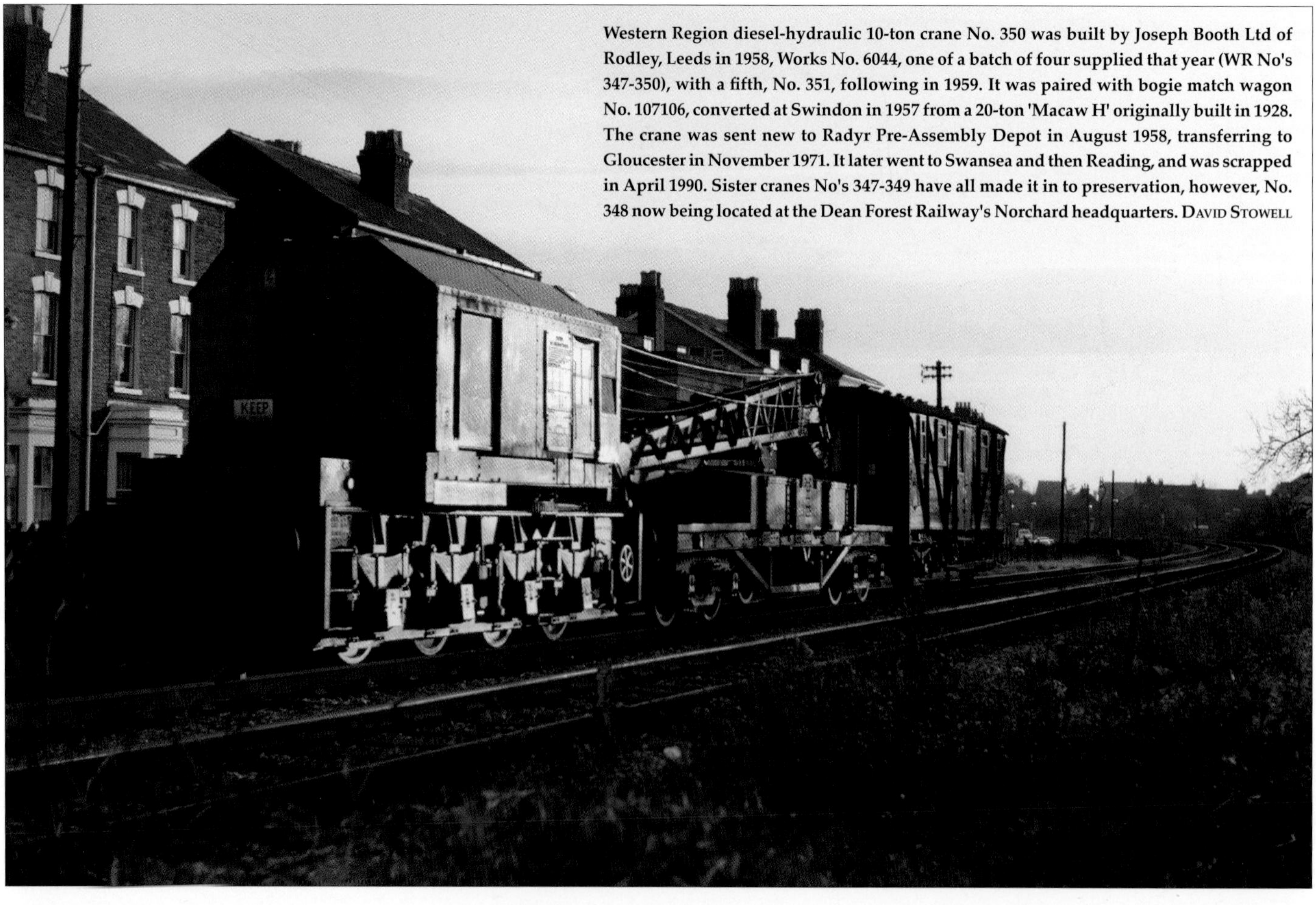

Western Region diesel-hydraulic 10-ton crane No. 350 was built by Joseph Booth Ltd of Rodley, Leeds in 1958, Works No. 6044, one of a batch of four supplied that year (WR No's 347-350), with a fifth, No. 351, following in 1959. It was paired with bogie match wagon No. 107106, converted at Swindon in 1957 from a 20-ton 'Macaw H' originally built in 1928. The crane was sent new to Radyr Pre-Assembly Depot in August 1958, transferring to Gloucester in November 1971. It later went to Swansea and then Reading, and was scrapped in April 1990. Sister cranes No's 347-349 have all made it in to preservation, however, No. 348 now being located at the Dean Forest Railway's Norchard headquarters. DAVID STOWELL

Left: On 1st November 1975, the route of the High Orchard Branch over Parkend Road is clearly delineated by the line of newer tarmac running from just behind California Crossing box. Today this is a busy section of road, part of the city's inner ring, where the four lanes of Trier Way divide, with two lanes going to the right here as Parkend Road, the other two following the docks branch alignment round The Park – and one would be well advised not to attempt parking where the red van – a Ford Escort Mk 1, the base 6cwt version, with a 1971-72 Oldham registration – is here! David Stowell

Right: With the rails all gone, California Crossing box is seen here being rescued by the Dowty Railway Preservation Society on Sunday 7th March 1976. It was winched sideways on to a Leyland Buffalo articulated low-loader belonging to E. Warner & Son Ltd of Tewkesbury and driven along the trackbed to Barton Street Crossing, visible in the left background, where the lorry turned on to the road for the journey to the DRPS base at Ashchurch, complete with police escort through Gloucester. With the demise of the DRPS, the box found a new home with the Gloucestershire Warwickshire Railway and now fully refurbished in Midland crimson and cream livery, is installed on the narrow gauge system at Toddington. A short film showing the loading and transport of the box can be found on YouTube. Peter Berry

Left: An unusual study of the line curving round towards Farm Street crossing on 11th November 1975, with Midland Road running parallel on the right and California Crossing visible in the background. The curve looks far sharper than it was in reality, the camera having a foreshortening effect on the picture. To the right of the line part way round the curve is signal G60R, a banner repeater for signal G60 on the approach to Painswick Road Crossing. The resignalling of the Tuffley Loop with colour lights was typical of the money wasted on modernising parts of the railways through the 1950s and '60s, which were then shut soon after – the colour light signals and equipment seen in these pictures had a life of just seven years! David Stowell

This picture and the one below give a far better impression of the easy nature of the curve south from California Crossing, turning the line south-east towards Tuffley Junction, whilst running parallel to Midland Road. This 1962 view is looking back to the crossing in the far right distance, as Stanier 'Jubilee" No. 45617 *Mauritius* of Crewe North shed powers away from its stop at Eastgate with train No. 1V26. The long rake of maroon carriages is broken by a single chocolate and cream vehicle two thirds of the way along. On the right, an Austin A40 rattles along Midland Road, which ends at the junction of Farm Street and Howard Street, a hundred yards or so behind the photographer. The back terrace of houses on the left still remains and several private garages have been built on the trackbed. No. 45617's career began in September 1934 and ended when it was withdrawn from Liverpool Edge Hill shed in August 1964, a month short of its thirtieth birthday. NPC

On the same day, another summer Saturday express was photographed in the same spot, with slightly more mundane motive power in charge in the form of one of the ubiquitous Stanier 'Black Five' 4-6-0s, Saltley shed's No. 45447. The vegetable allotments inside the boundary fence presumably belonged to Gloucester railwaymen living nearby. The 1937-built 'Five' lasted right up until the end of steam on BR, being withdrawn from Rose Grove shed in August 1968. NPC

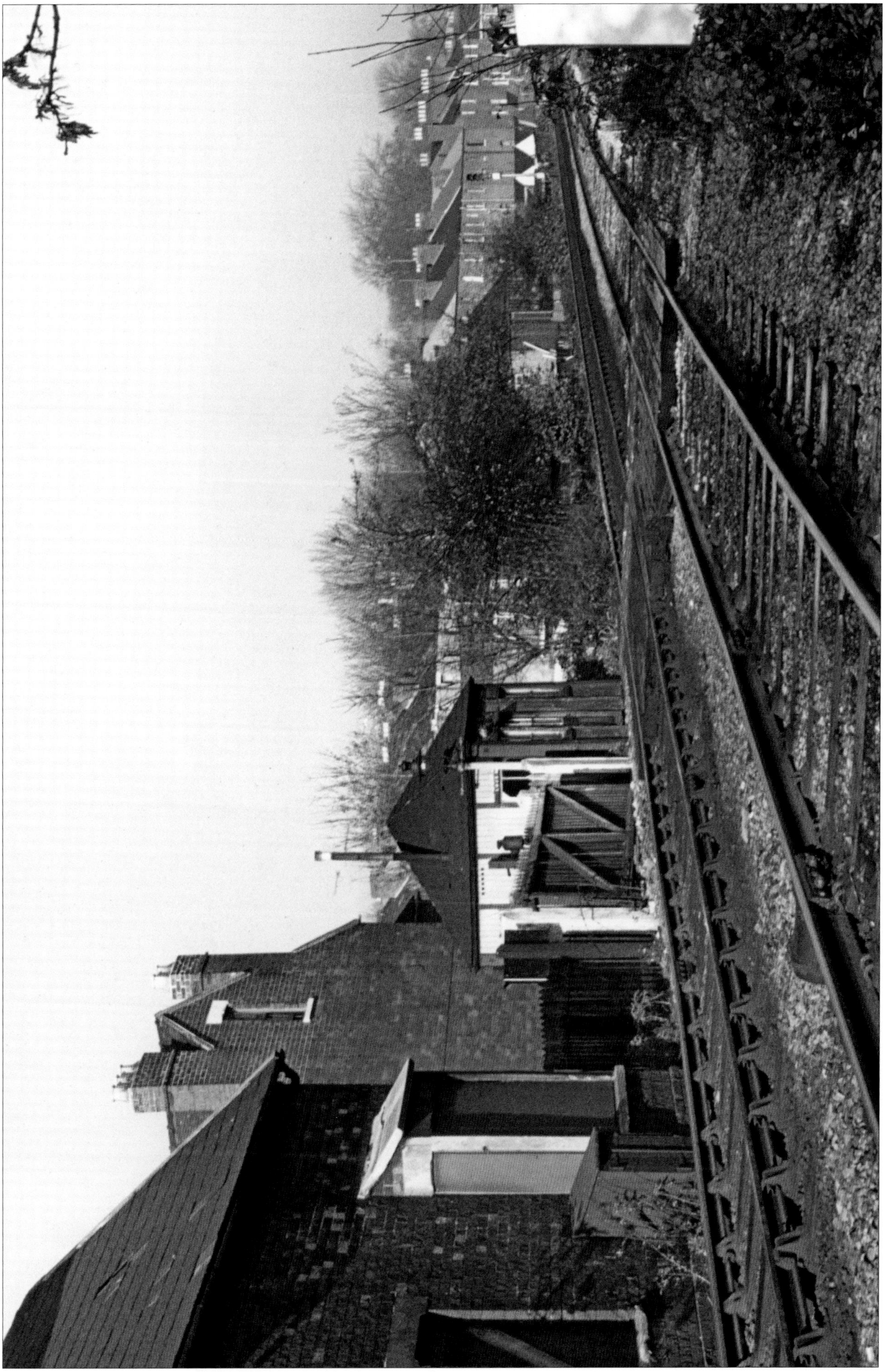

The most obscure of the level crossings on the Tuffley Loop was that at Farm Street, which had long been downgraded to foot crossing status. However, it still merited a small cabin for the crossing keeper, as the location, on the curve, was far from ideal. Taken in 1975, this view is again looking north, back towards Eastgate, with the houses in the right background being a continuation of the row seen in the previous two views. Originally known as Bowleys Crossing, possibly after the farm situated nearby when the line was first built, Farm Street was closed to road traffic some time during the first two decades of the 20th century. It seems British Railways tried to close it completely in the early 1960s but were prevented from doing so by Gloucester Corporation, who petitioned against its closure in the High Court. Ironically, ten years later the Corporation were glad to see the back of it, along with the other crossings on the loop. Note the colour light signal in the right distance warning of the approach to California Crossing. PETER BERRY

With closure imminent, Bill Potter also visited Farm Street Crossing to record it for posterity, on 1st June 1975. This first view is similar to Pete Berry's but shows a little more of the now demolished crossing keeper's house in the left foreground, which was out of use and boarded up. Bill Potter/KRM

The view south-east towards Tuffley Junction. Perhaps the most striking aspect is how rural the location still looked at this date, unlike today. Houses have been built on the trackbed here and the new development extends along the south side of Farm Street, replacing the terrace that was there. However, the 19th century terrace on the north side of the street, the end of which can be seen behind the cabin, still remains. The railway effectively divided Farm Street in two, the eastern portion (out of sight to the left here) being very short. Interestingly, the street was not joined back together after the railway closed, a steel barrier now taking the place of the set of wooden gates on the right. The western portion of the street was longer but still only stretched to around a hundred yards. On the corner where it met Parkend Road was the Empire Cinema, which closed in the 1960s but the building survives as Gloucester's Elim Pentecostal church. Bill Potter/KRM

ABOVE AND BELOW: Two final views of Farm Street taken on 16th November 1975. Although gated it had not been used for road traffic for many years, only as a pedestrian crossing supervised by a crossing keeper. Note the gas light still in use! The rear of the cinema can be seen between the houses in the lower picture. BOTH DAVID STOWELL

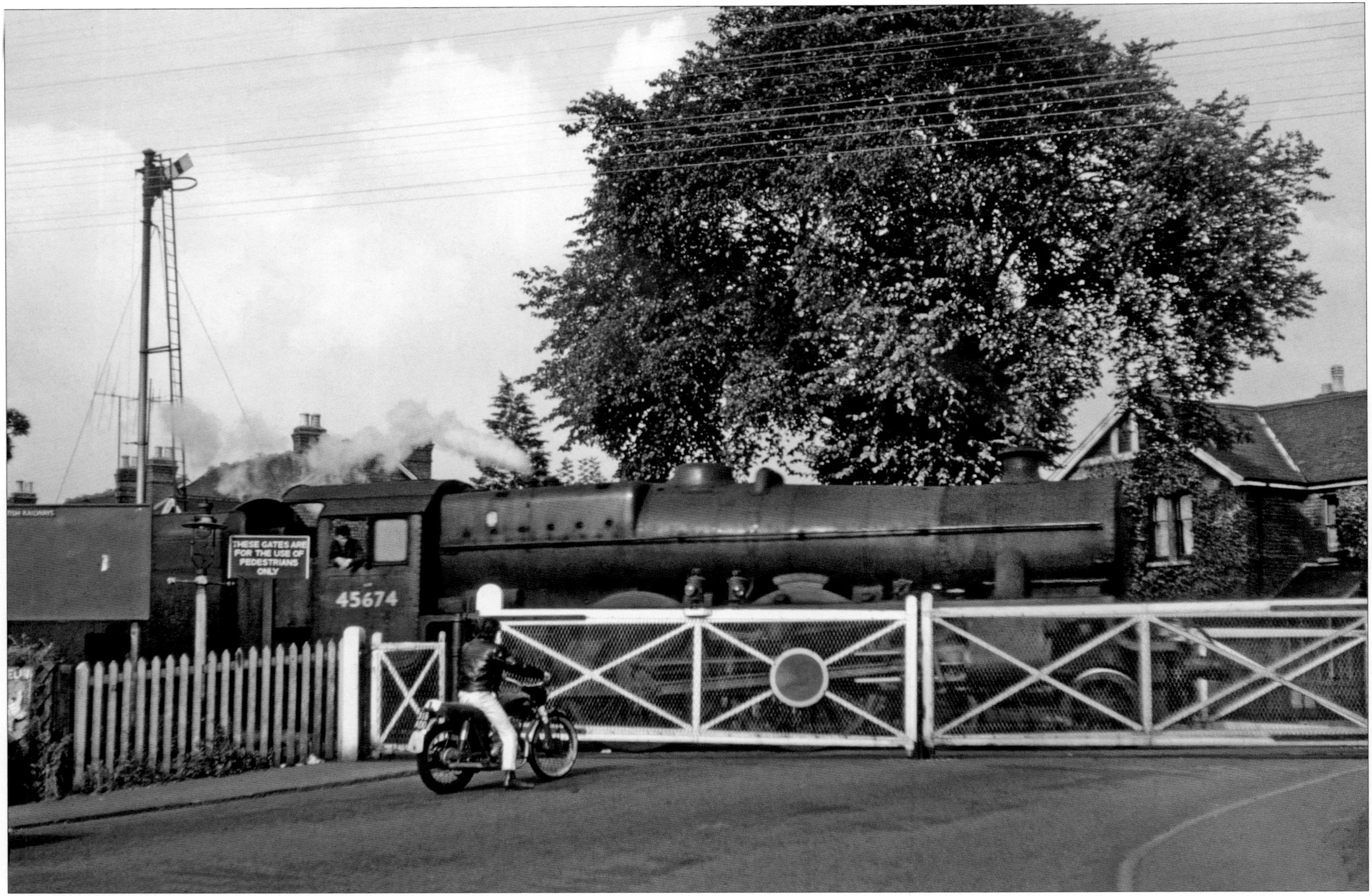

A rather splendid period view of Painswick Road Crossing, with a leather-clad 'Rocker' astride his motorcycle watching 'Jubilee' No. 45674 *Duncan* rumbling by in August 1964. The lad's carefully crafted image is just let down by the 'L' plate visible on the rear of the pillion seat. The bike is very interesting, being a Gloucester-built Cotton, probably the Villiers-engined 'Herald' model of circa 1959-66, which was derived from the 'Cotanza' model in 1959 and used the Villiers 2T twin cylinder 250cc engine. The 'leading link' front forks support the Cotton identification. The Cotton Company was based in Bristol Road and closed its doors in 1980, whilst the reversed 'OO' numberplate suggests Dagenham 1963 for the bike's first registration. Based at Saltley at the date of this view, No. 45674 had only weeks left in traffic, being withdrawn in early October, although it was despatched from Saltley to Crewe North for this to take place. The house facing on to Furlong Road in the right background has been replaced by a two-storey block of apartments. NPC

Right: Another from the large series of detailed notices that covered various aspects of the Gloucester area resignalling, this one relates to Painswick Road Crossing and Tuffley Junction and was published in summer 1968 for work to be carried out on Sunday 4th August. The Down Charfield line Starting signal referred to, which was to be recovered from Painswick Road Crossing following installation of the colour lights, is the signal which features on the left of the picture on the previous page. The diagram which accompanied this notice is shown across pages 104-105. NPC

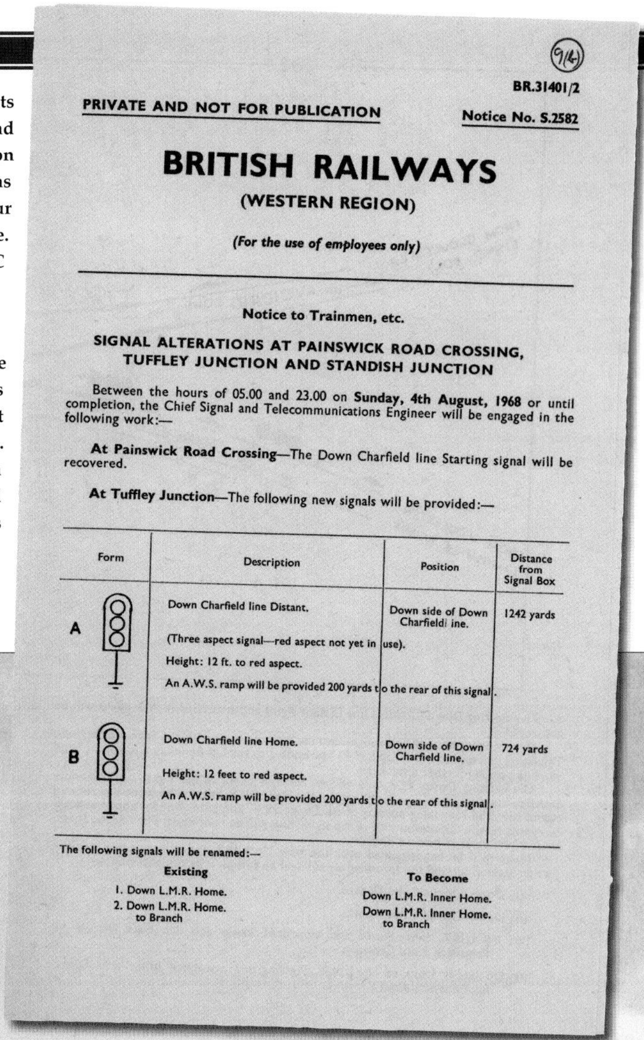

9/6

BR.31401/2

PRIVATE AND NOT FOR PUBLICATION — Notice No. S.2582

BRITISH RAILWAYS

(WESTERN REGION)

(For the use of employees only)

Notice to Trainmen, etc.

SIGNAL ALTERATIONS AT PAINSWICK ROAD CROSSING, TUFFLEY JUNCTION AND STANDISH JUNCTION

Between the hours of 05.00 and 23.00 on **Sunday, 4th August, 1968** or until completion, the Chief Signal and Telecommunications Engineer will be engaged in the following work:—

At Painswick Road Crossing—The Down Charfield line Starting signal will be recovered.

At Tuffley Junction—The following new signals will be provided:—

Form	Description	Position	Distance from Signal Box
A	Down Charfield line Distant. (Three aspect signal—red aspect not yet in use). Height: 12 ft. to red aspect. An A.W.S. ramp will be provided 200 yards to the rear of this signal.	Down side of Down Charfield line.	1242 yards
B	Down Charfield line Home. Height: 12 feet to red aspect. An A.W.S. ramp will be provided 200 yards to the rear of this signal.	Down side of Down Charfield line.	724 yards

The following signals will be renamed:—

Existing	To Become
1. Down L.M.R. Home.	Down L.M.R. Inner Home.
2. Down L.M.R. Home. to Branch	Down L.M.R. Inner Home. to Branch

Below: A timely view of Painswick Road Crossing on 19th July 1968, shortly before the removal of the semaphore signals here. The one just glimpsed on the right was the Painswick Road Inner Home, at the top of the post, with the Farm Street Distant arm below. Note that the box still had its nameboard facing the road at this date. When the loop first opened, a small gate cabin was provided here, on the Down side of the line but on the opposite side of Tredworth Road. This box, a Midland Type 1 15ft cabin, opened on 15th October 1893 and was also a block post. It was reduced to gate box status on 12th August 1968, during the major resignalling of the Gloucester area. Robinswood Hill in the right background was a favoured vantage point for postcard views across the city in the Edwardian era, many of which show the 'country' end of the Tuffley Loop to advantage. David Stowell

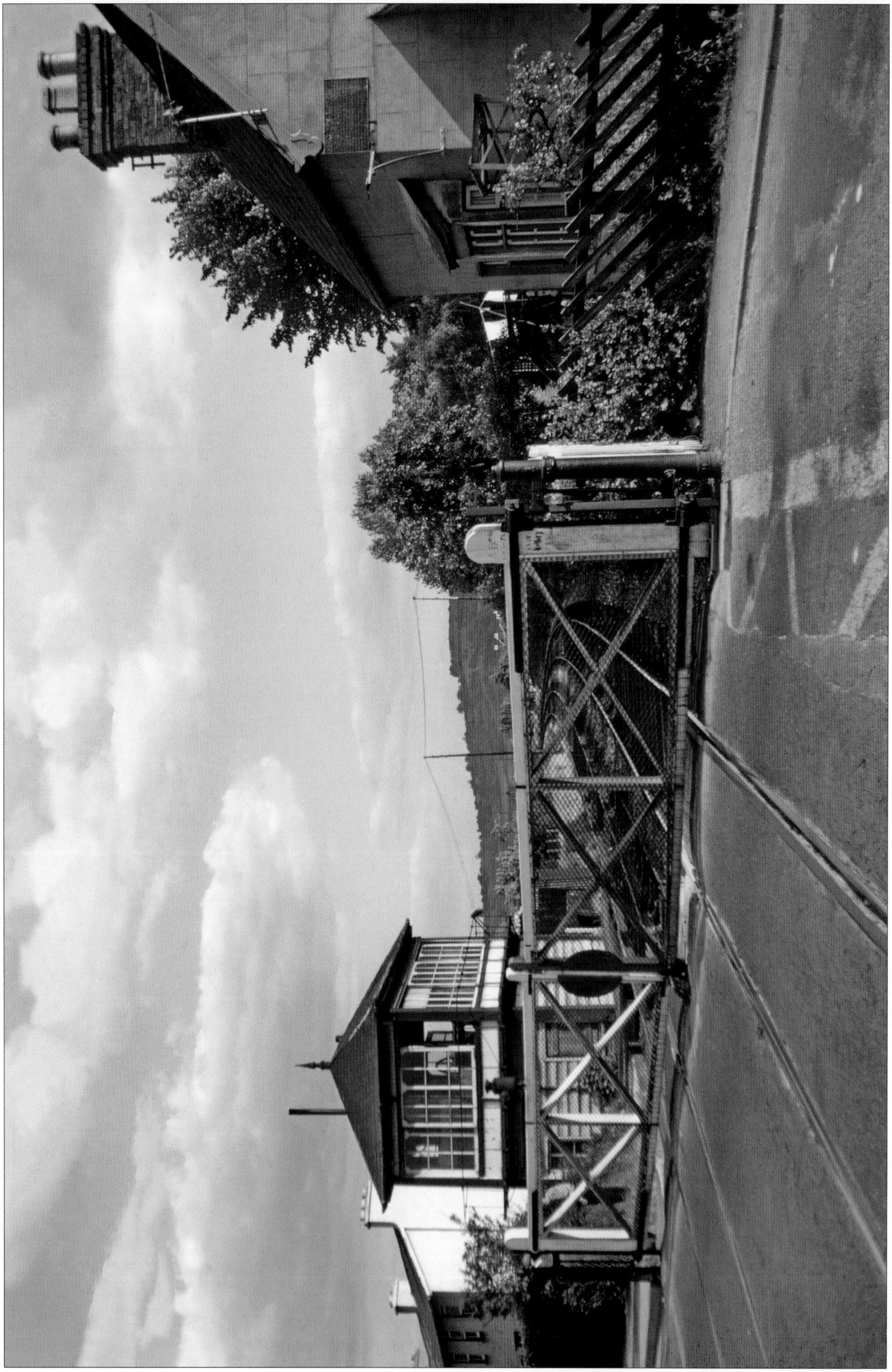

Painswick Road Crossing and signal box looking south-east towards Tuffley Junction on 31st May 1975. The thoroughfare passing over the crossing is actually Tredworth Road, which branches away from Stroud Road just a few yards off to the right. Tredworth Road runs for around half a mile in an easterly direction through the suburb of Tredworth before passing under the Gloucester to Bristol main line, after which it becomes Cotteswold Road. This carries on eastwards for a further half mile to meet Painswick Road. However, this would have been the main route into and out of the city towards Painswick from the Bristol Road area, with its docks and industries, which perhaps explains why it was named thus instead of Tredworth Road Crossing. The crossing keeper's cottage on the right survives today, although it has been substantially altered and expanded, so is largely unrecognisable from the building seen here. Note the Midland Railway cast iron notice high up on the end wall and the lamp bracket beneath it. Bill Potter/KRM

Class '47' No. 47258 rumbles over the crossing with an Up train in April 1975, watched by several pedestrians and road users. The green Austin A35 van has had a side-window conversion and possibly also a rear seat had been added but it would have been bought as a van to avoid the purchase tax on cars then prevalent. It dates from circa 1960 but they were made from 1956 to 1968 and this colour ran for the whole period. Behind is a Honda PC50 moped and a Vauxhall Victor FE estate of circa 1973. Again there is a gas light still in operation, by the pedestrian gates. DAVID STOWELL

The crossing on 16th November 1975, looking east with Tredworth Road stretching away in to the distance. The houses behind the box are no more, having been replaced in 2000 by the St. Catharine's Court assisted care apartments development. DAVID STOWELL

Looking west over the crossing, showing the rear of the box and the gas lamps lit by the pedestrian gates. Stroud Road Garage in the background was a fairly recent addition when these photographs were taken and it remains today, so is perhaps the easiest marker when looking for the site of the crossing. Fina petrol, the sign for which is partially obscured by the tree trunk, is no more, however, having merged with Total in 1999. DAVID STOWELL

Photographer Pete Berry also recorded Painswick Road Crossing signal box, on 29th November 1975, shortly before final closure. This view from the south shows the lamp hut and outside 'privy' provided for the signalmen who manned the box. The tiny crossing keeper's cottage again features on the left. PETER BERRY

These final two pictures were taken shortly after closure, with the rails already having a coating of rust. The first view shows the south end and entrance steps in more detail, whilst the interior shot below shows part of the lever frame, instrument panel and the gate wheel. Both Peter Berry

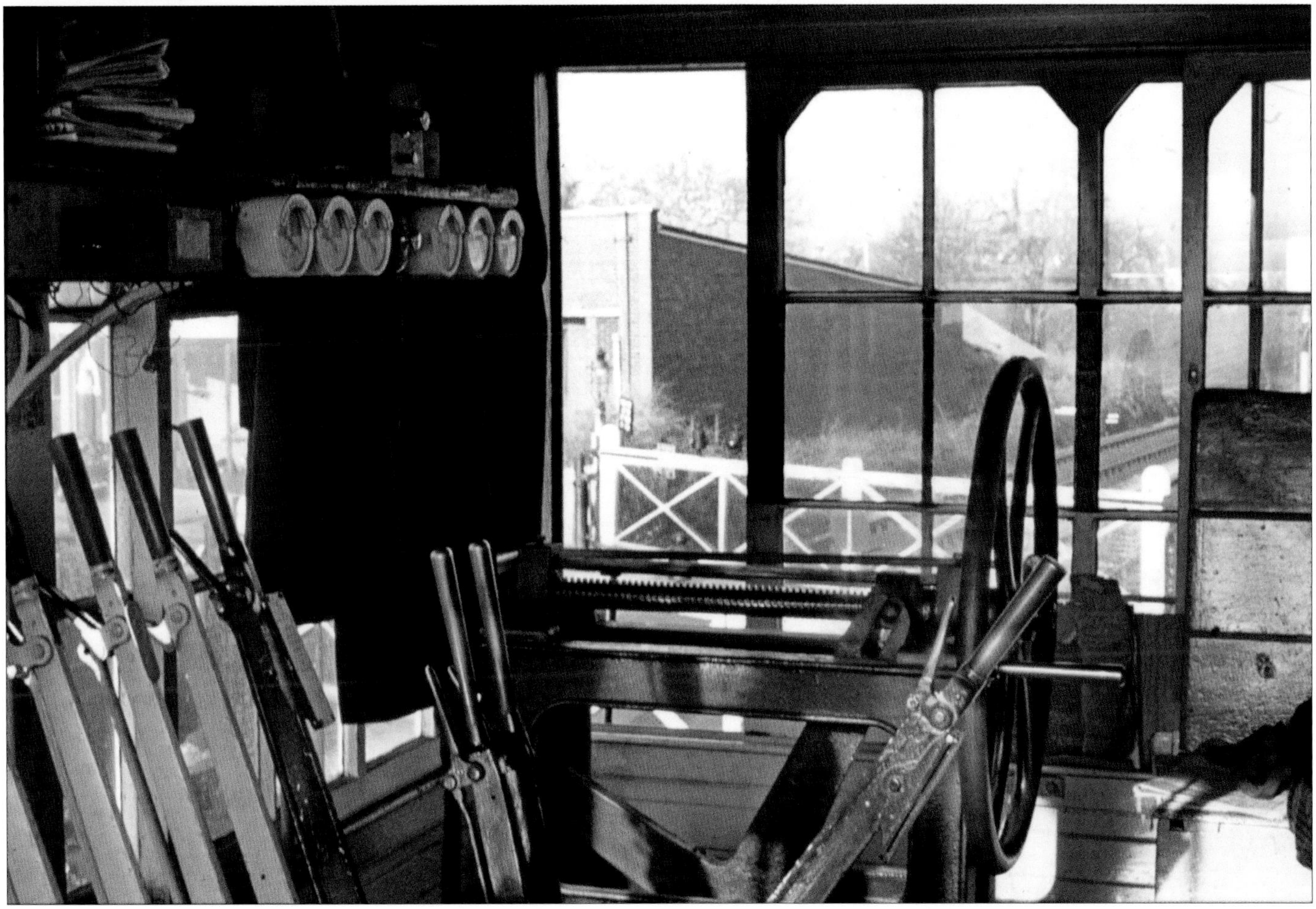

ABOVE: A footpath linking Southfield Road with Stroud Road crossed both the main line and the Tuffley Loop just before the two met at Tuffley Junction and this is the view from the footpath on 16th November 1975. In 1876, a siding was laid in on the Down side, which was controlled from a new cabin, Tuffley Siding signal box. The purpose of the siding (shown on the plan on page 107) is unclear but it would seem likely that it was used for dumping manure from the Midland's stables. The siding had gone by 1901, with new sidings for this traffic having been provided on the Hempsted or New Docks Branch opened in 1900. DAVID STOWELL

BELOW: This view of Class '45' No. 45044 *Royal Inniskillen Fusilier* heading south with a Bristol express was taken from the footbridge on 31st May 1975 (the main line can be seen in the right background). The 'Peak' had only received its TOPS number two months before, having previously been No. 63 from delivery on 29th March 1962. It was withdrawn from service on 15th June 1987. The allotments gave this end of the loop a rather rural feel and still remain today. BILL POTTER/KRM

ABOVE: Following on from the picture at the bottom of the previous page, photographer Bill Potter quickly turned round and caught the 'going away' shot of the train as it approached the junction. BILL POTTER/KRM

LEFT: English Electric Type '3' No. 6969 drifts past the allotments with train No. 6Z35, a trip working of loaded HAA hoppers bound for the coal concentration depot at Stonehouse on 18th March 1970. New in February 1965, in February 1974 the engine became Class '37' No. 37269 under TOPS and was then renumbered again in November 1985, becoming No. 37417 after a heavy refurbishment and fitting with electric train heating (ETH) equipment. It was withdrawn in late 2012 and scrapped early in 2013. CHRIS BALDWIN

BELOW: With Stroud Road bridge visible in the background, ex-LM&SR 'Jubilee' No. 45641 *Sandwich*, of Burton-on-Trent shed, takes the loop to Gloucester Eastgate at Tuffley Junction, bound for Derby with an Up holiday express from the south-west circa 1963. New in December 1934 and withdrawn in September 1964, this was another 'Jube' that just missed its thirtieth birthday.
PAUL RILEY/COURTESY THE RESTORATION & ARCHIVING TRUST/REF. PR8686

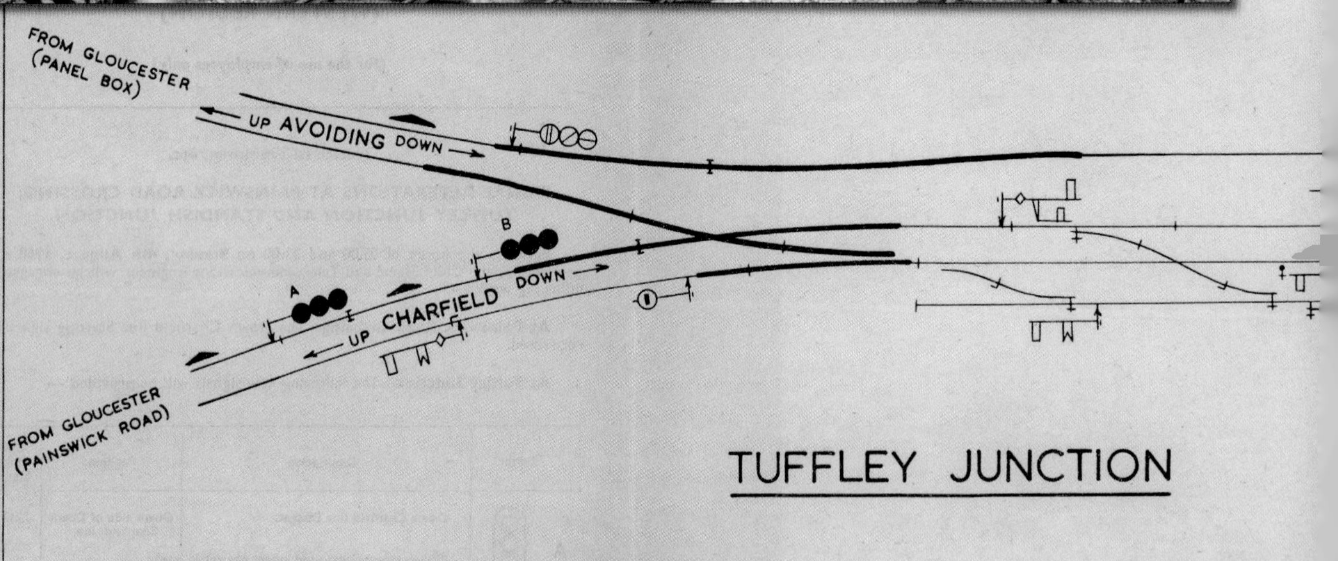

The existing Down Charfield line Distant signal and associated A.W.S. ramp will be recovered.

New connections will be brought into use in accordance with the enclosed diagram. The facing connection in the Up L.M.R. line leading to the Up Avoiding line will be hand worked pending further alterations.

The existing Down W.R. line will be severed opposite the signal box. Between Standish Junction Signal Box and this point the Down W.R. line will be taken temporarily out of use. The remaining portion of the Down W.R. line extending for approximately 600 yards on the Gloucester side of the signal box will be recovered. The revised layout is as shown on the enclosed diagram.

Trains will be handsignalled over the new Up L.M.R. facing connection pending further alterations and the following signals will be temporarily disconnected:—

(i) Down Charfield line Distant.

(ii) Down Charfield line Home.

(iii) Up L.M.R. Inner Home and associated lower arm Up Main Distant for Painswick Road Crossing.

(iv) Up Goods Loop to Up L.M.R. Starting and associated lower arm Distant for Painswick Road Crossing.

The track circuit to the rear of the Down L.M.R. Inner Home bracket signal will b extended in the rear as far as the new Down Charfield line Home signal.

A new independent telephone circuit will be provided between the Down Charfiel line Home signal and the signal box.

At Standish Junction—The following signals will be temporarily disconnected:—

(i) Down W.R. Distant.

(ii) Up L.M.R. to Down W.R. Distant.

(iii) Down W.R. Starting.

Levers in the locking frames at Painswick Road Crossing, Tuffley Junction an Standish Junction Signal Boxes will be bolted out of use as appropriate.

District Inspector George, Gloucester, to make all arrangements for the saf workingof the line in accordance with Rule 77 and provide the necessary hand-signalme

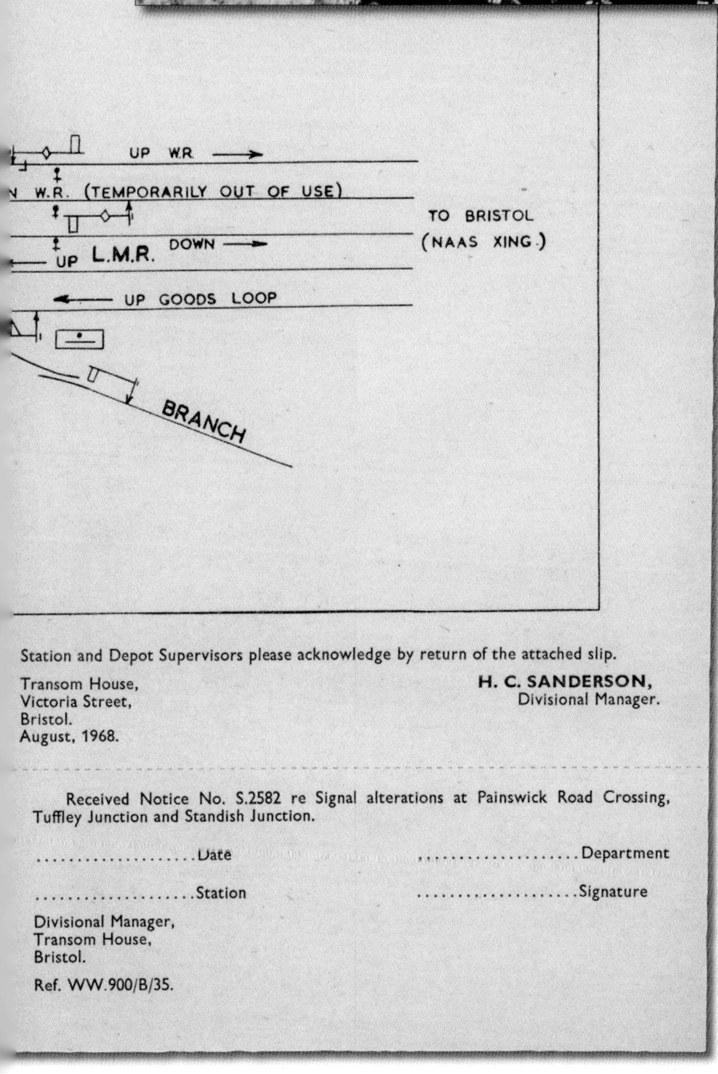

Station and Depot Supervisors please acknowledge by return of the attached slip.

Transom House,
Victoria Street,
Bristol.
August, 1968.

H. C. SANDERSON,
Divisional Manager.

Received Notice No. S.2582 re Signal alterations at Painswick Road Crossing, Tuffley Junction and Standish Junction.

....................Date ....Department

....................Station ....Signature

Divisional Manager,
Transom House,
Bristol.

Ref. WW.900/B/35.

PREVIOUS PAGE TOP: 'Black Five' No. 44805 heads a Down three-coach local through Tuffley Junction circa 1962. The locomotive was based at Saltley at this time but had been pressed in to action by the Barnwood shedmaster to cover this Bristol 'stopper'. A war-time build, at the LM&SR's Derby Works in June 1944, No. 44805 was withdrawn from Crewe South shed in September 1967. The view was taken from Tuffley Bridge (No. 102), which carries Stroud Road over the line.
PAUL RILEY/COURTESY THE RESTORATION & ARCHIVING TRUST/REF. PR3688

ABOVE: Over the Bank Holiday weekend of 4th-6th May 1968, Tuffley Junction was remodelled to provide a direct connection between the ex-Midland and GWR lines, as part of the process of removing the four-tracking between here and Standish Junction. This view from Tuffley Bridge shows that work in progress, with the Tuffley Loop closed whilst the new pointwork was laid in. A rail-mounted crane lifts track panels from a bogie bolster wagon in the foreground. The left-hand arm of the bracket signal controlled entrance to the Hempsted or New Docks Branch but the other arm (seen in the previous picture) had been removed as the loop to which it referred was now out of use. In the background can be seen the 'double bridges', from which a number of the pictures we have just seen were taken. Tuffley Occupation Bridge (No. 102) over the loop line has now gone but comprised brick arches either side with a wrought iron girder span over the tracks. We shall see more of the other bridge, which still remains today, in the next volume when we taken the ex-GWR route out of Gloucester to Stroud and Swindon. It does not, however, feature in the *Midland Bridge Register Gloucester District* from which the bridge numbers in this book are taken, as this line was GWR property. CHRIS BALDWIN

LEFT: Completion of the remodelling work at Tuffley Junction was in early August 1968. This is the diagram from the notice on page 97, illustrating the new connection and the signals which would control it. Tuffley Junction signal box was to close, with the hand operated connections to the Hempsted Branch and to the RAF Quedgeley depot becoming remotely operated from the new Gloucester power box, which replaced all of the mechanical boxes in the immediate area apart from those retained as crossing boxes. The Down WR line, of which the last 600 yards at this northern end were lifted, is marked '*Temporarily out of use*'. In fact it was merged with the Up LMR line as part of the reduction of this section from four tracks to two. NPC

Brush Type '4' No. D1935 in BR two-tone green sweeps past the new junction (see overleaf) on to the Tuffley Loop in August 1970 with train No. 5M20, oil tankers from the Fawley (Hampshire) refinery to Bromford Bridge in Birmingham. The locomotive had a long and varied history. Placed in to service in March 1966, it became Class '47' No. 47257 under TOPS in June 1974 but has been renumbered twice since then, as No. 47650 in March 1986 and No. 47805 in August 1989. In this latter guise and named *Roger Hosking MA 1925-2013*, it remains operational at Carlisle Kingmoor depot today, albeit in private ownership. It has also previously carried the names *Bristol Bath Road*, *Pride of Toton*, *Talisman* and *John Scott 12.5.45-22.5.12*. The view is from the footbridge over the Avoiding Line, with Tuffley Bridge (No. 102) in the background. Although a Midland bridge, it had been reconstructed by the GWR in 1907-08. Chris Baldwin

A rare combination here, as 'Peak' No. D156, in green livery with light grey lower body stripe and BR roundel, heads 'Warship' No. D845 *Sprightly*, in BR blue with the new double arrows emblem, round the curve at Tuffley Junction on 18th March 1970 with train No. 1E30 (10.40am off Bristol TM, bound for Newcastle). In spring 1970, the track layout at Temple Meads was remodelled in conjunction with the MAS resignalling. Cross-country services would normally have changed engines there, from a WR diesel hydraulic to a 'Peak' for the journey north of Bristol but between 22nd February and 3rd May the change was made at Gloucester instead. The train may have started from Plymouth and the 'Warship' would come off at Gloucester. However, the pilot would have been put on at Bristol (it was a Bath Road engine at this date), so it is possible that *Sprightly* had failed and the 'Peak' was attached to haul it to Gloucester. New in to service in April 1961, *Sprightly* was withdrawn in October 1971 and cut up at Swindon in May 1972. The 'Peak', meanwhile, became Class '46' No. 46019 in January 1973 and lasted in service until January 1980. Chris Baldwin

On 1st August 1970, Laira depot's No. D1005 *Western Venturer* takes the same route with train No. 1M22, a Plymouth to Nottingham express. No. D1005 had nearly a year and a half at Old Oak Common and twelve months at Swansea Landore, otherwise its fourteen year career, which ended in November 1976, was spent at Laira. If the station shown in the 19th century plan opposite had ever been built, it would have occupied the land around the rear of the train. Bill Potter/KRM

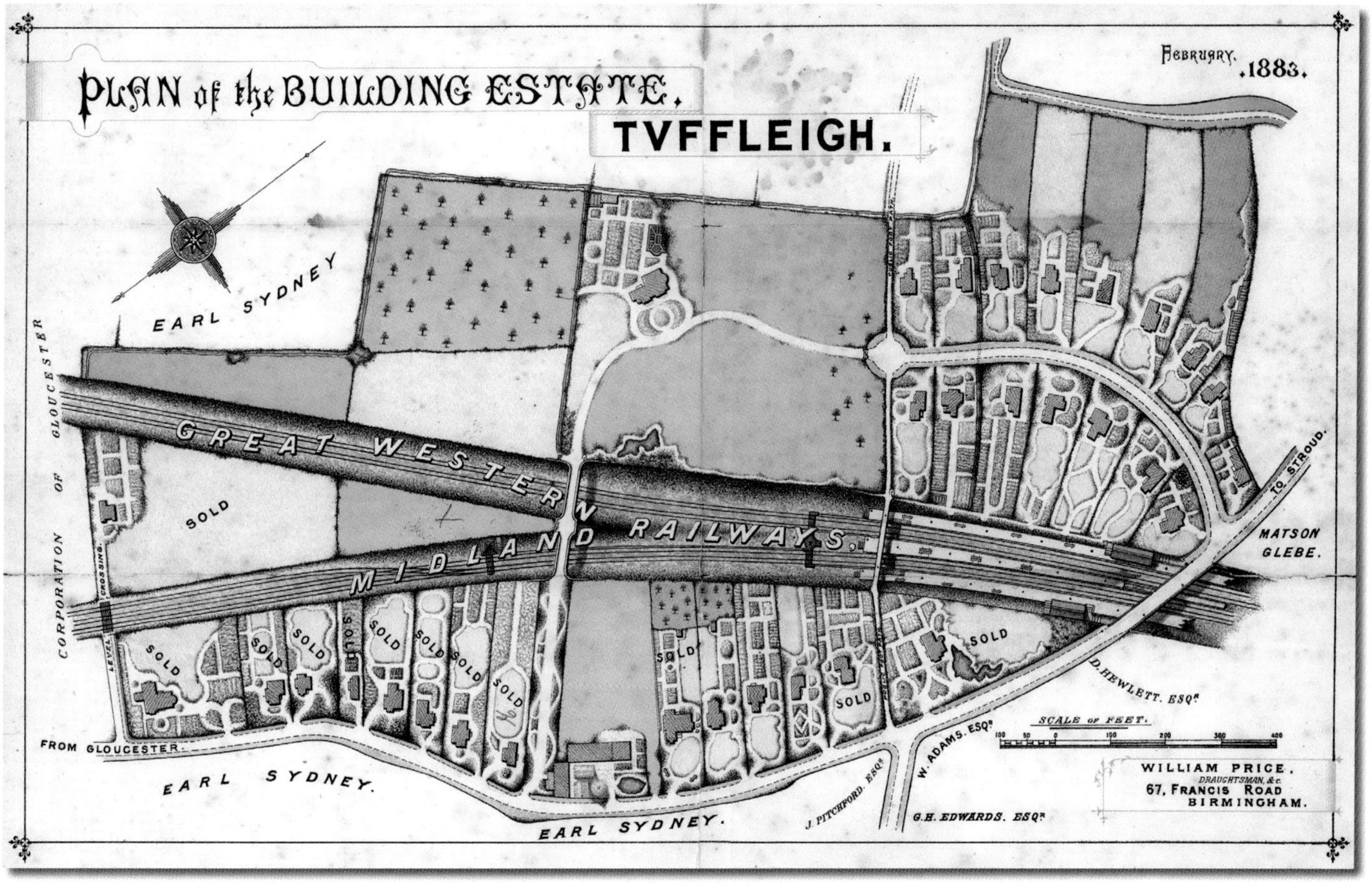

Although well outside the timeline of this book, this rare piece of ephemera is worth including here as an interesting 'what might have been' if this 19th century developer's plans for the Tuffley area had come to full fruition. The houses to the east of Stroud Road, many of which are marked here as 'Sold', did get built but the curved un-named avenue on the south-east side of the line did not. Nothing is known of a proposal for a four-platformed Tuffley Junction station here at the junction of the two lines in 1883, which may well have been just a figment of the developer's imagination. The platforms are shown running beneath Stroud Road bridge, from which steps ran down to platform level, whilst a footbridge at the north end also linked to Stroud Road and the proposed new development. Also shown on the Loop line on the left is Tuffley Siding and signal box, mentioned a little earlier, which was in existence from 1876 to circa 1900. With little in the way of pointwork except at the junction itself just to the south, the plan would make for an interesting 'through running' model railway layout. NPC

A BRCW three-car unit of Class '118' on a local service to Bristol comes off the loop in April 1975, having just passed beneath the footbridge (No. 103) that locals referred to as the 'Black Bridge', from which several of the previous pictures were taken. Under heavy magnification, the unit looks to be No. B478 again. The north end of the platforms for the proposed Tuffley Junction station would have been in the foreground, along with the footbridge that would have connected them directly with the new houses that were to be built on either side of the line. DAVID STOWELL

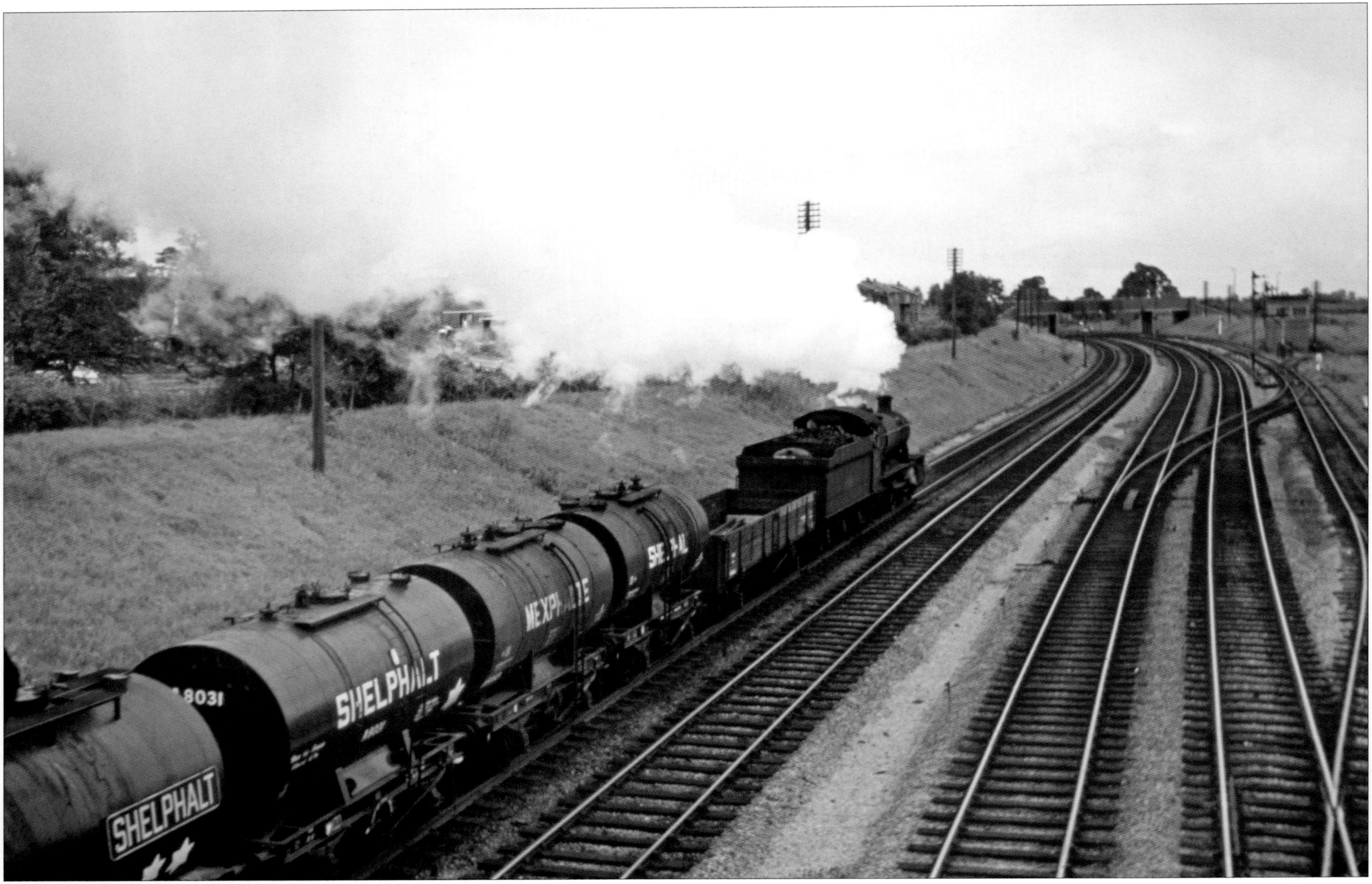

Featuring a WR goods hauled by ex-GWR 'Manor' Class 4-6-0 No. 7814 *Fringford Manor* along the WR Up Main at Tuffley on 30th July 1965, this view could easily been held over for the next volume. However, I decided to include it here as it shows the junction for the Hempsted Branch on the right, which is where we shall be heading shortly. New in to service in January 1939 and having previously been at Gloucester Horton Road shed from June 1964 to May 1965, the engine had been transferred back there in early July after a few weeks based at Didcot. Its return was short, however, as it was to be withdrawn in early September as steam on BR's Western region was brought to a premature close. The SHELPHALT and MEXPHALTE bitumen tank wagons were converted from Ministry petrol tanks shortly after the end of the war and are probably working out of Llandarcy, which was a base for bitumen until the refinery closed in the 1990s. The bridge in the background, built in 1959 and that carries Cole Avenue over the line between Tuffley and the Bristol Road, completed the last link in Gloucester's southern ring road. Don Mann

A fine view of Tuffley Junction from the aforementioned Cole Avenue bridge, showing the layout here as as it existed in the period from the Second World War up until the remodelling of 1968. 'Black Five' No. 44814 drifts southwards with a Down express circa 1962. The 'O' in the 1O53 headcode indicates that this was a working bound for the Southern Region, which would suggest that the train was heading for the Somerset & Dorset line, via Mangotsfield and Bath. However, Mike Arlett tells me that through trains on to the S&D, which finished in September 1962, carried numbers in the 80s and 90s, so the origin and destination of 1O53 are at present unknown. Saltley-based No. 44814 was another war-time build completed at Derby just four months after No. 44805 that we saw a couple of pages ago, in October 1944. Tuffley Junction signal box was only a little older, another of the classic war-time ARP builds of which there were several in the Gloucester area, as we saw in the previous volume. It opened on 7th December 1941, replacing an earlier box of 1898 which had been sited about a hundred yards further north. Although new sidings had been added nearby in 1940, the box's construction was probably more to do with its air raid withstanding abilities, due to its proximity to the nearby Quedgeley ROD depot. The lines here are from right to left: WR Down Main, WR Up Main, LMR Up Main, LMR Down Main, LMR Up Goods Loop (which led to the war-time sidings situated behind the photographer). The Hempsted Branch ran behind the box and then in a low cutting between the two post & wire fences on the left. Paul Riley/Courtesy the Restoration & Archiving Trust/Ref. PR3689

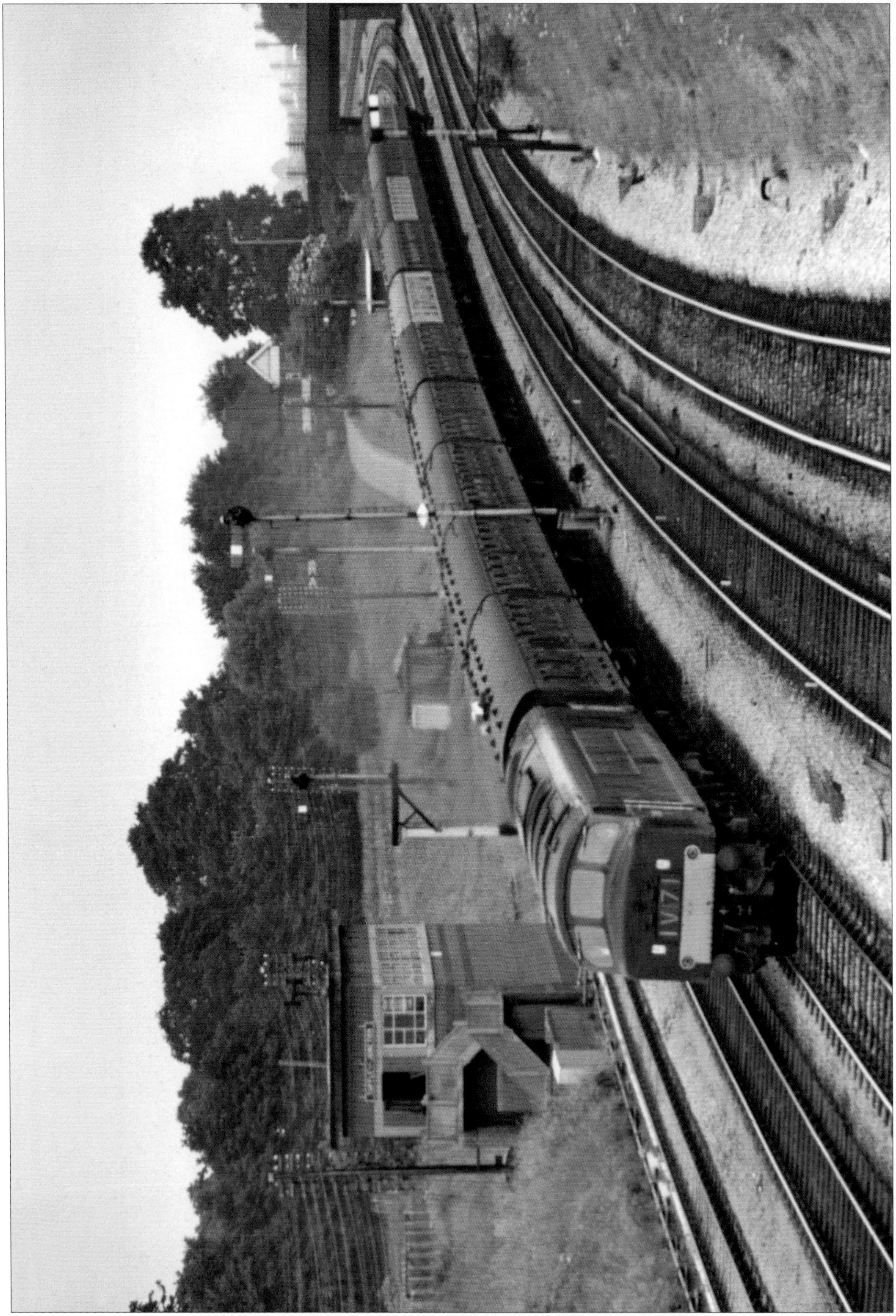

Tuffley Junction in the green diesel era, shortly before the remodelling that was to see the four running tracks here reduced to two. Taken on 4th May 1968, as work on constructing the new junction commenced beyond the Stroud Road bridge in the right background, an unidentfied 'Peak' Class Sulzer Type '4' heads south towards Bristol Temple Meads with train No. 1V71, a Sheffield to Paignton express. The ten coach train includes three carriages in the new BR corporate blue & grey livery, as along with mechanical boxes and semaphore signals, the railway history of the steam era began to be consigned to the past. Chris Baldwin

From the same Cole Avenue bridge vantage point but at a slightly different angle, this fascinating view of the Tuffley Junction remodelling, taken on 5th May 1968, shows a green liveried 'Hymek' in the left middle distance coupled to an engineers' coach and with a rail crane visible beyond, whilst a maroon 'Western' has just arrived with a train of loaded hoppers, carrying ballast probably from Whitecliff Quarry in the Forest of Dean, although with the closure of the Coleford Branch the previous year this would have been loaded from lorries at Parkend Marsh Sidings. Both carry 'Z' headcodes, indicating special workings but, unfortunately, neither of the locomotives are identified, although the 'Hymek' is likely to have been locally based at the time whilst the 'Western' had probably come up from Cardiff Canton, collecting the hoppers at Lydney Junction yard on the way. Note the temporary 15mph speed restriction signals positioned in between the running lines. Chris Baldwin

The 'Peaks' were regular performers on the Midland main line through the county in the 1970s and here, on 7th June 1975, another of the class, No. 46021 (formerly No. D158), comes off the Tuffley loop and through the simple double track junction installed here in 1968. Bill Potter/KRM

A pair of unidentified Class '25' Bo-Bo diesel electrics head a train of ballast wagons past the much simplified layout at Tuffley Junction on 28th September 1975. It remains the same today, although as elsewhere on the railway network, largely unchecked lineside tree and bush growth has obscured the view, whilst housing estates now cover the fields behind. Mike Spicer/Courtesy the Restoration & Archiving Trust/Ref. MSZZ4285

SECTION 4

THE NEW DOCKS OR HEMPSTED BRANCH

In the late afternoon glow of an early spring day, Class '4F' No. 43887 fights for grip as it struggles up to the junction at the top of the Hempsted Branch in March 1964. The engine had had to wait for the signal to be cleared by the Tuffley Junction signalman in order to join the main line and although only a train of empties from the gas works, the gradient and sharp curve combined to make restarting it something of an effort. The view provides a glimpse of the rear of the box, with the impressive outline of the Grade II listed St. Barnabas Church, built in 1938-40, on the skyline beyond it. David Bick/NPC

The Midland Railway obtained powers to build a new branch from Tuffley Junction to the Gloucester & Sharpness Canal at Hempsted in 1893, despite some fierce and probably justified opposition from the GWR. This was because as well as it stimulating (they hoped) industrial expansion southwards along the line of the canal, the Midland also intended to bridge the waterway and tap in to the traffic on the 'GWR side' at Llanthony. However, the company took their time in progressing it, with the result that the Hempsted or New Docks Branch finally opened for traffic on 24th September 1900.

The branch, which was a mile and a quarter in length from Tuffley Junction to where it met the GWR's Monk Meadow line at Hempsted, was built on a slight falling gradient towards the canal. It curved sharply after leaving the main line and then ran in a straight line north-westwards to Hempsted Sidings, before curving north as it crossed the canal via a swing bridge, meeting up with the GWR line a third of a mile further on. It was well built, with a three-arch, brick-built bridge (No. 1) carrying a farm track over the line near the junction and another (No. 3) lifting Bristol Road over the branch shortly before it reached the canal. A substantial swing bridge (No. 4), mounted on a new pier in the canal and controlled from a lofty, timber-built cabin with attendant semaphore signals (which included a cross-bar signal for canal traffic), was provided to take the branch across the waterway. About mid-way along the branch, one further bridge carried the line over a proposed extension of Podsmead Road, a somewhat incredible piece of forward planning as it was to be another thirty-five years before this was carried out to connect with a new estate at Lower Tuffley. No pictures of New Road Bridge (No. 2) have been located to date and nothing remains of it today but it was on a sharp skew and comprised a single steel girder span, with blue brick abutments and wings.

When built, the new branch had no connections to any industries at all, its principal traffic in the early years being manure from the Midland's stables in Gloucester, which was unloaded in the fields alongside the sidings at Hempsted Wharf. A third siding was later laid in for this traffic, presumably to allow dumping of the manure on fresh ground. In 1904, J.M. Collett & Co. Ltd moved their successful sulphur based chemicals business to a new factory alongside the new branch near Bristol Road and a siding was laid in to serve it. The Gloucester Gas Light Company built their Hempsted gas works on the Bristol Road between 1874 and 1877, served by a wharf on the canal, coal being delivered by coasters coming over from Cardiff. However, probably just prior to the First World War, a line was eventually laid in to supply the gas works by rail instead. Finally, one of the Hempsted Wharf sidings was extended southwards in February 1927, to serve the yard of building contractor W.T. Nicholls & Co.

However, this proved to be the peak of the Hempsted Branch's development, with little in the way of other new industry being attracted to the area it served. In addition, the connection to the GWR west of the canal failed to take anything much of the traffic away from that company and the swing bridge would have rapidly become an expensive luxury. Indeed, a report to an LM&SR Traffic Committee meeting in October 1937 stated that the swing bridge and the line beyond the canal had not seen any use since before 1923, further noting that the swing bridge had been hit and damaged by a steamer in 1932; the recommendation to formally close and remove this section of the line was approved, the official closure of it being from 21st May 1938.

The Second World War did generate some additional traffic on the line, with two further sidings being laid in at Hempsted Wharf in 1942. After the war, coal to the gas works was the chief source of revenue for the final twenty-five years of the line's existence, supplemented by traffic from the chemical works up until the mid 1960s. The sidings at Hempsted Wharf were closed on 1st August 1967 and the line was then worked as a long siding to the gas works but after this ceased production in 1970, the branch was closed on 14th January 1971.

The course of the branch curving away from the junction can still be traced today, running behind The Crypt school. Bridge No's 1 and 3 survive but New Road Bridge has gone and the site of Hempsted Sidings is now slowly being hidden beneath new industrial development. The gas works site has been cleaned and redeveloped, whilst west of the canal there is little sign that the New Docks or Hempsted Branch ever existed.

Top & Above: Two more views of No. 43887 with its train of empty coal wagons in March 1964. Held by the signal to come off the branch, the photographer thankfully had time to get three shots of what was a very rarely recorded working. Reallocated from Barnwood to Horton Road shed when the former closed a few weeks after these pictures were taken, the 1919-built '4F' was not to see out the year, being withdrawn in early October. The Crypt school playing fields feature on the left of the top view and the occupation bridge in the one below it. Both David Bick/NPC

Left: 'Jinty' 0-6-0T No. 47308 at Hempsted Sidings on the inward journey of the GRS's Nailsworth & Stroud rail tour of 7th July 1963. The centre siding where passengers are climbing down had been removed two months earlier. Bristol Road bridge can be seen in the background, through which the branch had originally carried on across the canal, whilst in the left middle distance a line can be seen curving round to Hempsted Wharf Sidings. Bill Potter/KRM

RIGHT: No. 44045 shunts a brake van in Hempsted Wharf Sidings, at the very end of the branch, on 16th May 1964. Built at Derby Works under the LM&SR in March 1925, this was another of Horton Road's complement of Class '4F' 0-6-0s which had transferred over following the closure of Barnwood shed just twelve days earlier, on 4th May. It too was to be withdrawn before year's end, in November 1964. The piles of sleepers indicate that some of the sidings had been lifted by this date. NPC

ABOVE: Hempsted Sidings looking north-west towards Bristol Road bridge on 4th August 1967. The polished line of rails heading across and off to the left led to the gas works, the rust on all of the other lines indicating that this was the only traffic now remaining on the branch. BILL POTTER/KRM

GLOUCESTER HEMPSTED BRANCH

Gas Works Siding

The scotch block with padlock which is provided at the entrance to the Gas Works Siding must always be kept locked across the rails except when necessary to be unlocked to enable vehicles to be placed in or removed from the siding. The key of the padlock is attached to the train staff.

Gardenside Sidings

Spring points set normally towards the spur are provided at the Canal End of the Gardenside Sidings at Hempsted and trains on arrival at Hempsted must first be run into one of the Gardenside Sidings.

INSET ABOVE LEFT: Instructions for working the Hempsted Branch, from the *Sectional Appendix to the Working Time Table, October 1960.* There were allotment gardens on the north side (right in the picture above) of the sidings just before the Bristol Road, which I presume is why they are referred to here as Gardenside Sidings.

LEFT: A month after the view above, on 8th September, the photographer returned to take this view of the overgrown track at the start of the gas works line. BILL POTTER/KRM

A final view of the rusting and overgrown end of the branch at Hempsted Sidings, looking south-east from the Bristol Road bridge towards Tuffley and Robinswood Hill on 4th August 1967. On the left is the chemical works of J.M. Collett & Co. Ltd, the connection serving which can just be made out running back in from the short siding on the left. A stub siding serving the end loading ramp on the right, which had probably been provided during the Second World War, had been lifted during rationalisation here in 1963. Beyond the pile of scrap the route of the connection round to Hempsted Wharf can be made out, with the gas works line heading off to the right at the far end of Hempsted Sidings. The girders of Podsmead Road bridge can just about be discerned in the middle distance. Bill Potter/KRM

SECTION 5

THE BRISTOL & GLOUCESTER LINE
TUFFLEY JUNCTION TO STONEHOUSE

Few people realise today that the Midland line between Gloucester and Bristol was originally built to the broad gauge. This was due partly to the persuasive powers of Isambard Kingdom Brunel, engineer of the GWR, who had also been appointed engineer to the Bristol & Gloucester Railway (Br&GR), and partly to their wish to use the broad gauge rails of the proposed Cheltenham & Great Western Union Railway from Standish north to Gloucester, thus saving the cost of building their own line over this section. Brunel's involvement in the Br&GR can also be seen in the designs of the stations.

The Br&GR was incorporated in 1839, to rebuild as a main line the standard gauge Bristol & Gloucestershire Railway, a colliery railway running from the north of Bristol to the city docks and to extend it north to Gloucester. The decision to change the proposed new railway to broad gauge was taken in 1842, the line opening as such to regular passenger services on Monday 8th July 1844 and to goods traffic on 2nd September. In the event, this preceded the commencement of services on the GWR line, as the section between Kemble and Standish was not completed until the following year, opening on 12th May. In 1845, the Bristol & Gloucester and Birmingham & Gloucester companies merged to form the short-lived Birmingham & Bristol Railway, which was absorbed by the Midland Railway in 1846 but the Act permitting this also required the MR to retain the broad gauge rails and so they had to purchase a small fleet of broad gauge locomotives and rolling stock to operate it. In 1848, the Midland were granted permission to convert their line to mixed gauge but the work was not completed until 1854, when they were able to sell off their broad gauge stock, whilst the

Top: A poor quality but rare view of a Brush Type '4' passing Tuffley Junction in August 1970 with train No. 1E01, a Newton Abbot to Sheffield car carrying service which comprised five Mk1 TCV Motorail vans at the front and seven coaches. Above the roof of the engine, the track of the Hempsted Docks Branch is still in place; it was lifted the following year. Chris Baldwin

Above: No. D1047 *Western Lord* with the weedkiller train in 1975, on the short branch to Quedgley RAF depot, formed partly of the old Up Goods loop here at Tuffley and further south the Up LMR line. The headcode should be 6Z07, which was that used for the Fisons weedkiller train. The 'Western', which was to be withdrawn from Laira depot in February 1976, would have to propel the train back along the single line. Rail-Online

Left: The much simplified layout at Tuffley on 1st June 1975, showing the start of the Quedgeley line and the course of the lifted docks branch on the far right. The crossovers remain today. Bill Potter/KRM

broad gauge rails were finally removed in 1872.

The line between Tuffley Junction and Stonehouse is largely level and straight, running along the lower slopes on the eastern side of the wide valley of the lower Severn, which lies between the southern Cotswold escarpment to the east and the hills of the Forest of Dean to the west. With the meeting of the two main lines at Standish, north from there to Tuffley had been four tracks possibly from opening but certainly by 1873. There was one intermediate station between Stonehouse and Tuffley, at Haresfield, opened by the Midland in 1854 when they converted the line to mixed gauge and which only ever had platforms on their side; it closed in early 1965. The line was reduced to two tracks in 1969, although staggered Up and Down loops or lie-bys were constructed at Haresfield by retaining a short length of the two lifted lines on either side. The level crossings at Naas and Haresfield were closed to road traffic at the same time.

During the First World War, No. 5 National (shell) Filling Factory was opened on the Up (west) side of the line at Quedgeley in 1915-16, served by a short branch with several loops and sidings, and a platform enabling workers – at its height 6,364 people (mainly women) were employed here filling shells – to travel to and from Gloucester by train. A signal box, opened in conjunction with the factory in 1915, closed when all of the track was lifted in late 1925 and the buildings demolished. However, the site, which had first been taken over by the War Department in 1914, remained in Ministry of Defence ownership and in early 1939, No. 7 Maintenance Unit, RAF Quedgeley was established there. New sidings were laid in to serve the depot which were brought in to use on 9th April 1939, the connection from the main line being worked by a ground frame. The depot remained in use after the war and the rail network serving it was extensive, with more sidings and other alterations being carried out in 1963. Rail traffic in and out continued until 1976 and the depot closed in 1995, the site now lost beneath the Kingsway housing estate. Being a restricted area, photographs of the railway at Quedgeley depot are practically non-existent and nothing in colour but the merest glimpse has been found.

The other major rail feature on this section of the Br&GR main line was and still is the junction at Standish. The four-track section was always operated as two separate twin-track main lines; there was a physical connection between them at Standish, although it only allowed Bristol-Gloucester trains to cross from the Midland to the GWR lines and *vice versa*; it was not until 1964 that a new crossover was laid in permitting Up and Down Stroud Valley line trains to directly access the LMR lines. Five years later, in 1969, when the four tracks from Tuffley Junction were reduced to two, a simple double track junction was all that was required here, situated just to the north of the B4008 Gloucester Road bridge at Standish. The half mile or so before the grade separation starts, where the ex-GWR line then climbs gradually as it curves away towards Stroud whilst the Midland line drops gently towards Stonehouse, is now the only section of four-track line remaining in the county.

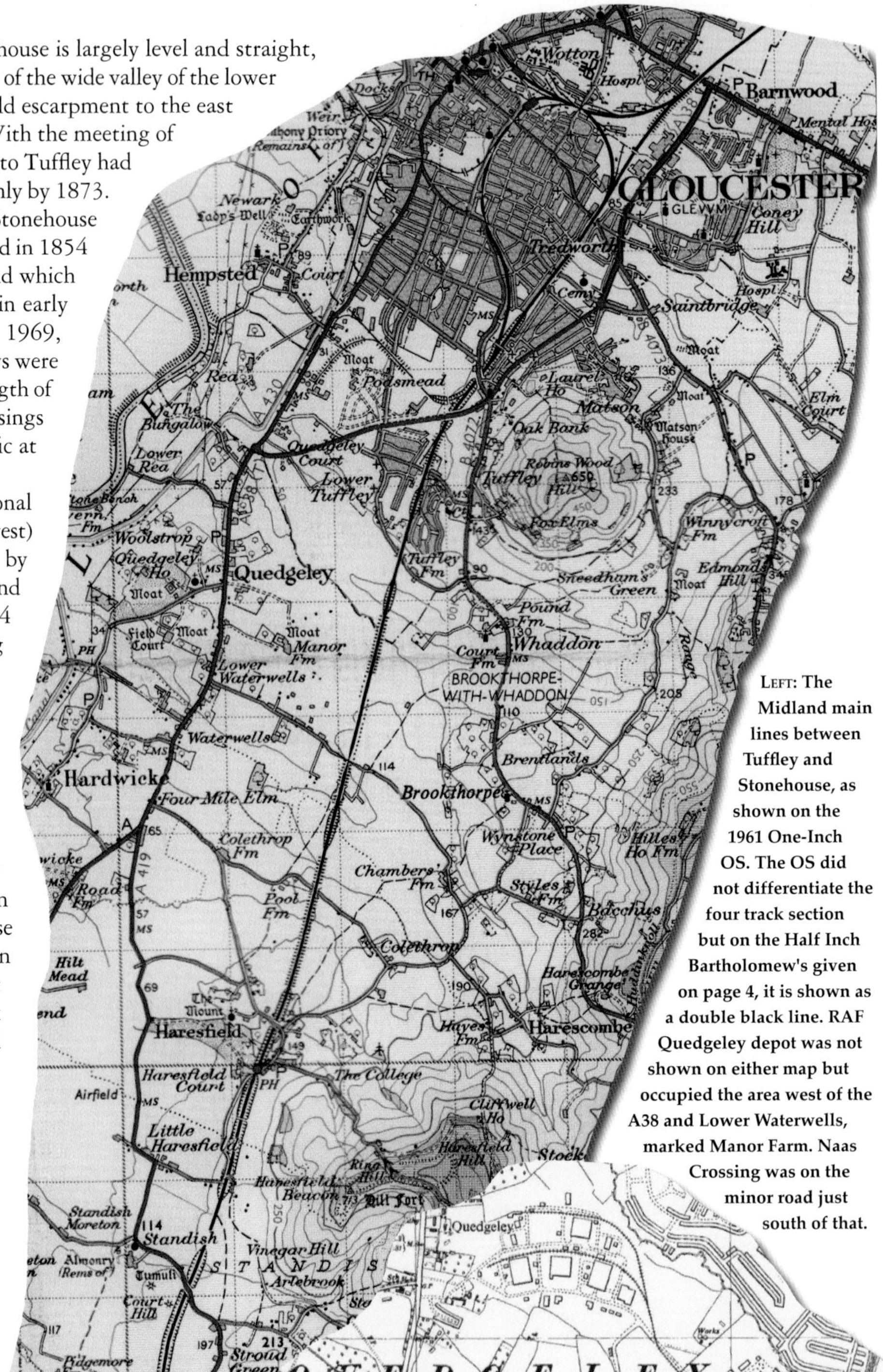

Left: The Midland main lines between Tuffley and Stonehouse, as shown on the 1961 One-Inch OS. The OS did not differentiate the four track section but on the Half Inch Bartholomew's given on page 4, it is shown as a double black line. RAF Quedgeley depot was not shown on either map but occupied the area west of the A38 and Lower Waterwells, marked Manor Farm. Naas Crossing was on the minor road just south of that.

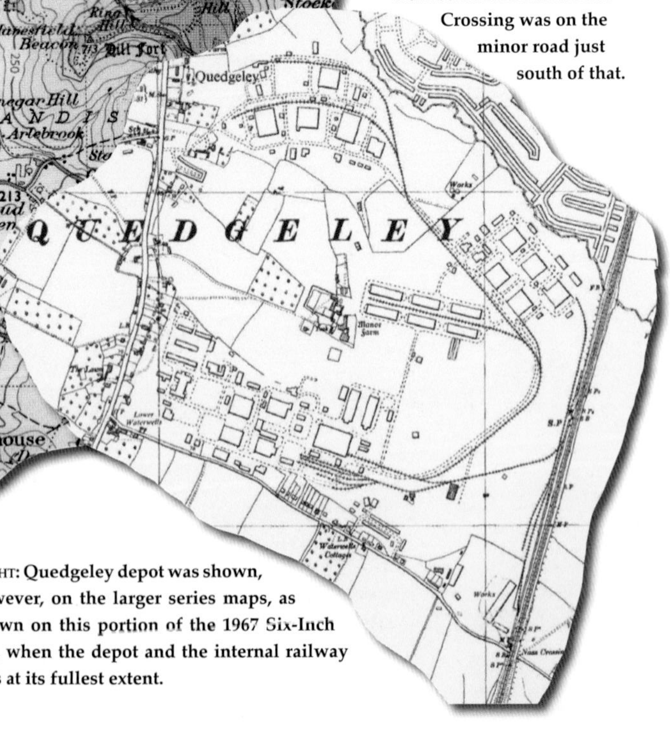

Right: Quedgeley depot was shown, however, on the larger series maps, as shown on this portion of the 1967 Six-Inch OS, when the depot and the internal railway was at its fullest extent.

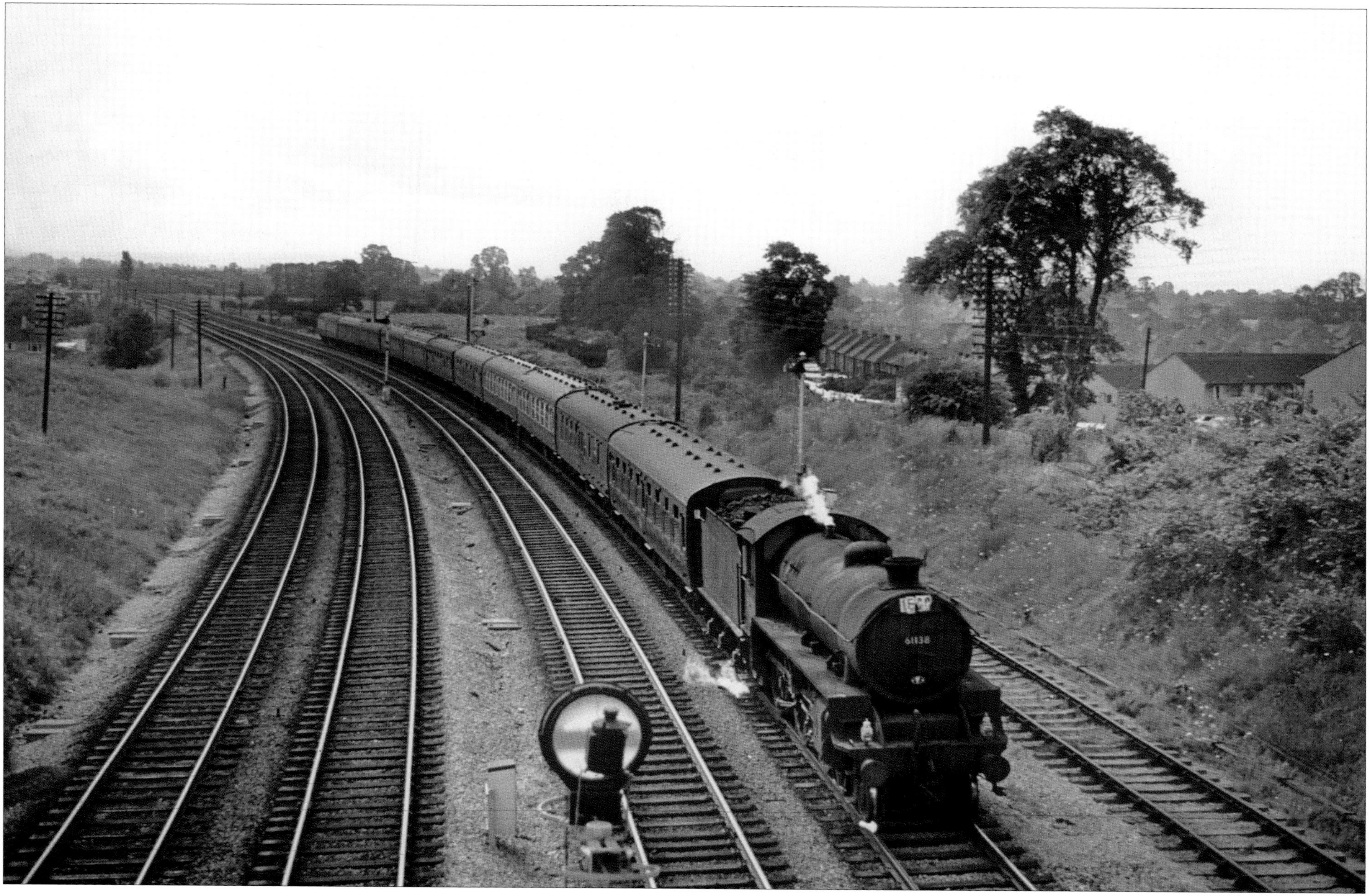

Looking south from Cole Avenue bridge, as ex-L&NER 'B1' Class No. 61138 approaches Tuffley Junction with an Up Express circa 1962. The reporting number is not clear but this is likely to be a Bristol to Sheffield train, No. 61138 being based at Sheffield Darnall from April 1961 to September 1962, after which it transferred to nearby Mexborough shed until January 1964. Built for the L&NER by the North British Locomotive Co. in March 1947 as No. 1138, it was given its BR number in December 1948 and lasted in service until early January 1965. On the right there is a rare glimpse of Tuffley Sidings, which were laid in during 1940 and accessed off the Up Goods Loop line, on the right. It would appear by this date that they were in use only for the storage of redundant wagons. Paul Riley/Courtesy the Restoration & Archiving Trust/Ref. PR2682

This is our 'merest glimpse' of the sidings serving Quedgeley depot, on the extreme left of this view looking north from Naas Crossing on Sunday 24th January 1965. The crossover served the southern connection into the depot, the rails turning in to it just being visible on the edge of the picture, the main focus of which was 'Dub-Dee' 2-8-0 No. 90069 slogging southwards in late afternoon sunshine on the Western Region lines with a heavy train of BR-built 21-ton coal hoppers, some of which are quite new. Built by the North British Locomotive Co. in June 1944 and originally WD No. 854, the engine became No. 60854 six months later and then passed in to L&NER stock in 1946, becoming No. 3069. Renumbered by BR as No. 90069 in September 1950, it passed in to WR stock in August 1951, serving at Shrewsbury, Pontypool Road, Ebbw Junction and, at the time of this view, Cardiff Canton shed. Moving to Southall in autumn 1962, it was then transferred to the Eastern Region and was withdrawn from Langwith Junction shed in January 1966. Roy Denison

Swinging round, the photographer took this second view of the 'Dub-Dee' as it headed towards Haresfield. As well as providing us with a fine view of this now long lost section of four track main line, we also get a partial glimpse of Naas Crossing signal box, which was reduced to ground frame status in 1968 with the removal of two of the lines and renamed Brookthorpe Crossing (probably to distinguish it from Naas Lane level crossing near Lydney). The ground frame has now gone completely and the crossing is pedestrian only; road traffic can use a short detour via an underbridge a couple of hundred yards to the south, which was only opened as a through route around 1980 despite the bridge having been built with the line. Approximately half a mile in the distance, beyond the low cutting, a bridge now carries the remaining two lines over the M5 motorway, this section of which was opened in 1971. Roy Denison

Photographs of Naas Crossing box are rare, so although not of the greatest quality, this view taken on 12th August 1968 fully merits including. Also shown is the crossing gate on the Up side, with a group of schoolboys perched on it, and the crossing keeper's cottage beyond. The box was another Midland Type 1 and may date from the mid-1870s but was certainly here by 1883. Behind is one of the large factory buildings that formed the RAF Quedgeley depot. These are the only colour views seen which give any sort of glimpse of it at all but if anyone can assist with any other pictures before the next volume comes out, I can include them in that. As it will cover the GWR line from Gloucester to Swindon via Stroud, we will pass along this section of railway again. A total of sixteen different locomotives worked the depot railway system, over the years, all diesels. David Stowell

Viewed from Dunn's Bridge (No. 94) just to the north of Haresfield station, No. 45232 heads south with an 'all stations stopper'; to Bristol in August 1964. The 'Black Five', built for the LM&SR by Armstrong Whitworth in August 1936, was allocated to Burton-on-Trent shed at the date of this view, so having previously arrived at Gloucester, had presumably been pressed in to service by the Horton Road shedmaster to cover this working. Further allocations followed in 1966 to Warrington Dallam and then Birkenhead Mollington Street, before withdrawal from Liverpool Speke Junction in November 1967. JOHN STRANGE/NPC

Photographed working northwards tender first on the Western Region lines though Haresfield on 26th June 1963, Class '4F' 0-6-0 No. 44123 had been a Gloucester-based engine for many years. Built at the ex-London & North Western Railway Crewe Works in the early part of the LM&SR era, in July 1925, the engine had been transferred to Barnwood shed in September 1950. It then moved across to Horton Road in May 1964 when Barnwood closed and was withdrawn from there in early June 1965. LMR trains that were heading straight on at Tuffley Junction, rather than running via the Tuffley Loop, gained the WR lines at Standish Junction, whilst the tender first running suggests that the train may have been a trip working from the ex-Midland Nailsworth & Stroud Branch. NPC

A filthy '4F' 0-6-0, No. 44605, leaking steam and clearly burning some very poor quality coal, heads a Bristol to Gloucester local away from Haresfield station on 25th July 1964. New in February 1941, this Saltley-based engine's time left in service was not long, withdrawal occurring two months after the picture was taken, in late September. Dunn's Bridge (No. 94), which carries Haresfield Lane over the railway, comprised four cast iron rib plates supporting cast iron floor plates and mounted on blue brick abutments and wing walls. The corrugated iron parapets have since been rebuilt in red brick. There are still three tracks here at this point, the line the '4F' is on was being in place as the Up loop or lie-bye, although both it and the Down lie-bye, south of the station site, look to have seen little use in recent years. Tony Bowles/Courtesy the Restoration & Archiving Trust/Ref. ARC00273

A quiet moment at Haresfield in April 1964, looking south from the Down platform. The uneven boards would have made walking along it hazardous, particularly at night given the poor lighting. Note too how narrow it was, having been slotted in between the two sets of double track main lines when the station first opened on 29th May 1854. John Strange/NPC

Left: An unidentified Stanier 'Mogul' hurries north through Haresfield station with an Up holiday express – possibly a relief working given the motive power – in August 1964. The camera has not managed to 'stop' the locomotive's front end, so nothing about the train can be gleaned. NPC

Right: The Up platform buildings and signal box from a Down 'stopper' circa 1962. Haresfield was at one time staffed by a station master and two porters, as well as a signalman. However, the platform staff had been reduced to just one person by the end, who may have still held station master status. It is clear from the pictures that whoever was here on a full time basis took some care with the platform gardens, in between his other less than onerous duties. NPC

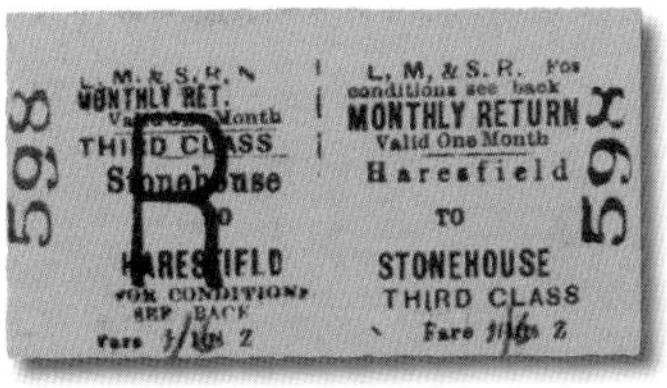

A Down train scampers through Haresfield and over the crossing in August 1964, headed by a 'Jubilee' Class 4-6-0. Again the camera has failed to 'freeze' the locomotive's smokebox but, under heavy magnification, the cabside number appears to be No. 45557 *New Brunswick*, which had recently transferred from Burton to Derby at the date of this view. Courtesy of the BristolSteam64 website, this could therefore be train No. 4V44, the 5.50am from Washwood Heath to Bristol on Friday 14th August. Later that day, No. 45557 worked back to Derby with train No. 5M27. However, its career of just over thirty years was drawing to a close and it was to be withdrawn just four weeks later. There is another partial view of the signal box on the left. NPC

Looking back through the platforms towards Gloucester from the foot crossing at the south end in April 1964. Most trains did not stop here and this was a fast section section of line, so great care had to be taken using the crossing. However, the lack of space between the LMR Down line and the GWR Down line precluded the provision of a footbridge, whilst the Down platform, having been squeezed in to the available space, was not wide enough to accommodate any form of shelter. Indeed, standing on this platform as a Down WR express thundered northwards just feet behind must have been a somewhat disconcerting experience for some passengers. The train service comprised five trains each way Mondays to Saturdays, generally time tabled for those going to and from work or coming home late, and there was no Sunday service. JOHN STRANGE/NPC

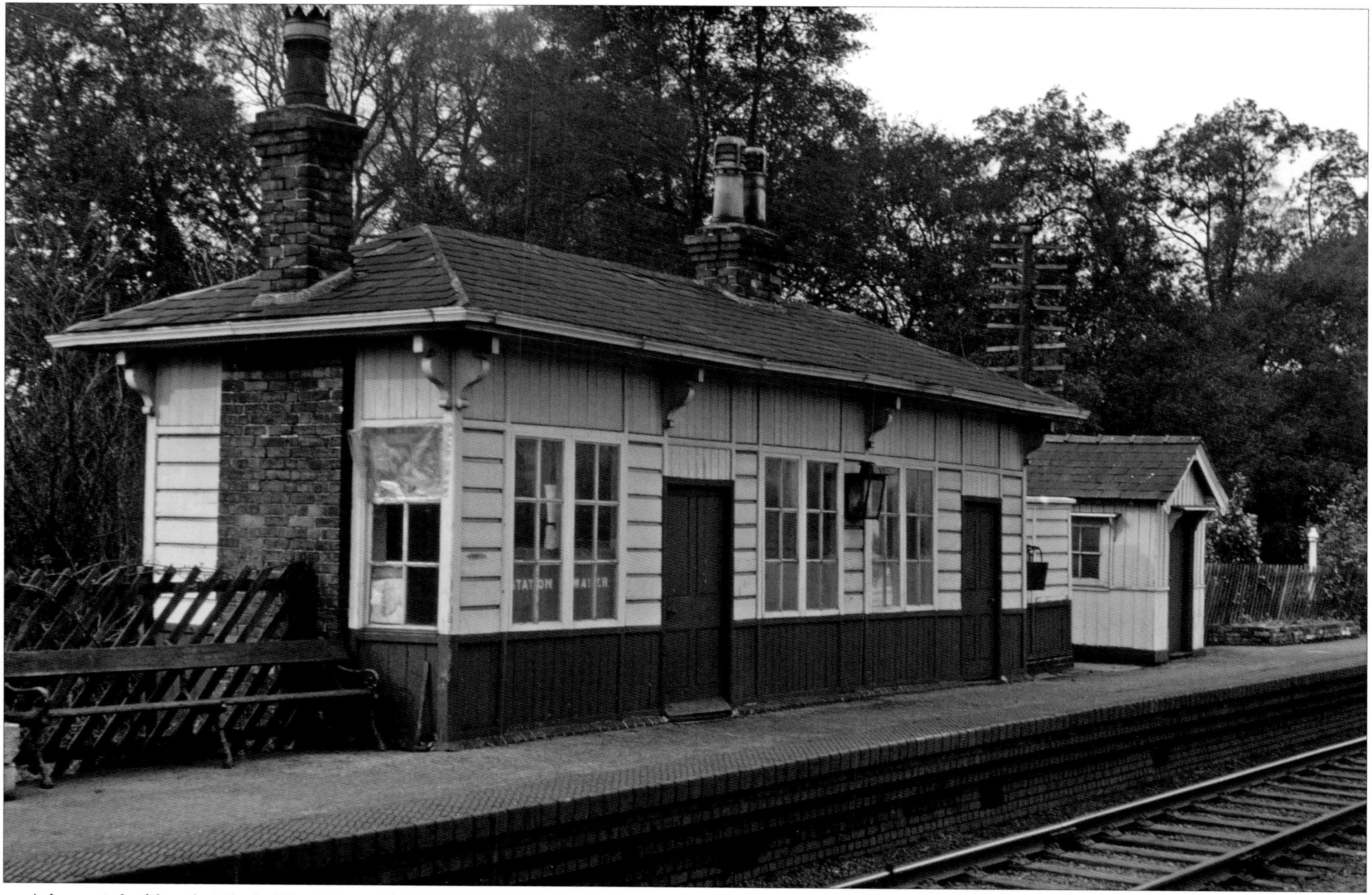

A close-up study of the main station building on the same day. The wooden building probably dated from the opening of the station by the Midland Railway in 1854 but the brick faced Up platform was originally of wood as well and remained so into the 20th century; it was rebuilt in brick as seen here probably after the First World War. The building had a hipped slate roof with brick chimneys serving the fireplaces in the station master's office and the waiting room. There was a gents urinal at the far end but whether there was any provision for ladies is not known – they were often not catered for in the Victorian era and it may not have been considered worth the expense later on. The smaller hut at the north end may have been a parcels office. This is not a well documented station so any further information about it would be welcome. John Strange/NPC

LEFT AND BELOW: This ex-Somerset & Dorset Joint Railway sack barrow had somehow found its way north to Haresfield from an unknown S&D line station. Having an interest in such items, the photographer had it posed so he could capture it for posterity. With closure less than a year away, doubtless it would have been thrown away, along with the ancient Midland platform trolley, below, which had clearly reached the end of its useful days. JOHN STRANGE/NPC

BELOW: A final view of the station and the rear of the Down platform from a train passing by on the WR Up line circa 1962. The only additional protection for passengers on the Down platform was the wooden screen nailed to the fence. NPC

RIGHT: Haresfield crossing on 12th August 1968, shortly after the resignalling which saw the four track main line reduced to two and the signal box reduced to gate box status. The tracks remaining here were the former Up Midland nearest to the box, which was now out of use and awaiting lifting; the former Down Midland which was now the Up Charfield, the former Down Western which was now the Down Charfield and the former Up Western which, courtesy of a new point off the Down Charfield, was now the new Down Goods Loop. DAVID STOWELL

ABOVE: Haresfield level crossing circa 1971, after the box had been reduced to the status of a ground frame controlling the crossing gates and associated locking. This was under Stage 3B of the Gloucester MAS scheme, which covered the section from Tuffley Junction to Standish Junction and was brought into use between 10.00pm on 14th September 1968 and 8.00pm on 15th September 1968. The box remained in use until the level crossing was closed to vehicular traffic and was replaced by a pedestrian foot crossing, controlled by miniature red and green warning lights. Note the end of the old carriage body in use as a storage shed on the right. DEREK J. JONES

LEFT: Gloucester S&T Installers Ray Jones, Peter Whitcomb and nineteen year old Roger Phelps, who had just started on the railway, take a break from their duties at Haresfield circa 1971. In the doorway is Den Gainey, the signalman here who was now demoted to crossing attendant. Roger Phelps is today general manager of the Dean Forest Railway and a qualified signalling examiner. Note the outside toilet at the far end of the box. DEREK J. JONES

Celebrity Class '9F' 2-10-0 No. 92220 *Evening Star*, the last steam locomotive built by British Railways, in March 1960 at Swindon Works, heads north towards Haresfield with a mixed freight. The slide is undated but is likely to be either the late summer/autumn of 1962 or the late summer/autumn of 1963, when No. 92220 was based at Bath Green Park shed. Its final posting was to Cardiff Canton in October 1963, from where it was withdrawn on 12th April 1965 after a month less than five years in service. Earmarked for preservation when built, it was the only '9F' to be painted in BR lined green passenger livery. After a number of years running in preservation on various lines, *Evening Star* is today a static exhibit at the National Railway Museum in York. The train is passing beneath Butt's Bridge (No. 92), carrying a farm track and access lane to Dowager Cottage over the line. Of similar construction to bridge No. 94 at Haresfield but utilising only three cast iron rib eye girders instead of four, it remains today but now has a mesh fence parapet in place of the corrugated iron one seen here. Just glimpsed though it in the distance is Martin's Bridge, of identical construction and carrying a farm access track, which was demolished circa the early 1970s. All three bridges were a single 72ft span. NPC

Class '9F' No. 92151 of Saltley shed drifts by just south of Haresfield with a long train of steel mineral wagons probably carrying Warwickshire coal on 23rd May 1964. Having skirted Gloucester via the Avoiding Line, No. 92151 and its train will cross to the LMR lines at Standish Junction to head towards Bristol, probably bound for St. Philips Yard. The '9F' spent nine years of its short career at Saltley, the final five months being at Birkenhead Mollington Street. NPC

Heading the opposite way on 25th June 1964 was another Saltley engine, Class '4F' No. 44137, with train No. 8M49, the 11.15am mineral empties from St. Philips Yard to Washwood Heath. New in October 1925, the '4F' just fell short of reaching forty years in service when it was withdrawn in February 1965. NPC

'Black Five' No. 44765 heads train No. 1V31 (number not visible but this was a Nottingham to Bristol holiday relief) between Haresfield and Standish just before midday on 25th July 1964. This engine was one of two of the class (No. 44766 was the other) experimentally fitted with a double chimney late in the LM&SR era, whilst retaining standard Walschaerts valve gear. No. 44767 was given a double chimney and outside Stephenson link motion, whilst twenty of the first BR-built members of the class were given double chimneys and Caprotti valve gear. No. 44765 had been allocated to Crewe North since it entered traffic in December 1947 but transferred to Crewe South in early June 1965 and was withdrawn from there in September 1967. Tony Bowles/Courtesy the Restoration & Archiving Trust/Ref. ARC05388

Looking in the opposite direction but a couple of days later on 27th July, the photographer captured 'Jubilee' Class No. 45608 *Gibraltar* passing at the head of a northbound holiday relief, train No. 1N48 from Bristol to York. New in 1934, the locomotive was based at Leeds Holbeck at this date. It was withdrawn at the beginning of September 1965. Tony Bowles/Courtesy the Restoration & Archiving Trust/Ref. ARC05389

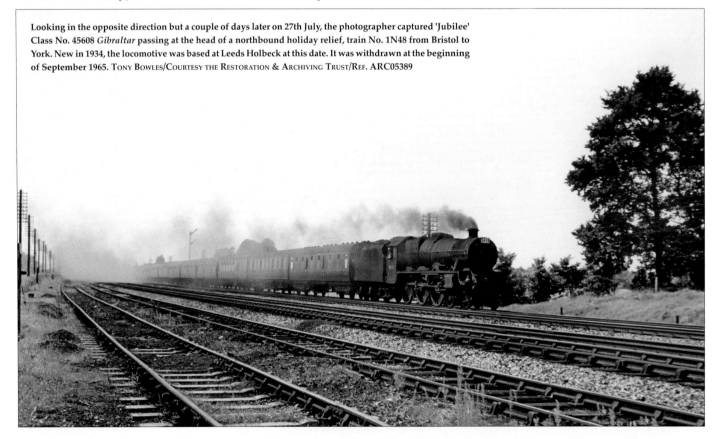

Between 1943 and 1969, there existed a short section of six track railway between Haresfield and Standish Junction, courtesy of two goods loops laid in on the Up GWR/WR side of the line. They appear incidentally in the pictures that follow over the next few pages and we shall see more of them in the next volume – *The Gloucester to Swindon Line and Branches*. Here, on 25th July 1964, as another 'Black Five' 4-6-0, No. 44666, whips by with train No. 1V42, a York to Bristol summer Saturday holiday relief, we get a view of the north end of the loops and the connection in to them off the WR Up line. The sheen on the rails indicates that they were still well used as this time but they were to be removed when this section was reduced to two tracks. A British Railways build at Crewe Works in the summer of 1949, No. 44666 was based at Saltley when seen here so may have taken over the train at Birmingham. Alternatively, it may have worked north from its Midlands base a day or so before and then been turned around to bring this train south. The engine moved to Tyseley in October 1965 and was withdrawn from Liverpool Edge Hill in September 1966. TONY BOWLES/COURTESY THE RESTORATION & ARCHIVING TRUST/REF. AR05219

RIGHT: An unidentified 'Jubilee' Class 4-6-0 speeds north through Standish in June 1961. The train reporting number is also not readable, so the destination of this summer Saturday express can only be guessed at but the leading vehicle, an ex-L&NER Brake Composite, would probably suggest that it was bound for somewhere in the north-east. JOHN STRANGE/NPC

LEFT: The Summer 1961 Time Table saw the introduction of diesel-hauled services on the Birmingham-Bristol main line from 12th June and the last Saturday of full steam working was in early July. Sadly, whilst the photographer returned here to record some of the workings on that day, he did not make a note of the actual date as well. With little information to go on, I have tried to put these pictures in what I think is the likely sequence of trains passing. I think that these first two views, under a somewhat overcast sky, probably begin proceedings. No. 43887 hurries past the loops with a southbound van train. Built at the Midland's Derby Works in late 1919, the '4F' had been on Barnwood shed's allocation from at least 1946, so the first thought was that this was a Gloucester to Stoke Gifford freight, running late as there were only two in the working time table, one at 4.55am and one at 8.55pm. More likely perhaps is the 5.00am Washwood Heath to Westerleigh, which arrived at Gloucester at 8.37am and departed at 9.12am, probably having changed engines; it was due past Standish at 9.27am. JOHN STRANGE/NP

RIGHT: I have surmised that next in John Strange;s sequence of pictures came classmate No. 44263 of Saltley shed, scampering by with a five-coach Birmingham to Bristol service, possibly the 8.10am ex-New Street which had called at Barnt Green, Worcester Shrub Hill, Ashchurch and Cheltenham Lansdown on the journey to Eastgate. Departing from there at 10.01am after a five minute stop, calls would then be made at Stonehouse Bristol Road, Charfield and Wickwar only on the run to Temple Meads, where arrival was scheduled for 11.01am. The train was due past the photographer at about 10.15am. No. 44263 was transferred to Horton Road in May 1964 but its time there was brief, withdrawal taking place at the end of January 1965. JOHN STRANGE/NPC

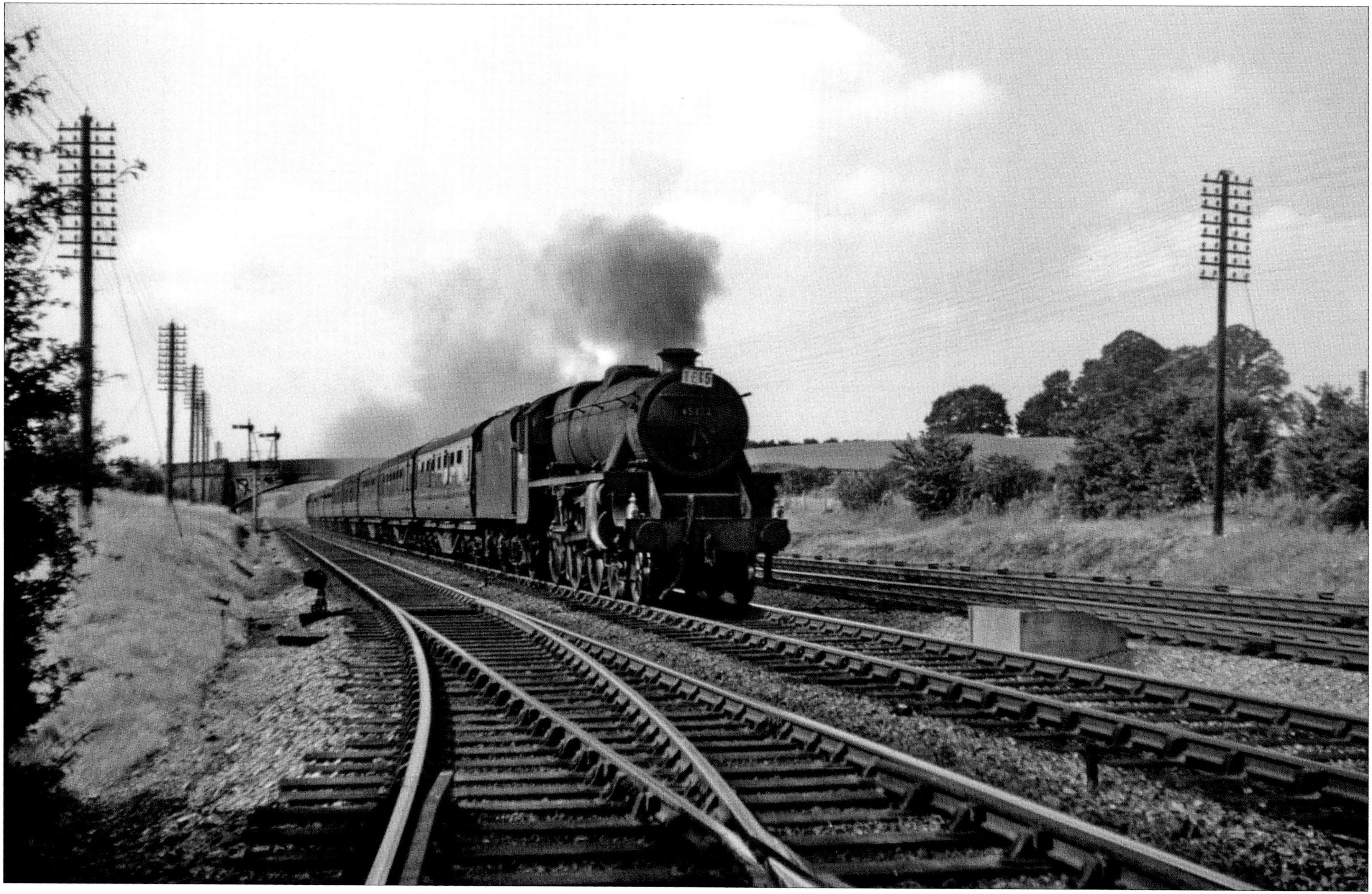

With the day clearly starting to warm up as the sun broke through the cloudy haze, another of Saltley's vast stable of engines, 'Black Five' No. 45272, was then photographed heading north past the southern exit from the loops at Standish with train No. 1E65, a summer Saturday holiday express from Weston-super-Mare to Sheffield. Off Bristol Temple Meads at 9.55am, it was due past here at 10.37am and in to Birmingham New Street at 12.18pm. The train had crossed over to the WR lines at Standish Junction, to then run non-stop past Gloucester on the Avoiding Line. Built for the LM&SR by Armstrong, Whitworth in Newcastle in November 1936, No. 45272 ended a near ten-year sojourn at Saltley when it transferred to Shrewsbury in late April 1964, a brief stay there being followed by equally short visits to Crewe North and Mold Junction, before returning to Saltley and then on to Wolverhampton Oxley for its last six months in service, prior to withdrawal in October 1965. John Strange/NPC

ABOVE: 'Royal Scot' Class 4-6-0 No. 46106 *Gordon Highlander* speeds south past a northbound express. The 'Scot' was in the midst of a three month allocation to Derby, so whilst the train reporting number is not fully readable, this looks to be 1V30, the 8.00am off Derby, calling Birmingham New Street at 9.15am, Eastgate at 10.35am, due past Standish Junction at 10.51am and in to Bristol Temple Meads at 11.39am. If that is the case then the Up train is likely to be No. 1N65, the 6.50am from Paignton to Bradford, due past Standish at 10.52am. New in September 1927 and unique in being the only 'Scot' fitted with BR 'Standard' smoke-deflectors, No. 46106 was to be withdrawn from Carlisle Upperby shed in December 1962. JOHN STRANGE/NPC

RIGHT: Also heading south shortly afterwards was this rather grimy unidentified BR Standard Class '5' 4-6-0 with train No. 1V36, the 7.32am from Bradford to Bristol, which was due past Standish at 12.48pm. JOHN STRANGE/NPC

LEFT: Ex-GWR Class '14XX' 0-4-2T No. 1424 was also photographed, heading 'light engine' back to Horton Road, after a time working the Berkeley Road-Sharpness branch shuttle. I think this move is unusual, as I can find no number for it in the 1961 WTT, whilst the branch engine would normally have spent the full day there, so perhaps there was a problem; the 0-6-0PT which we shall shortly see heading south on page 149 is likely to have been its replacement. The truncated run to Sharpness was what remained of the Berkeley Road-Lydney Town service following the accident which had severely damaged the Severn Bridge in October 1960 (see *Vol. 2: Forest of Dean Lines and the Severn Bridge*), which ultimately led to its official closure and demolition. New in November 1933 to Goodwick shed near Fishguard, No. 1424 moved to Gloucester in 1942 and then spent most of the rest of its career working from there, prior to withdrawal in early December 1963. JOHN STRANGE/NPC

Class '4F' No. 44560 heads south with a train of loaded ballast hoppers on 7th August 1965. The ballast is likely to have come from Whitecliff Quarry in the Forest of Dean, with the train having been assembled for onward movement at Gloucester New Yard (see *Gloucester Midland Lines Part One: North*, page 218). The locomotive was built by Armstrong, Whitworth in 1922 and spent a fair part of its career on the Somerset & Dorset Joint line, being stationed at Bath Green Park in 1948 and then moving to Templecombe in 1960. However, it had moved to Horton Road in November 1964 and was to be withdrawn from there a fortnight after this picture was taken. Note that No. 44560 was still carrying the Whitaker token catching apparatus on the tender side that was fitted to S&D locomotives. DON MANN

In July 1964, 'Grange' Class 4-6-0 No. 6819 *Highnam Grange* heads south through Standish Junction on the Midland lines with a Wolverhampton to Torquay summer Saturday express. New in to service in December 1936 and having spent much of its BR era career working from sheds in South Wales, No. 6819 transferred to Worcester in June 1964, not long before this picture was taken. It looks in desparate need of a clean here, with little sign of its BR passenger lined green livery showing through a thick coating of dirt and grime. Nevertheless, it still had another sixteen months of service left, being withdrawn from Worcester shed in mid-November 1965. Note the unusual design of the Down Home signal which the engine has just passed, with the arm raised and centrally positioned above the post to allow for the limited clearance between the Down LMR and WR lines. NPC

An unidentified ex-LM&SR Class '8F' 2-8-0 assists with relaying work at Standish in autumn 1964, when a new double junction was laid in. Tony Cooke, in one of the early editions of his GWR/WR track plans series, *Section 35 Gloucester and Cheltenham*, noted that the work was carried out over the weekend of 24th-26th October 1964; if that is correct, the warm colours of the surrounding vegetation suggests that there was something of an Indian summer that year. The new junction was laid in so that services between Cheltenham, Swindon and London could be diverted to run via Eastgate and the Tuffley Loop from 31st October 1964, thereby cutting out the reversals required at Gloucester Central station. The change also meant that trains were now diesel operated throughout, as it also did away with the need for tank locomotives to haul the coaches between Gloucester and Cheltenham. Here at Standish, these trains could now run directly to and from the WR line. Note that the signal seen in the previous picture had been taken out and is on the ground alongside the '8F's tender. NPC

Three years earlier, prior to the new junction being laid in, Class '8F' 2-8-0 No. 48183 throws a trail of thick, claggy smoke across the tracks as it powers towards the Whitminster Bridge (No. 91) with a train of steel mineral wagons loaded with coal on 17th March 1962. As this selection of pictures indicates, the bridge, which carries the B4008 Gloucester Road over the line, was a popular location for photography. A war-time build, by the North British Locomotive Co. in April 1942, the '8F' was based at Saltley at the date of the view, so this is likely to be Warwickshire coal heading south. Withdrawal was from Leicester Midland shed in July 1965. NPC

Again sending a plume of dirty black smoke high in to the air, 'Black Five' No. 44919 grinds its way past the new North Junction with a trainload of coal on 17th October 1965. The locomotive had transferred from Saltley to Wolverhampton Oxley earlier in the year and was withdrawn from there in December 1966. Built by the LM&SR at Crewe Works shortly after the end of the Second World War, in December 1945, the highlight of No. 44919's career came on 11th July 1964, when it hauled the Royal train with HM The Queen Mother on board, on her way to reopen the southern section of the Stratford upon Avon Canal. As can be seen, just over a year later, it was in a far less well cared for state than it had been on that day. Colour-Rail

LEFT: Following the reduction of the four tracks between Tuffley and Standish to two in 1968, the layout here was much simplified, a simple double junction between the two twin track main lines sufficing. An unidentified 'Peak' Class '45' speeds through on to the Bristol line at Standish Junction with a Down express in August 1976.
MIKE SQUIRE/COURTESY THE RESTORATION & ARCHIVING TRUST/REF. MSZZ4232

RIGHT: A three-car set in all over BR blue livery takes the Bristol line on 23rd August 1976. This looks like a BRCW unit of Class '118', which would fit with the body style (with roof-mounted headcode box) and the WXXX24 number. The candidate would be No. 51324 (which is a DMS) and the unit for that car was No. B467 but it could well be reformed into unit No. 470 displacing car No. 51328, according to the 1976 RCTS book with WR unit formations. Unit No. 470 was allocated to Laira at this time, so would be an unusual candidate for a Gloucester to Bristol service but not impossible. BILL POTTER/KRM

LEFT: In the first of four views all taken within an hour or so in bright sunshine on 13th November 1976, Class '46' No. 46030 heads a Down express on to the Bristol line. The 'Peak' was new from BR's Derby Works in May 1962 as No. D167, being renumbered under TOPS on 2nd February 1974. It had five more years left in service when seen here, withdrawal taking place on 1st November 1981. Note that by this date BR had dispensed with train reporting numbers and the headcode boxes either displayed all zeroes or, for certain classes such as the 'Western's which had four digit numbers, the locomotive's number.
MIKE SQUIRE/COURTESY THE RESTORATION & ARCHIVING TRUST/REF. MSZZ4189

RIGHT: This is probably the train that the photographer postioned himself here to capture. Class '52' diesel hydraulic No. D1013 *Western Ranger* heads 'The Cornishman' rail tour south through the junction, bound for Penzance. Under train reporting No. 1Z68, the tour had set out from Nottingham at 5.50am behind 'Peak' No. 45041, double heading with No. 44006 between Derby and Birmingham. The 'Western' then took over for the run to Cornwall. Departure from Penzance was at 4.40pm but timings from there back to Nottingham are not known. No. D1013 was withdrawn from Laira depot at the end of February 1977.
MIKE SQUIRE/COURTESY THE RESTORATION & ARCHIVING TRUST/REF. MSZZ4192

LEFT: The sequence of these views has been ascertained by careful study of the shadows, which move slightly between each picture. Thus next came Class '50' No. 50017 heading a Down express taking the Bristol line at Standish Junction. The class gained the nickname 'Hoovers' due to the body shape resembling said domestic appliances. No. 50017 was built by English Electric at their Vulcan Foundry works in spring 1968 and was originally No. D417. At the date of this view it was allocated to Bristol Bath Road. On 24th April 1978, it was named *Royal Oak* at Laira depot, a name it carried until withdrawal in September 1991.
MIKE SQUIRE/COURTESY THE RESTORATION & ARCHIVING TRUST/REF. MSZZ4188

RIGHT: Lastly on the same day, Class '31' No. 31251 was seen heading a long train of box vans towards Bristol. Built by Brush Traction in Loughborough and new in to service as No. D5679 in December 1960, the Class '31' was allocated to March depot in Cambridgeshire at the date of this view, so was some way from home. Renumbered in 1973, it was withdrawn on 1st September 1993 and scrapped eleven years later, in September 2004 by Booths of Rotherham. The trackbed to the right of the train had previously carried the other pair of lines, whilst the Up WR loop sidings had occupied the land just beyond the hedge in the right middle distance.
MIKE SQUIRE/COURTESY THE RESTORATION & ARCHIVING TRUST/REF. MSZZ4187

Now well known 'Modified Hall' Class No. 6998 *Burton Agnes Hall* works north beneath Gloucester Road bridge with a parcels train from Bristol on 14th August 1965. An early BR build, in January 1949, the locomotive was based at Southall shed in west London, transferring to Oxford a month after this picture was taken. Withdrawn from there at the end of WR steam, No. 6998 achieved lasting fame when it became the last steam locomotive to haul a passenger train on the Western Region of BR in January 1966. The engine is today preserved at Didcot Railway Centre, albeit currently awaiting overhaul for a return to steam again. Don Mann

Same day, same location! Green-liveried No. D1002 *Western Explorer* heads north with train No. 1A15, from Paddington to Gloucester. Running via Kemble and Stroud, this could also be a picture for the next volume but the train had been retimed to run to and from Eastgate the previous summer, which is why it is here seen crossing over to the LMR Up line via the new North Junction. No. D1002 had been in service since March 1962 and was withdrawn in January 1974. Although of similar construction to the previous few pages, No. 91 had red brick abutments supporting five rib eye girders and the span is 83ft on the skew. The corrugated iron parapets have been rebuilt in red brick and Network Rail now refers to it as Standish Overbridge BGL2. Don Mann

After passing beneath bridge No. 91, Gloucester Horton Road's heavily work stained BR 'Standard' Class '2' 2-6-0 No. 78006 ambles across the South Junction crossover from the WR Up line to the LMR Down, watched by the Standish Junction signalman on 31st October 1964. This Midland Railway Type '4C' box was opened on 25th July 1908, replacing an earlier box which had stood adjacent just to the south. The opposing Up and Down directions of the GWR/WR and MR/LMR running lines required the signalmen here to maintain two train registers. The box was closed on 14th October 1968, following the removal of one of the pairs of tracks to Gloucester and the consequent simplification of the junction, with control transferred to the new Gloucester power box. The new North Junction, installed a few days previously, can be glimpsed through the bridge arch and the view again indicates that the UK was enjoying an Indian Summer in 1964. New in March 1953, No. 78006 was withdrawn at the end of December 1965. Roy Denison

'Black Five' No. 45280 heads north past Standish Junction with a long train of vans in June 1962. Based at Saltley shed from June 1958 to June 1965, the train is most probably bound for Washwood Heath yard, so could perhaps be the 2.40pm from Westerleigh. Built for the LM&SR by Armstrong, Whitworth in November 1936, No. 45280 later had stints at Holyhead, Chester, Birkenhead Mollington Street and Liverpoool Speke Junction prior to being withdrawn in November 1967. DAVID BICK/NPC

Although probably only around nine years old when seen here passing Standish Junction box circa 1965, the filthy, rust stained condition of '9F' No. 92086 shows how many locomotives were suffering from neglect as the end of steam grew near. New from Crewe Works in June 1956, the picture probably dates from the summer of 1965, No. 92086 having transferred to Birkenhead Mollington Street shed at the beginning of July. Despite its appearance here, the engine was to complete over two more years in service, being withdrawn from Liverpool Speke Junction shed in November 1967. The train, again of vans, is likely to be perishables from Avonmouth Docks, bound probably for one of the yards in the Birmingham area. D.B. SWALE/COLOUR-RAIL

On 2nd January 1965, 'Black Five' No. 44888 was seen scampering north with a Bristol to Gloucester 'stopper' calling all stations to Eastgate. The photographer's visit here so early in the new year was timely, as the stations at Yate, Wickwar, Charfield, Berkeley Road, Coaley Junction, Stonehouse Bristol Road and Haresfield were all closed to passengers from Monday 5th January (Frocester had closed in 1961). With no Sunday service, this was therefore the final day for these stopping trains. Shortly to be transferred to Stockport Edgeley, No. 44888 was based at Burton-on-Trent at the date of this view but presumably Horton Road had pressed it in to service to cover this working. The cessation of all of the local branch and secondary line passenger services covered by the shed two months earlier on 1st November 1964 had seen the wholesale withdrawal of many of the small and medium size locomotives from Horton Road's allocation. Built at Crewe Works in August 1945, No. 44888 survived until the end of steam on BR, being withdrawn from Lostock Hall shed, Lancashire in August 1968. The connection here between the two main lines became Standish South Junction in 1964, after the installation of the new North Junction crossover. Prior to that, from 1873 this had been the only junction between the GWR and Midland main lines, there having been no call for trains from the Stroud direction to run to or from Eastgate. John Strange/NPC

RIGHT AND BELOW: Two views of the site of the junction in 1976, after it had been moved north of the Gloucester Road bridge and the line from there to Gloucester reduced to two tracks. This short length is now the only section of four track main line in the county. Both also show unidentified Class '45' 'Peak' diesels powering north with Up expresses, the picture right taken on 13th November 1976 and that below earlier the same year, on 23rd August. Locomotive hauled passenger trains through here are now a rarity, except on the occasional special. The wooden pw shed seen in both views is also now a memory but the brick building in the foreground below, which houses power equipment for the junction, now has a hipped tiled roof. The 40mph speed restriction sign also seen below was for trains approaching the junction from the Stroud direction.
RIGHT: MIKE SQUIRES/COURTESY THE RESTORATION & ARCHIVING TRUST/REF. MSZZ4191
BELOW: BILL POTTER/KRM

BELOW: Stanier Class '8F' 2-8-0 No. 48456 has just passed Standish Junction and is now starting to drop down below the level of the ex-GWR route, as the two main lines part company, as it heads towards Bristol with a trainload of coal in October 1964. With the locomotive based at Nuneaton, this would once again be coal from the Warwickshire coalfield. Apart from a few weeks on loan to Stockport Edgeley in 1956, No. 48456 spent most of its BR career at Nuneaton, first being allocated there in October 1949. It looks in smart condition here for a freight engine at this date, so may have just had a light overhaul. Transferred to Buxton in early June 1966, it was withdrawn a month later.
TONY BOWLES/COURTESY THE RESTORATION & ARCHIVING TRUST/REF. ARC00405

From the opposite side of the cutting to the previous picture but again looking back towards the junction, '9F' 2-10-0 No. 92236 drops down towards Stonehouse on 21st December 1963. With the sun shining brightly on what was clearly a cold crisp day, No. 92236 is producing a fine plume of clean white steam despite being on a downward slope with its heavy train. This includes a rake of nine fairly new looking tanks at the front; they are ICI G (for glycol) tanks hired from Tank Rentals and working from Severnside to Wilton. They were 40T glw vacuum braked vehicles and some appear to have a nameplate at the left-hand end of the tank, which looks like an RIV plate but which is actually an ICI plate. Typically they are a raft in this train but there were also dedicated company services later in the decade.. No. 92236 was built at Crewe Works in September 1958 and spent its career allocated to sheds in South Wales, starting with Pontypool Road, before transfers then to Ebbw Junction, Cardiff Canton, Cardiff East Dock (at the date of this picture) and finally Severn Tunnel Junction, from where it was withdrawn in early March 1965 – a service life of less than six and a half years. Trevor Owen/Colour-Rail

An unidentified Class '57XX' 0-6-0PT heads 'light engine' down the bank bound for Berkeley Road and a stint on the Sharpness Branch in July 1961. The shadows suggest an afternoon view, so perhaps the pannier tank was taking over from No. 1424, seen heading in the other direction back to Gloucester on page 136. This move would normally have been made under train reporting No. 0B57 at this date. John Strange/NPC

'Jubilee' Class No. 45626 *Seychelles* storms up the bank beneath Standish Black Bridge (No. 90) with a northbound express in July 1961. As with the picture above, although the photographer had not marked the mounts as such, I suspect that these may be more of his 'last Saturday of full steam haulage' slides. Built at Crewe Works and new in to service in November 1934, *Seychelles* was based at Burton-on-Trent when seen here, so this is likely to be a working off the S&DJR line, possibly 1M06, the 10.05am Bournemouth to Derby train, which was due past here at 1.44pm. No. 45626 was withdrawn from Leeds Holbeck in November 1965. John Strange/NPC

Once again we are probably lineside on the last full Saturday of steam haulage on the Birmingham to Bristol main line, in July 1961, with the livery of the coaching stock providing the clue as to the identity of the train. This is the Down 'The Devonian', bound from Bradford to Paignton, a journey on a summer Saturday which took nearly nine and a half hours from end to end, albeit with numerous intermediate stops and an engine change at Bristol Temple Meads. Sadly, photographer John Strange did not record the identity of the 'Jubilee' at the head of the train. The difference in height between the two lines is well illustrated, with the cutting spanned by the wrought iron girders forming Standish Black Bridge, which carriesa public road, albeit mainly a farm access. As built this was a triple span wooden bridge carried on two timber trestles, the *Bridge Register* noting that the GWR side was reconstructed in 1904, so the Midland obviously waited a while then before tackling their side. John Strange/NPC

I am fairly certain that photographer David Pollard's vantage point here is the bracket signal seen overleaf, carrying the Up Distants for the junction. Even in the less officious environment of the early 1960s, this would surely have been frowned upon but as a Swindon Works apprentice it is entirely possible that David had gained a permit to cover his activities lineside. The '9F' at the head of this fairly lightweight freight for an engine of this size is only partially identifiable as one of the Swindon-built members of the class, its number starting '922'. The date was also not recorded but is circa 1964. DAVID POLLARD/NPC

With the locomotive number usefully chalked on the smokebox door, in between the two representations of the train reporting number, BR-built 'Modified Hall' No. 7912 *Little Linford Hall* powers up the bank towards Standish Junction on 3rd July 1965. The engine was based at Banbury, whilst train No. 1M35 was the 11.10am from Ilfracombe to Wolverhampton, so it was not working back home. New in March 1950, No. 7912 was to be withdrawn three months after the picture was taken. Bill Potter/KRM

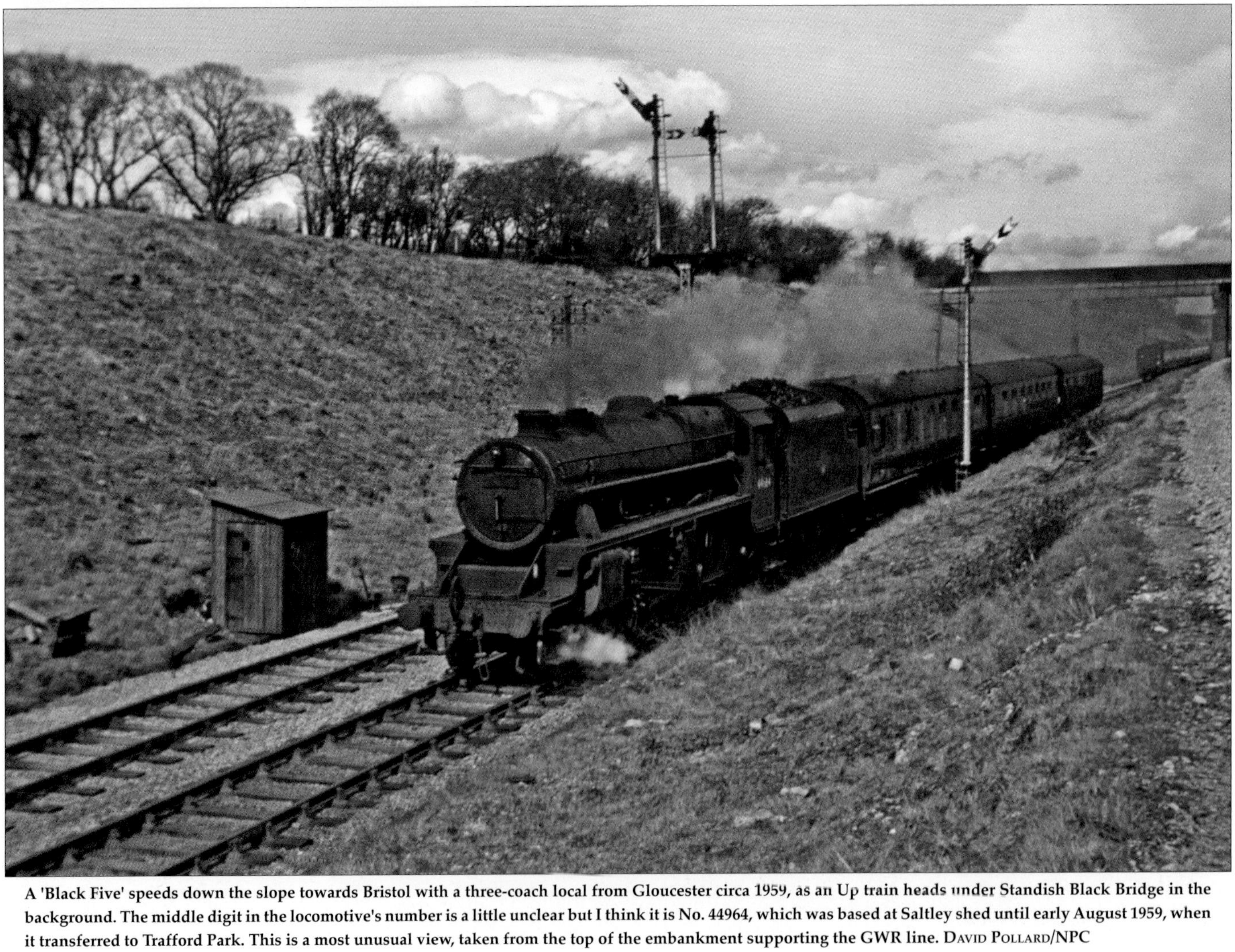

A 'Black Five' speeds down the slope towards Bristol with a three-coach local from Gloucester circa 1959, as an Up train heads under Standish Black Bridge in the background. The middle digit in the locomotive's number is a little unclear but I think it is No. 44964, which was based at Saltley shed until early August 1959, when it transferred to Trafford Park. This is a most unusual view, taken from the top of the embankment supporting the GWR line. David Pollard/NPC

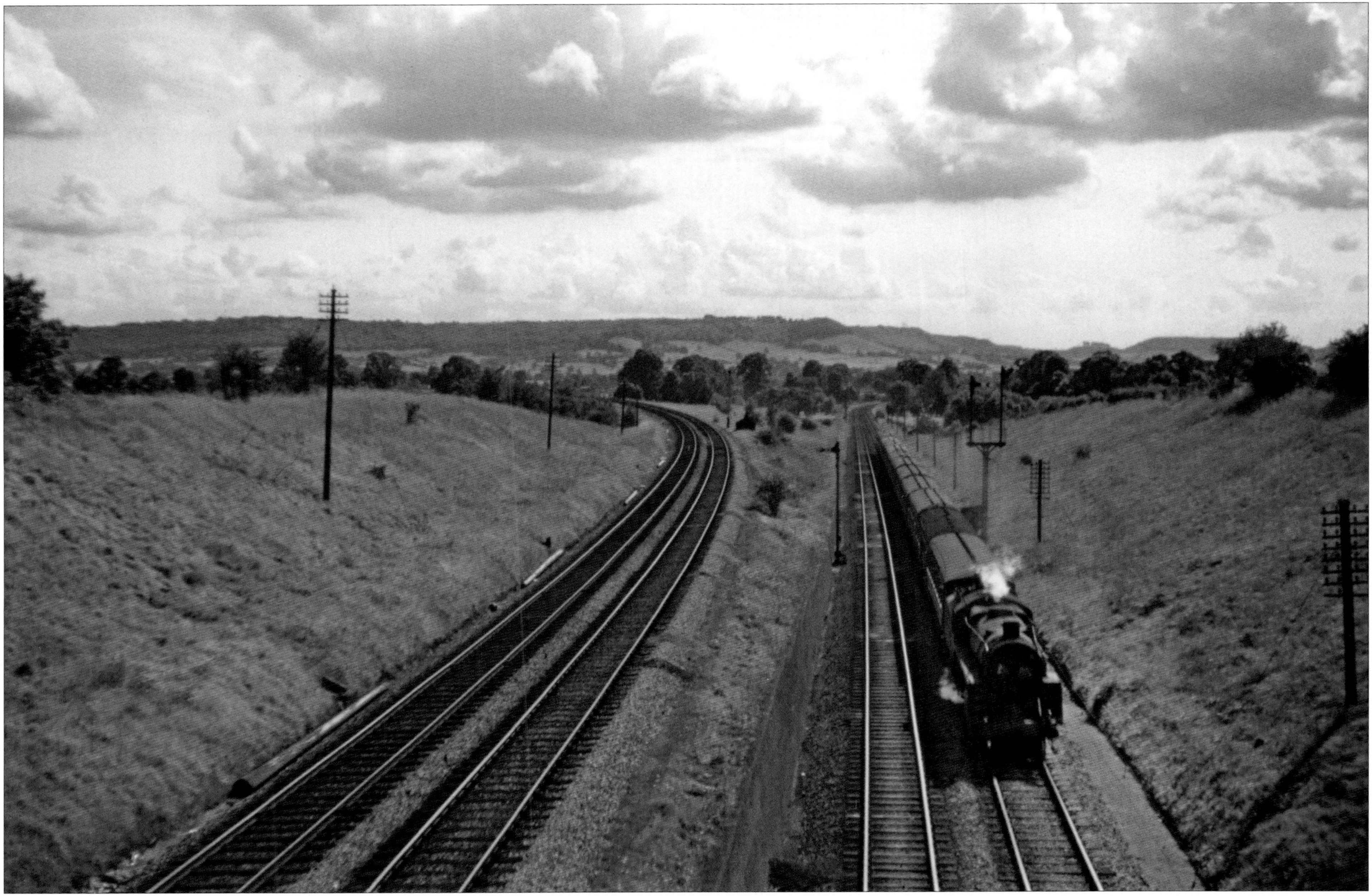

Photographs from Black Bridge are not as common as one might suppose, probably due to the height of the girder parapets making it awkward to see over, so presumably the photographer was using something to assist him in getting a leg up to see over here. Whatever, as the view clearly shows, the effort was worth it. An unidentified BR 'Standard' Class '5' 4-6-0 heads north with a holiday express circa 1962. The bracket signal on the right is the vantage point from where the previous picture was taken, whilst the Distant signal on the Down side was for Oldends Lane level crossing, just round the curve in the distance. As the Midland line drops gently down towards Stonehouse, round the curve in the distance, the WR line climbs gently and sweeps round to the east to head towards Stroud, Kemble and Swindon, a journey which we will follow in the next volume. Stanley Woods covers the hillside in the background, part of the southern end of the Cotswolds Hills. David Bick.NPC

At the north end of Stonehouse Bristol Road station, Olden's Footbridge (No. 89) carried a public footpath over the line. In steam days, when the station was still open and the branch still had a goods service, it provided a useful vantage point for operations. On 30th June 1965, Class '4F' No. 44264 was photographed arriving from Gloucester with a short train comprising thirteen steel mineral wagons loaded with coal for Stroud and Nailsworth. As we shall shortly see, the train would have to continue for a short distance and then reverse back through the yard on to the siding to the right of the Down Home signal to access the branch. This had always been the case and the remains of a point in the centre foreground, which hints at a direct connection, had actually only permitted trains to run off the branch to the Up main line; it had been taken out in November 1960. In the days of the passenger service, the train had remained on the branch for the day, with the single coach that sufficed latterly being brought down every morning from Gloucester. Oldends Lane level crossing can be seen just beyond the end of the train, with the crossing keeper's cottage, visible on the right. The footbridge and the cottage are all that remain today, with plain double track running through the station site. Bill Potter/KRM

SECTION 6

THE NAILSWORTH & STROUD BRANCH

The very last passenger train to call here at Stonehouse Eastington Road platform was on 7th July 1963, with the running of the GRS's 'Tour to Nailsworth & Stroud' which had ex-MR 'Jinty' No. 47308 in charge. The overgrown branch platform at Stonehouse had been sufficiently removed from the main line station to be separately named, whilst a covered walkway ran from the forecourt of the main line station to the branch platform, which was removed, along with the wooden station building, in the mid 1950s. The tour was an afternoon trip and the call here was at around 1.45pm. John Ryan

Whilst the Midland main line between Birmingham and Gloucester mostly deliberately missed all the large centres of population in between when built, in order to have as direct a route as possible, southwards to Bristol the route to be followed was very much dictated by the terrain. The larger towns, such as Stroud, Dursley and Thornbury, were effectively cut off from any direct route, either situated up valleys that ran off at a tangent, as with the first two, or the other side of a high escarpment, as was the latter. Thus the only way that the company could tap in to the potentially lucrative traffic offered by these places was to build branches off the main line serving them. Having already passed the main line junctions at Tuffley and Standish, the stations south from there to Yate thus comprised a series of branch line junctions, with the odd way-side station in between. The first was at Stonehouse, where there was a single track branch leading off to the east, which divided again at Dudbridge to serve both Stroud and Nailsworth.

The Stroud Valley was well served for the transport of goods by the Stroudwater and Thames & Severn canals, opened throughout in 1779 and 1789 respectively. Meeting at an end on junction in Stroud, the two waterways provided a through route between the River Thames in the south and the River Severn in the west, and thus outlets in both directions for the goods produced in and around the Stroud area. This monopoly on the transport of goods was finally threatened by the opening of the GWR line through the Stroud Valley in 1845 but this still left the Midland Railway some distance from the mills and other industries of the area, and its inhabitants. A horse-drawn omnibus service was running from Nailsworth to Stroud station by 1854, whilst the MR had opened an office in Stroud by 1864, from where another bus service was run to Stonehouse station. Clearly, however, there was a demand for something better and the first proposal was for a branch to Nailsworth.

The Stonehouse & Nailsworth Railway gained its Act in 1862, for a $5^3/_4$ mile line linking the two places of its name. The finance was quickly raised and construction began apace, with the branch opening amidst great excitement to goods on 1st February 1867 and to passengers three days later, intermediate stations being provided at Ryeford, Dudbridge and Woodchester. However, all was not well with the railway company's finances and the Midland, which was taking 50% of the receipts to operate the line in any case, was approached to bale the S&NR out. Reluctantly, they covered the losses for several years

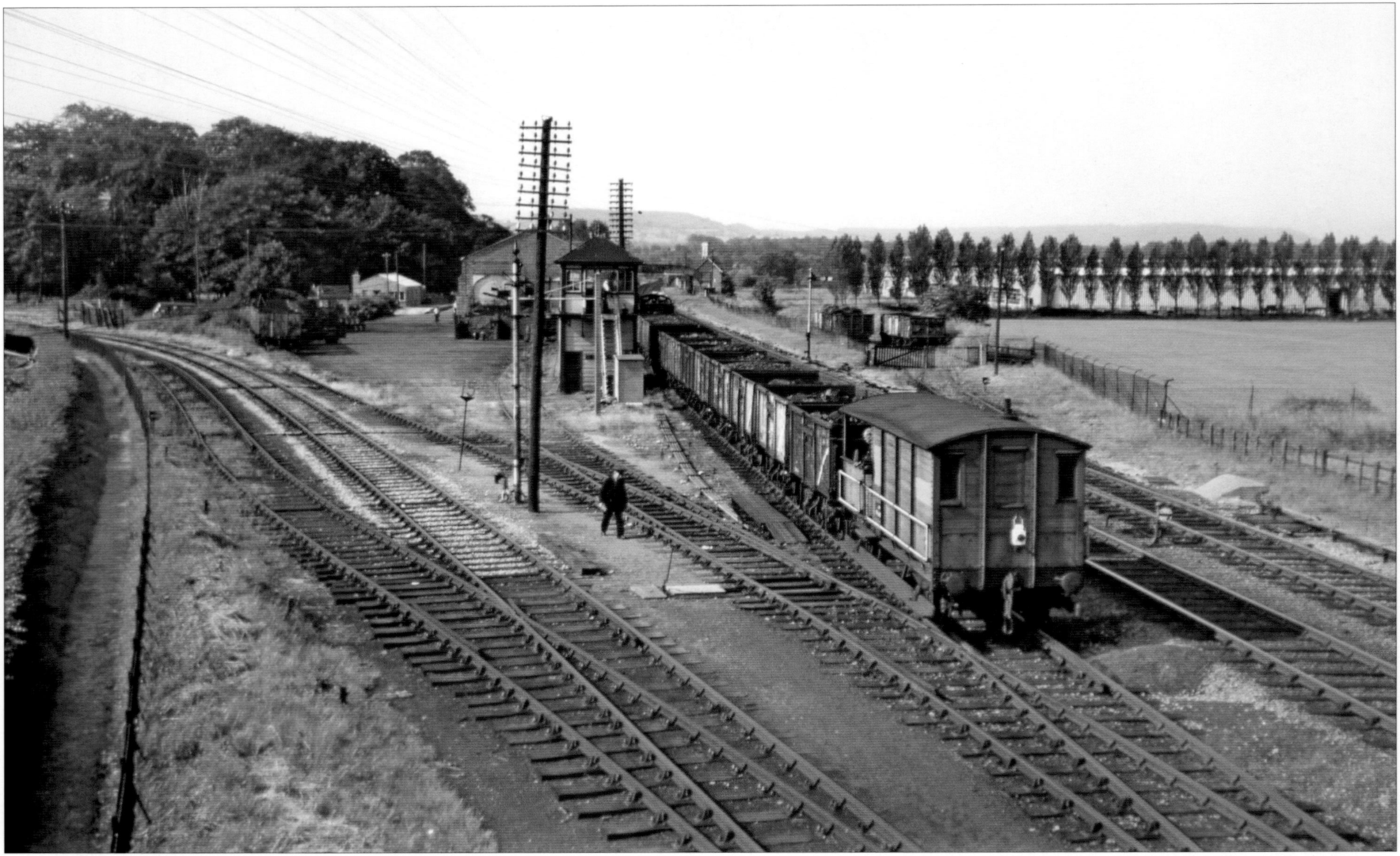

A short while after the picture seen on page 146, No. 44264 shunts its train back past the goods yard in order to access the connection to the branch, seen heading off to the left. From opening, a turntable had been provided here for branch locomotives to turn; situated near the end of the branch platform, between the running line and the siding where some coal wagons are bing unloaded by a mechanical shovel, it was removed on 21st January 1934. To the right of the main line can be seen the engineering works of Hoffman (Gloucester) Ltd, which had opened in 1938 and made bearings for the aircraft industry. The gated private siding serving the factory was opened under a Private Siding Agreement (PSA) dated 8th May 1940, which was terminated on 18th November 1966, with the rails being lifted two months later. The factory is today owned by the SKF Group and the whole area to the right of the line between Oldends Lane and the A419 is now covered with industrial premises. The siding can be seen curving sharply to the right beyond the wagons, to run along the southern side of the factory. The company had their own shunting engine, a 4-wheeled diesel-mechanical built by Muir Hill Engineering Ltd in Manchester, Works No. 29 of 1927, and bought second-hand from AEC Southall. It was not named as such but carried the initials 'HG' for Hoffman Gloucester and was scrapped circa 1969. The goods yard at Stonehouse was officially closed on 1st June 1966 but latterly had only been in use for coal traffic, with the goods shed doors blocked off and the rails through it lifted in October 1963. A rail supplied coal concentration depot was then opened in the yard in October 1966. Bill Potter/KRM

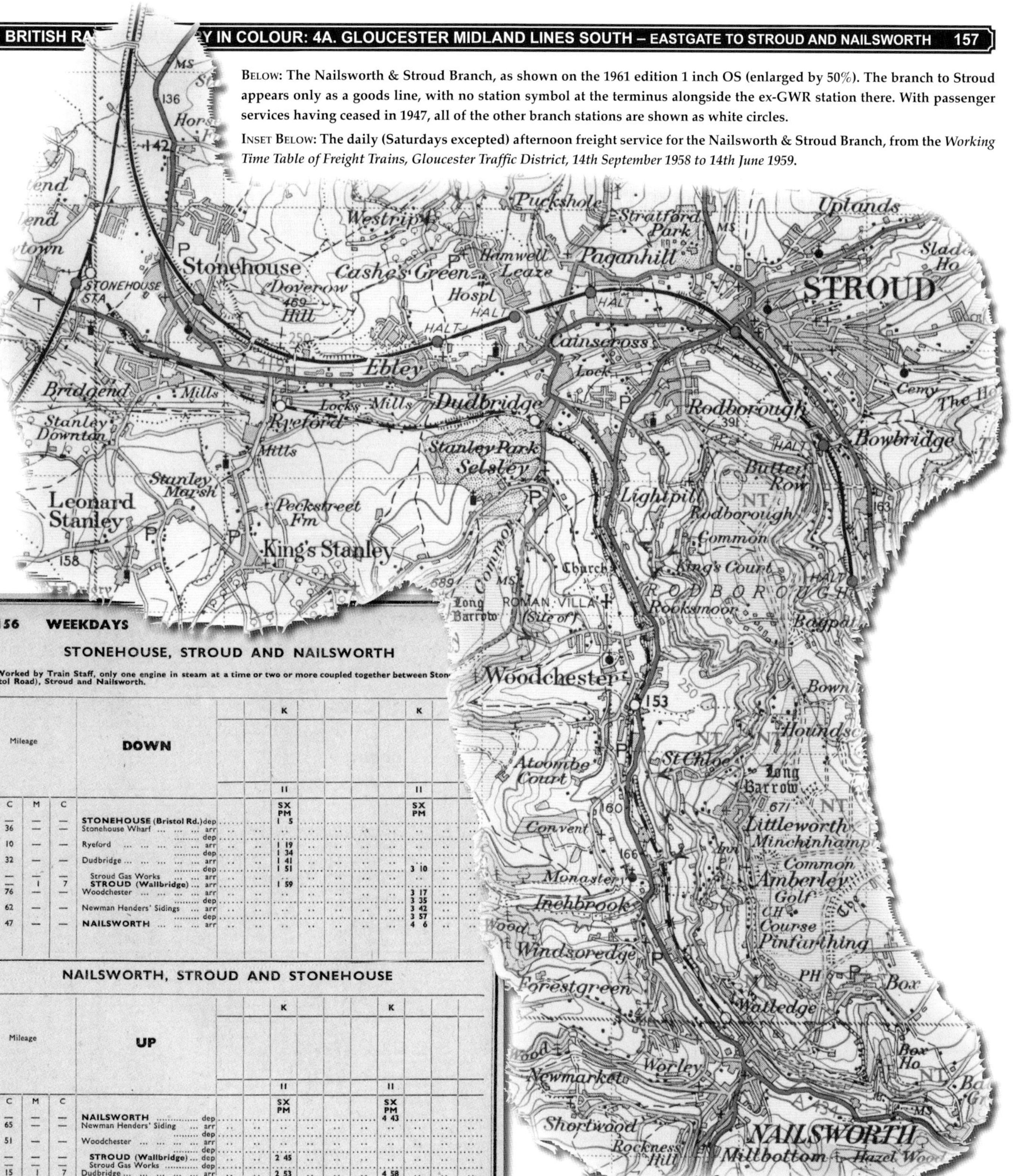

Below: The Nailsworth & Stroud Branch, as shown on the 1961 edition 1 inch OS (enlarged by 50%). The branch to Stroud appears only as a goods line, with no station symbol at the terminus alongside the ex-GWR station there. With passenger services having ceased in 1947, all of the other branch stations are shown as white circles.

Inset Below: The daily (Saturdays excepted) afternoon freight service for the Nailsworth & Stroud Branch, from the *Working Time Table of Freight Trains, Gloucester Traffic District, 14th September 1958 to 14th June 1959.*

K156 WEEKDAYS

STONEHOUSE, STROUD AND NAILSWORTH

Worked by Train Staff, only one engine in steam at a time or two or more coupled together between Ston[e]house (Bristol Road), Stroud and Nailsworth.

Mileage M	C	M	C	DOWN		K 11 SX PM	K 11 SX PM
—	—	—	—	**STONEHOUSE (Bristol Rd.)**	dep	1 5	
0	36	—	—	Stonehouse Wharf	arr	..	..
					dep		
1	10	—	—	Ryeford	arr	1 19	..
					dep	1 34	
2	32	—	—	Dudbridge	arr	1 41	..
					dep	1 51	3 10
—	—	—	—	Stroud Gas Works	arr	..	..
—	—	1	7	**STROUD (Wallbridge)**	arr	1 59	
3	76	—	—	Woodchester	arr	..	3 17
					dep		3 35
4	62	—	—	Newman Henders' Sidings	arr	..	3 42
					dep		3 57
5	47	—	—	**NAILSWORTH**	arr	..	4 6

NAILSWORTH, STROUD AND STONEHOUSE

Mileage M	C	M	C	UP		K 11 SX PM	K 11 SX PM
—	—	—	—	**NAILSWORTH**	dep		4 43
0	65	—	—	Newman Henders' Siding	arr	..	..
					dep		
1	51	—	—	Woodchester	arr	..	..
					dep		
—	—	—	—	**STROUD (Wallbridge)**	dep	2 45	..
—	—	—	—	Stroud Gas Works	dep		
3	15	1	7	Dudbridge	arr	2 53	4 58
					dep		5 8
4	37	—	—	Ryeford	arr	..	..
					dep		
5	11	—	—	Stonehouse Wharf	arr	..	..
					dep		
5	47	—	—	**STONEHOUSE (Bristol Rd.)**	arr	..	5 18

to keep the line running and in the end, in 1877, they were forced to absorb the S&NR Company than let it close.

The Midland had deliberately supported a branch to Nailsworth that by-passed Stroud, already served by the GWR but this had proved to be a mistake. With by far the larger population, the Stroud Valley was also the centre of an extensive cloth manufacturing industry, with numerous mills in the area. However, whilst several schemes had been put forward over the years for another line serving the town which would link with the Nailsworth Branch, for various reasons nothing had been done. The MR's absorption of the S&NR, however, brought matters to a head and a firm proposal was made as a result to build a branch from Dudbridge to Stroud. The necessary land was acquired, although this took some time to complete as certain properties on the route were bought by private purchase. It was also an expensive section of line to construct, as although it was only $1^{1}/_{4}$ miles in length, a high curving embankment, a deep cutting, a long, curved, double-track viaduct and numerous other under and overbridges had to be built, all being reflected in the contractor's final bill of £13,000, which also included the station and goods buildings at the terminus. The line finally opened for goods on 16th November 1885 and to passengers on 1st July 1886.

Initially, receipts were high, passenger numbers at the Midland

Moving on a few minutes once again from the picture on page 156, No. 44264 has now accessed the branch and is heading past the old Eastington Road platform with its trainload of coal. The covered walkway that protected passengers transferring between the main and branch platforms apparently had glazed sides and a corrugated iron roof; it joined the platform here between the trees to the left of the engine but passengers still faced a dash across the forecourt of the main line station in inclement weather to reach the platforms on that side. Although several early 20th century views of the station are known, they do not show the walkway, so no picture of it has been seen to date. No. 44264, which had had its reversing lever painted in buffer beam red, was new from Derby Works in October 1926 and was allocated to Gloucester Barnwood in May 1948. In the autumn of 1962 it was at Bristol Barrow Road and stayed there until around a month before this picture was taken, when it was transferred to Horton Road, where it spent its final few months in service before being withdrawn in November 1965. Note the engine was still carrying its 82E Barrow Road shedplate on the smokebox door – it was probably never changed. Bill Potter/KRM

Again taken on 30th June 1965, Bill Potter simply noted that No. 44264 was at Stonehouse on the slide mount. I am fairly certain that the view is looking north-west across the fan of lines at the start of the branch and the yard sidings, with the locomotive standing on the Up main line, having collected the three wagons seen on the left of the loop at the start of Hoffman's private siding, on page 156. This may have been the final manoeuvre of the day here, the relaxed nature of the crew suggesting that they have assembled their train and are waiting for the road back to Gloucester but we shall now head off to Stroud and Nailsworth. Bill Potter/KRM

station actually exceeding those at the larger GWR facility by a small margin but two factors were to combine in the early years of the 20th century to severely impact on those figures – the commencement by the GWR of rail motor services through the valley between Chalford and Stonehouse in 1906, with the opening of several new halts, and the advent of the motor bus, with a service between Stroud and Nailsworth starting in 1908. In 1889, nearly 82,000 passengers were recorded at Stroud MR, nearly 400 more than at the GWR station but by 1913 the respective figures were just over 63,000 for the MR and over half a million for the GWR. Passenger numbers on the branch were declining. By 1922, the total number for all six stations was just over 105,000 and by the end that figure had dropped to an unsustainable 6,000 passenger annually. Even the running of a non-stop Stroud-Stonehouse service, taking just seven minutes, could not compete with the GWR's auto trains running direct from the Stroud Valley to Gloucester.

The passenger service on both branches was temporarily suspended from 16th June 1947, as part of the Government's drive to restrict passenger mileage during a period of severe post-war fuel shortages. It was stated to be for the summer months at least but the local press clearly thought it would never be reinstated, publishing an account of the last train commencing *'the obsequies of the 'Dudbridge Donkey', which made its last trip from Stroud LMS station to Nailsworth on Satuerday night'* and highlighting the phrase *'temporary suspension'*. They were right not to be fooled; the service was never reinstated, being made permanent two years later, on 8th June 1949.

Both branches still enjoyed a healthy goods traffic, however, with incoming house and gas works coal in particular being important, along with other commodities such as animal feedstuffs, livestock, pig iron, coke, roadstone and building materials incoming, and trout, aluminium scrap and timber outgoing. Again much of this had dwindled away by the end. Some of the intermediate stations were closed to goods traffic in 1964 and the last trains serving the yards at Stroud and Nailsworth ran on Wednesday 1st June 1966, the track being lifted shortly afterwards. Locomotives appearing on the branch during the later BR period included Class '3F' and '4F' 0-6-0s, ex-GWR 0-6-0PTs, BR Class '2' 2-6-0s and finally 'Class '14' 0-6-0 diesel-hydraulics and even at least one visit by an 0-6-0 diesel shunter.

Initially much of the infrastructure of the line remained intact but gradually, over the fifty years following closure, with a couple of notable exceptions, most of it has been lost. Development and road realignment has obscured everything at the Stonehouse end, the first significant survival thus being the skew girder bridge over the Stroudwater Canal. Ryeford station building remained until circa 1990 but was demolished when the route of the line at that point was used for the construction of the A419 Ebley by-pass, which opened in 1994; part of the embankment and an occupation underbridge survive between there and Dudbridge, the trackbed having become a cycle path. Dudbridge station was also demolished around 1990 and the site now lies beneath the realigned Selsey Hill road and a roundabout serving a supermarket. The 'temporary' wooden station building provided at Stroud for the opening in 1886 was never replaced, surviving for a century before being demolished, as did the goods shed and other buildings in the yard. All remained in commerical use for many years after closure but, again, re-routing of the A419 at this point has seen the obliteration of the station site along with partial demolition of the viaduct, although around half a dozen arches remain, several still enclosed and in commercial use as they had been long before closure. The gem, however, is Nailsworth station building, which is now a private residence and Grade II listed since 1975. Additionally, whilst the goods shed has gone, a red brick warehouse that belonged to C.W. Jones & Co., builders merchants, still stands in the old yard, complete with its owner's lettering, and the nearby Railway Hotel also remains, albeit converted as apartments.

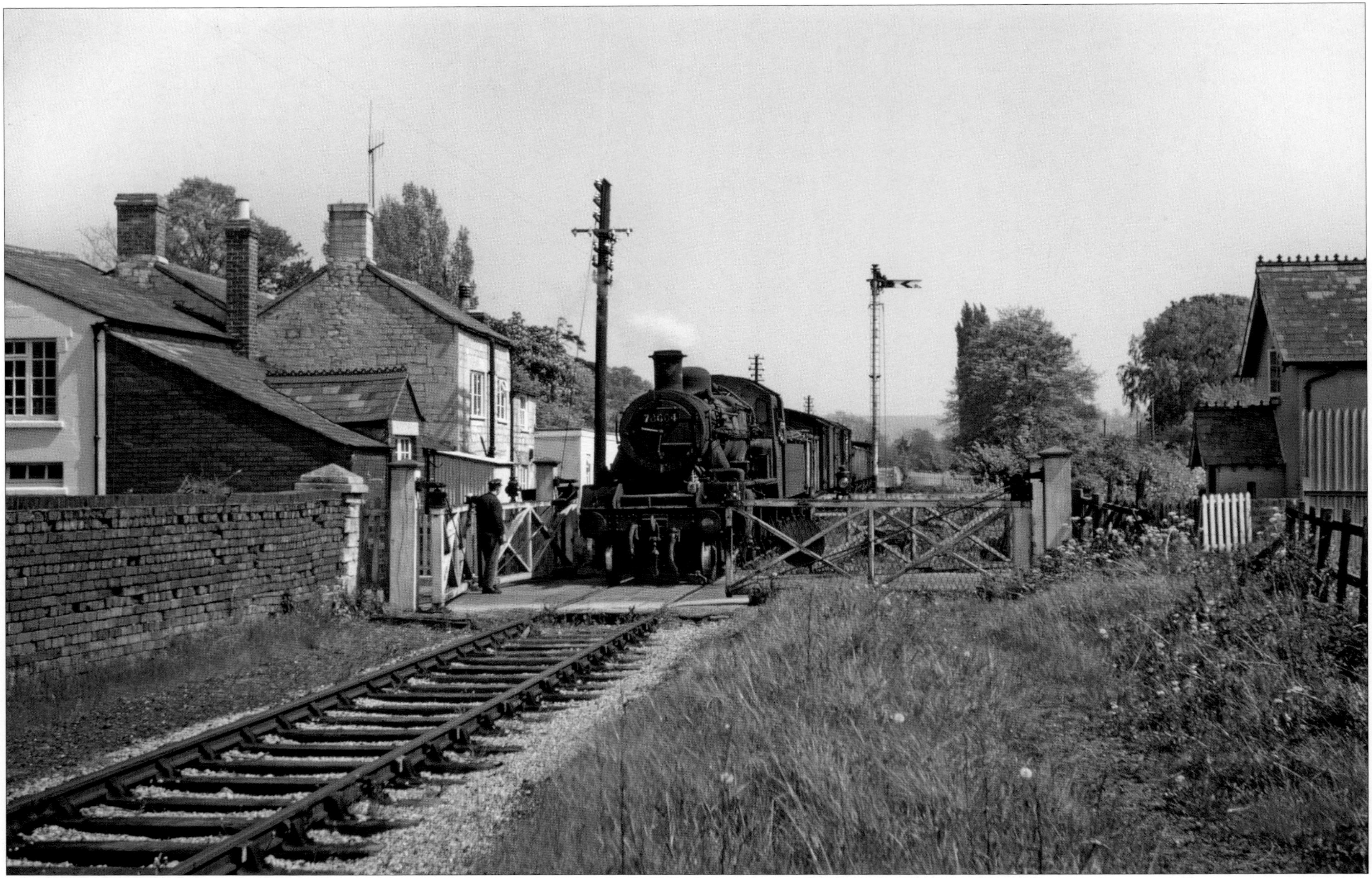

In a county filled with picturesque areas, the Stroud and Nailsworth valleys were certainly up there with the best. They still are in many respects but undoubtedly the huge development that has taken place over the five decades or so since these pictures were taken has turned them in to crowded corridors in many places. The route of this railway is now mostly lost and rural locations such as Stonehouse Wharf and crossing are no longer recognisable. As such, I am including all three of the delightful pictures Bill Potter took here on 12th May 1965, as BR 'Standard' Class '2' No. 78004 made its leisurely way back down the branch on its journey back to Gloucester. The fireman has climbed down from the cab to open the gates – just the one pair note, no need to open them both! – and I'm guessing that he would then get back up on to the footplate. Once the rear of the train had cleared the crossing, the guard would then come down from his van to close them again. Teamwork! The crossing keeper, in the days when the service had comprised more than the one train on Mondays, Wednesdays and Fridays only, lived in the cottage on the right, the property on the left being The Ship Inn. Sadly, nothing in this picture remains today. Bill Potter/KRM

Moments later, No. 78004 draws slowly through the part opened gates, past the Fixed Distant signal for Stonehouse. Bill Potter/KRM

Stonehouse Wharf, originally provided as an interchange point with the Stroudwater Canal, consisted of a single siding trailing back from a point near the middle of the train. Probably built with the line, latterly it had been used only for some local coal traffic and it was lifted in early September 1958, with Stonehouse Wharf Crossing ground frame which controlled it being closed and removed at the same time. The property on the right may have been the wharfinger's cottage or a warehouse. This area is now covered by a new development, Boakes Drive, built in 1992 and named in honour of the late David Boakes, one of the early campaigners for the regeneration of the Stroud Valley canals. Bill Potter/KRM

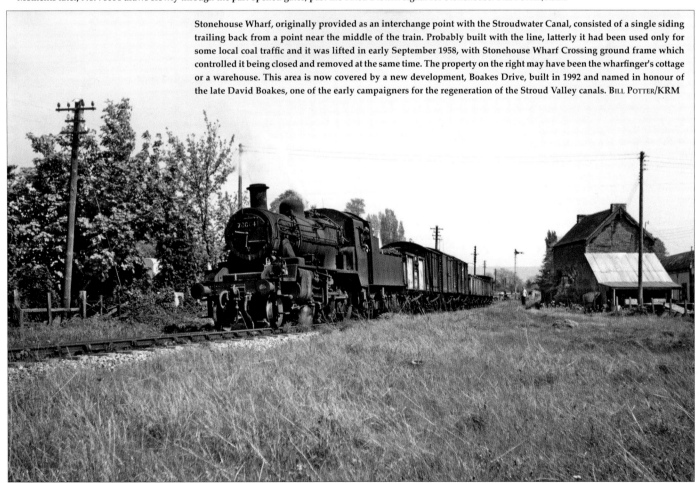

A wonderful view of the rural steam railway at its best – but let's not get carried away too much because there will be quite a few more to come before we end our journey along this branch – and what a duty for the crew to draw on a fine sunny day like this. With No. 78004 due to stop at Stonehouse Wharf Crossing, or Ship Inn Crossing as it was more commonly known, Bill had time to capture this shot and then nip back over the canal bridge to take the pictures seen on the previous two pages. The house in the centre background is part of Wycliffe College – was it the headmaster's house? – whilst the canal here has now been landscaped, dredged and is once again navigable. This section of the line and the cultivated plot between it and the canal is now wild scrub but may yet prove ripe for another desirable waterside development. No. 78004 was one of several of the first-built members of the class to feature at Gloucester and to venture along this branch. New from Darlington Works in January 1953, it was withdrawn from Horton Road in November 1965. Bill Potter/KRM

DELIVERING A NEW TRANSFORMER
FOR RYEFORD ELECTRICITY SUB-STATION

It was rather ironic that around fifteen months before final closure the branch was to prove hugely useful for the delivery of a new transformer manufactured by GEC for Midlands Electricity, who needed to install it at a new sub-station being built just to the west of Ryeford station. The site was on the south side of the Stroudwater Canal and it was thought likely that the low loader lorry required to carry it would ground on the hump-backed bridge over the waterway. It was therefore agreed with British Railways that they would carry the transformer for the last few hundred yards of its journey from GEC's works at Witton near Birmingham. The operation was undertaken on 27th March 1965 and only a very short section of the branch was used, with Class '4F' No. 44123 being sent down from Gloucester Horton Road to provide the motive power for the move. Fortunately for us, John Strange clearly got to hear about the operation and along with at least one other local photographer travelled down from his Shropshire base to record it in colour, on what was clearly a warm and sunny early spring day, for us to enjoy. Quite how he found out about it, when other more locally based photographers seemingly did not, we shall now never know. As the pictures show, it was clearly the railway side of the move that interested him and it would seem that he arrived when loading of the transformer on to the bogie well wagon had been almost completed and then left again shortly after the train had arrived at where it was to be unloaded.

LEFT: Having positioned its short train adjacent to the little used Davis or Brushworks level crossing, which led to a swing bridge over the canal, No. 44123 drew back whilst the transformer was loaded. There is no evidence of a crane being present here, so was it loaded by means of the lorry trailer being positioned butting up to the wagon and the transformer then carefully winched across on to the bed of sleepers?

Below: With The Ship Inn as a backdrop, the driver of No. 44123 lets off a little steam from the boiler as the crew wait for loading to be completed. BOTH JOHN STRANGE/NPC

Right: Taken from a similar point across the canal to Bill Potter's picture on page 154, No. 44123 has now moved forward and coupled up to the train, the puffs of white smoke indicating that it had begun the gentle shunt towards Ryeford. Colin Maggs, in his book about the branch (see Bibliography), reports that the section of track traversed was strengthened with the addition of extra sleepers, which presumably were slipped beneath the rails and between the existing sleepers, probably at intervals rather than every gap. There is also some evidence that fresh ballast was laid on this section at the same time. John Strange/NPC

Right: The total length of the transformer's rail journey was a mere 650 yards but this did include crossing the canal on the wrought iron girders of Ryeford canal bridge. The men in the brake van keep a watchful eye as the train creaks over the bridge. The timber span at the far end had then recently been damaged by fire and was propped up using steel trestles. John Strange/NPC

Left: Having crossed the canal, the line then dropped down slightly and curved round towards the station at Ryeford. Just prior to the station was a road overbridge, from which this final picture of the move was taken. The sub-station, which has been enlarged over the intervening years and is still in operation today, was on the south side of the line and the concrete pad seen here was laid in to assist with the unloading of the transformer. Colin Maggs stated that a crane was used to lift it off at this end of the journey but a photograph in his book on the branch shows the sleepers seen here stacked to form a bed to winch it on to and then on to a lorry again for the last few yards of the journey in to the sub-station site. Perhaps that is where the crane was used. Maggs also refers several times to more than one transformer being delivered but is that because they were joined as a pair? There is certainly no evidence that this operation had to be performed a second time. In earlier times, a siding serving Stanley Mill had curved sharply away to the left but this had been removed in the summer of 1930. The view here today has changed completely, with the trackbed now lost under the A419 Ebley By-Pass. The bridge from which this picture was taken has gone but the hump-backed bridge over the canal a hundred yards to the north, which led to this unique move, still remains. John Strange/NPC

LEFT: No. 44123 caught neatly in the centre of the span whilst crossing the canal in April 1965. The steel trestles propping the charred timbers at the western end can be clearly seen. Although final closure was only fourteen months away, the bridge was repaired with a new concrete span put in place. COLOUR-RAIL

BELOW: A view of the derelict bridge on 11th August 1981, looking along the canal towards Stroud and showing the replacement concrete span on the left. Happily, this section of the waterway has been brought back in to use, as part of the multi-million pound scheme to restore the whole length of the Stroudwater and Thames & Severn canals through the Stroud Valley, which continues to make exciting progress. The span and other ironwork has been cleaned and painted green, the vegetation cut right back and the towpath has been repaired. This view today also now includes the new bridge carrying the A419 Ebley By-Pass over the canal around 100 yards in the distance. BILL POTTER/KRM

BELOW: Moving back in time again, this fine view across the deck of the bridge was taken on 5th October 1962, as Class '4F' No. 44045 headed back towards Stonehouse with the branch goods. Note the Midland Railway bridge plate, No. 3, on the abutment pillar at the far end. Bridge No. 1 was a metal public footbridge near Stonehouse and Stroud Road Bridge was No. 2, which carried what was in fact Bristol Road over the line but neither remain today, although the latter survived in to the 21st century. BILL POTTER/KRM

Above: Ryeford station slumbers in early summer sunshine on 2nd June 1962. In the left distance the point leading in to Ryeford Saw Mills Siding can just be seen; opened with the line in 1867, the PSA was terminated in 1964. Just beyond that can also be discerned the point for the single yard siding, which ran through the wooden goods shed and ended alongside a short loading dock behind the platform fence; the rails still remained, hidden in the grass. Ryeford signal box, the site of which was beyond the foot crossing and to the right of the line, had closed in September 1958 and when it was removed it is likely that the edge of the unusually wide platform was taken up at the same time. There is also a glimpse of the weighbridge hut on the far right. R. Patterson/Colour-Rail

No. 78004 heads past the station with the branch goods on 12th May 1965. Rail traffic from Ryeford saw mills had ceased by this date but latterly had comprised sawn timber being despatched, the cut logs being delivered by road. Bill Potter/KRM

Left: The original grandiose plans for the branch intended it to be part of a through route to the GWR at Chippenham, running via Tetbury and Malmesbury, hence the three original stations at Ryeford, Dudbridge and Nailsworth being of a high architectural standard. This study of the portico entrance to Ryeford, taken on 29th May 1973 as it quietly awaited its ultimate fate, illustrates the care and the detail with which it was built. When it was demolished circa 1990, all that was saved were the panelling and some of the equipment from the booking office, which can now be found in the Dean Forest Railway's museum at Norchard. NPC

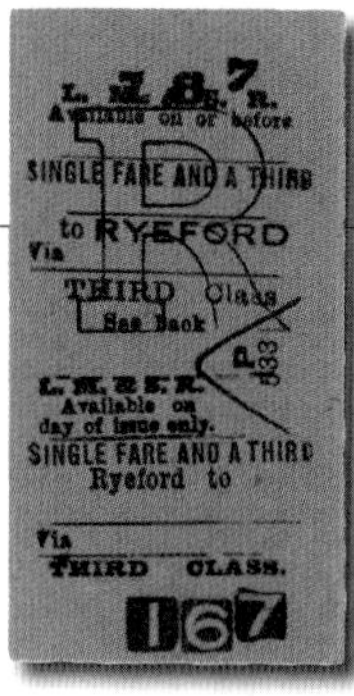

Above: The east elevation of the station building, as seen from a rail tour passing by. The slide is undated but it will have been taken from one of the two trips that traversed the line in July 1963, one on 7th and the second on 21st, both of which we shall see more of in this section. There is a glimpse of the road overbridge with the remains of a wooden post signal just in front. NPC

Left: A final view of Ryeford, taken in the late summer or autumn of 1966, after closure and with evidence of some rails having been removed in the middle distance. The site of the saw mills is today a builders merchants. John Strange/NPC

Class '4F' No. 44264 shunts the yard at Dudbridge on 16th March 1962, collecting empty mineral wagons for return to Gloucester. The station can be seen in the right background, with another wagon alongside the old cattle dock. When the Nailsworth Branch first opened, the station had a single platform and the passing loop, the only one on the branch, was the line on which the two wagons are standing. A second platform was added when the Stroud Branch opened to passengers in 1886, with the line on the right serving this and thus forming a new longer loop, with the goods yard also being extended at the same. In 1958, the line on the right was severed short of the second platform and became a long siding, although the rust on the rails shows that it clearly saw little use. Roy Denison

This fine panorama of the goods yard was taken a short while later and shows No. 44264 about to couple back up to the brake van after collecting the three empty mineral wagons; the two loaded coal ones at the front will be dropped off at Newman, Hender's siding or Nailsworth. When the line was first built, turntables had been provided at Nailsworth and Stonehouse but these had long since been removed, so tender engines generally worked backwards from Gloucester in order that they could head smokebox first on the return journey. These views of No. 44254 at Dudbridge facing towards the branch terminii are therefore more unusual. In the left background is Ebley Mill, a cloth mill built on the site of earlier mills between 1820 and 1823 for the Marling family. Latterly trading as Marling & Evans, the company pulled out of the site in the 1970s, although they are still in operation, now based in Huddersfield as manufacturers of high quality cloth. In 1989, Ebley Mill was extensively refurbished for use as the offices of Stroud District Council. Roy Denison

Right and Below: Two views of the GRS trip of 7th July 1963 during the stop at Dudbridge. This afternoon tour from Gloucester became the last passenger train to call at the intermediate stations on the Nailsworth & Stroud Branch. The RCTS ran a Gloucestershire Rail Tour two weeks later, which we shall also see more of shortly, but this was a widespread tour of lines in the south of the county so the only calls were at the two terminii, where the locomotives had to run round anyway. The stop here at Dudbridge, which was timed for 2.15pm, was followed by the run to Nailsworth, with the visit to Stroud then being made on the way back. As we have seen, the day ended with both of the ex-MR Gloucester docks branches being traversed on the return to the city. Note the substantial retaining wall behind the second platform in the picture below. The alcove had originally housed a wooden fronted waiting shelter, which had survivd until circa 1961. Right: John Ryan / Below: Bill Potter/KRM

Below: A shaft on sunlight pierces the gloom of a very damp rainy afternoon in the Stroud Valley on 5th June 1964. Note the rather stylish weighbridge hut in the right background. Another siding, recently lifted at the date of this view, had run at the rear of the station terminating near the hut; it had served a narrow gauge hand-worked tramway, which carried coal on a trestle bridge over a stream a short distance to Kimmins flour mill, which it entered at first floor level. This traffic ended in 1931 and milling here ceased in 1935 but the mill survives today, more recently in use as the Stroud Mills Heritage Centre but they have recently been forced to vacate in order that owners Sainsbury's can carry out vital refurbishment work. Note the old Midland Railway covered goods wagon body on the platform, which had been placed here for use as a parcels store. The exceptionally tall TV aerial was necessary to get any sort of signal close to the steep side of the valley. Howard Burchell

ABOVE AND BELOW: After the closure of Dudbridge Junction signal box, the train staffs were kept in a locked box in the station and the exchanges with the footplate crew were handled by either the porter in charge of the goods yard or the train guard. Here, on 30th July 1965, the porter collects the Stonehouse-Dudbridge staff from the fireman of No. 78001 and exchanges it for the Dudbridge-Nailsworth one; there was also a third staff for the Dudbridge-Stroud section. Selsey Hill bridge, below, from which Ben Ashworth's picture on page 6 was taken, has also not survived the redevelopment of this area. BOTH BILL POTTER/KRM

First built member of the Type '1' (later Class '14') diesel-hydraulic 0-6-0s, No. D9500, passes through Dudbridge with just a brake van in tow on Friday 27th May 1966, *en route* to Nailsworth to collect empty wagons. With just five days to go before services ceased altogether, on Wednesday 1st June, this was part of the process of clearing the line of wagons. The final trip on that fateful day was to be see a rare appearance on the branch by a 'Type '1' 0-6-0 diesel shunter (later Class '08'), No. D3994. Bill Potter/KRM

Later that day, after returning from Nailsworth with a short rake of empty coal wagons, No. D9500 stops at Dudbridge again to exchange the train staff. New from Swindon Works in July 1964, No. D9500 was officially based at Bristol Bath Road at the date of this view although was clearly working from Gloucester. It was put in to store at Worcester a month after these pictures were taken (and following closure of the branch) but was then reinstated six months later. After withdrawal in April 1969 it was bought by the National Coal Board (NCB) and sent to Ashington Colliery in Northumberland, becoming their No. 1. Bought for preservation in 1987 after the colliery system had closed the previous year, it is owned by Andrew Briddon and is currently awaiting overhaul and a return to operation at his Peak Rail base at Darley Dale. Bill Potter/KRM

Having photographed the train heading in both directions through Dudbridge, Bill persuaded the train crew to let him climb aboard the brake van for a trip back down the branch and this is his view of the station as they departed. Coal merchants' lorries line the yard on the left but all future inward deliveries would now be by road. Notice the double slip point at the entrance to the goods yard, with the overgrown stub siding which it led to running to a loading dock with cattle pens by the Bedford lorry. Coal was it seems always the principal traffic here at Dudbridge and hence probably why the yard was unusual in never being provided with a goods shed. The merchants' lorries are a varied selection: On the left is a Fordson Thames 502E 3-ton dropside, possibly a tipper and powered by Ford's 4-cylinder diesel engine, as evidenced by the rectangular badge in the grille which bore the '4D' legend, and current from 1952 to 1957. Next to the right are two Bedford 'TK' models, introduced in 1960 and carrying on the immense popularity of the Bedford marque established in the 1930s. The one on the left is an example of the lowest load-rated TK as evidenced by its small wheels and short wheelbase, and updated derivations of the original 'TK' carried on up to the sad demise of the Bedford name in 1987. The old Up line serving the second platform had become even more overgrown but the buffer stops showing where it had been cut back to can be seen in this view. The building behind the coal pens, of which just the upper storey is visible here, was an engineering works. BILL POTTER/KRM

A final view through the platform, looking through the span of Selsey Hill bridge, showing the line heading straight on towards Nailsworth in the background. The slide mount is dated June 1966 but the rails are still shiny from use, so the view is likley to be at the end of May, a day or so before final closure. NPC

A rare colour view of the station forecourt circa 1961, showing the old (parcels?) coach body on the right which had been placed here for use as an office by one of the coal merchants. The main building was another architectural gem, sadly now swept away by a supermarket development. NPC

ABOVE: No. 44045 winds its way off the Stroud line at Dudbridge Junction on 5th October 1962. Having opened twenty years later, the Midland regarded the short line to Stroud as a branch off the Nailsworth Branch and this was to an extent reflected in the way that the passenger service was operated, latterly a mix of Stroud-Stonehouse, Nailsworth-Stonehouse, Dudbridge-Stroud and Dudbridge-Nailsworth trains, mostly single coach motor services. The Stroud-Stonehouse motors ran direct, taking just seven minutes to complete the journey but still could not compete with the Chalford autos, due to the change of trains involved at Stonehouse. After the passenger service was withdrawn in 1947, under British Railways the goods service continued to serve various private sidings and works, including Stroud Gas Works until 1956, as well as the station goods yards. However, as the number of places served declined, the service came down to a single daily train, which ran first to Dudbridge, then serviced Stroud before finally making the run down to Nailsworth. The *Working Time Table* extract for the branch for 1963 is given at the end of the Nailsworth section on page 200 and shows that 4 hours 10 minutes was allowed for the thrice weekly operation, which included servicing Ryeford Saw Mills sidings, the yards at Dudbridge, Stroud and Woodchester, Newman, Hender & Co's siding and the yard at Nailsworth. As we shall see, that still left time for the odd other stop! BILL POTTER/KRM

K169

Engine Restrictions—continued

WORKING OF ENGINES BETWEEN CHARFIELD AND CHELTENHAM LANSDOWN (INCLUDING GLOUCESTER EASTGATE)—continued

Route colour, **Red**—continued.

STROUD—DUDBRIDGE—Route colour, **Blue.**				
None...	2-6-2T 82XXX 84XXX 2-6-0 76XXX 77XXX 2-6-4T 80XXX	8200–8236 200 h.p. B.R. 204 h.p. B.R. 10800	0-4-4T 41900 0-6-0T 41702–41879, 47200–47681 51371–51498 4-4-0 40396–40700 0-6-0 43185–44606 52095–52526, 58115–58305 2-4-2T 50721–50850 2-6-2T 40001–40209 2-6-0 43000–43161, 43112–43121 2-6-0 46400–46527 2-6-4T 42050–42299, 42425–42494, 42537–42699	
NAILSWORTH—STONEHOUSE (BRISTOL ROAD)—Route colour, **Blue.**				
*22XX	2-6-2T 82XXX 84XXX 2-6-0 76XXX 77XXX 2-6-4T 80XXX	8200–8236 8400–8409 200 h.p. B.R. 204 h.p. B.R. 10800	0-4-4T 41900 0-6-0T 41702–41879 47200–47681 51370–51498 4-4-0 40396–40700 0-6-0 43185–44606, 52095–52526, 58115–58305 2-4-2T 50721–50850 2-6-2T 40001–40209 2-6-0 43000–43161, 43112–43121, 46400–46527 2-6-4T 42050–42299, 42425–42494, 42537–42699	*—W.R. 22XX Class Engines may work over all running lines and to Engine Stop Board on the Oil Cake Store road at Ryeford. All other Sidings prohibited.

NAILSWORTH BRANCH

The speed of trains over this Branch must not exceed 40 miles per hour, and must be further restricted to lower speeds as shewn.

Stonehouse (Bristol Road)	Between Stonehouse and 102¾ m.p. All	Down and Up Trains	25
Dudbridge Station	Through Junction and up to end of Dow	n Loop. All Down and Up Trains ...	15
Birds Crossing	Dudbridge	Nailsworth—All Down Trains	25
Nailsworth Station...	Nailsworth...	Dudbridge—All Up Trains	25

STROUD BRANCH

The speed of trains over this Branch must not exceed 25 miles per hour and must be further restricted as shewn below.

At Dudbridge	All Up Trains through Junction... ...	... ...	15

ABOVE AND LEFT: Extracts from the *Working Time Table of Freight Trains, Gloucester Traffic District, 12th June to 10th September 1961*, showing the locomotive and speed restrictions for the branch. In effect, the only section where 40mph running was permitted was the short length between Ryeford and Dudbridge, so it is unlikely that this speed was ever reached.

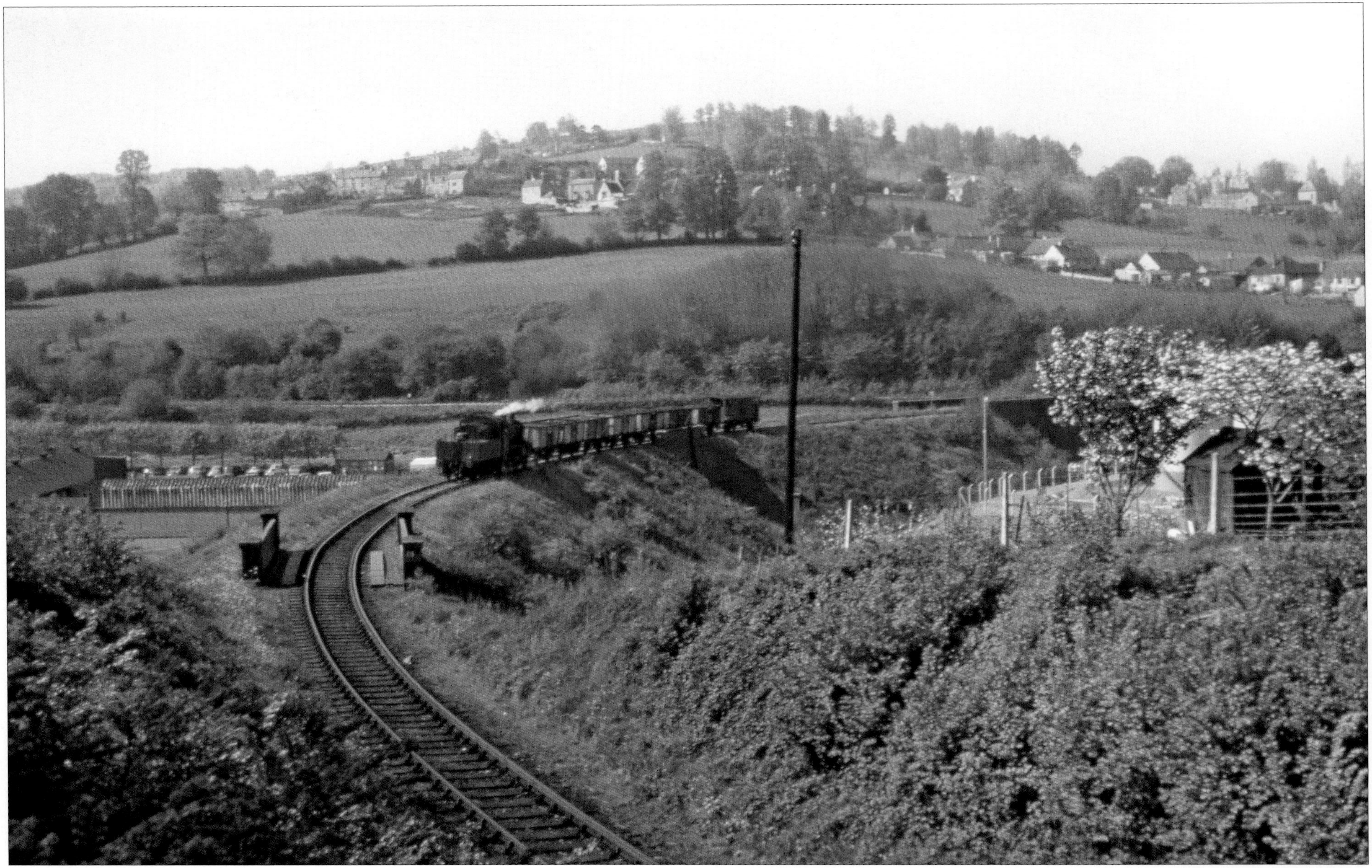

On 12th May 1965, No. 78004 negotiates the embankment carrying the sharply curved – note the check rail – start of the short branch from Dudbridge Junction to Stroud. It was whilst trying to make sense of the bridge numbers on the Nailsworth & Stroud Branch that an internet search fortuitously led me to the Midland Railway Study Centre website, where I found a downloadable PDF containing the *Midland Railway Bridge Register Gloucester District*, which covers all of the lines in this volume. In the right distance, partially hidden by the blossom, is the blue brick arch of Nailsworth Brook Bridge, Stroud Branch No. 1. The brook flowed in a culvert beneath the grounds of Dudbridge House and served various mills along the Nailsworth Valley. Inside the arch was South's Bridge, No. 2, a timber trestle occupation footbridge which spanned the brook on the diagonal. The train is just passing over Smith's Bridge, No. 3, an occupation arch again built of blue brick, whilst a little nearer out of sight at the base of the embankment was Smith's Flood Arches, No. 4. The wrought iron girders of Nailsworth Road Bridge, No. 5, which were supported on blue brick abutments with matching wing walls, are prominent in the left foreground. Bill Potter/KRM

Above: A second view, with No. 78004 and its train of six loaded coal wagons and brake van about to pass the photographer beneath Rodboro' Road Bridge, No. 6. The houses on Selsey Hill in the background gaze down on a scene which today has changed beyond recognition. The embankment and its bridges have been flattened, replaced by a small housing estate, whilst a large factory has been built on the site of the sports grounds on the left. Bridge No. 6 still stands, albeit largely hidden by tree growth, at the start of a footpath that follows the old trackbed all the way to Wallbridge. Bridge No. 7, a water pipe and footbridge spanning the cutting a short distance behind the photographer, has also gone. Bill Potter/KRM

Above: Colour views of the section of line between Dudbridge and Stroud are scarce, so although not sharp, both this and the picture left merit using here. On 27th May 1966, five days before the goods service ceased on 1st June, diesel-hydraulic 0-6-0 No. D9500 heads away from Stroud beneath Bath Road Bridge, No. 8, with a rake of empty coal wagons. Stroud Gas Works siding, a loop installed in November 1924, had been on the right just round the curve; out of use in 1956 when the works switched to road delivery of coal for its final two years, it was not removed until 1964. Bill Potter/KRM

Left: Back to 12th May 1965 for this shot of No. 78004 departing Stroud with a short train of box vans. The picture was taken from Bridge No. 9, which slightly confusingly was named Rodboro' Road Bridge No. 2. Both of these bridges survive today, as does part of Stroud Viaduct, No. 10, the end of which can just be glimpsed in the background behind the train. Bill Potter/KRM

0003
(7586)
2nd · SPECIAL ARRANGEMENT
The Gloucestershire Railway Society
TOUR TO NAILSWORTH & STROUD
SUNDAY, 7th JULY, 1963
Gloucester (Eastgate), Standish Junction
Stonehouse (Midland), Nailsworth and
Stroud (Midland), Hempsted and High
Orchard Lines and Return to
Gloucester (Eastgate)
(W) For conditions see over
0003
2Z10

Above: The GRS afternoon rail tour of 7th July 1963 travelled first to Nailsworth, which was reached at around 2.30pm, and then back to Dudbridge to cover the Stroud Branch. As can be seen, the weather had turned by the time the train arrived at Stroud Midland station about an hour later, with the light having faded amidst the falling of a heavy drizzle and most of the colour views that were taken here suffered as a result. Of those I have seen, this is by far the best, with No. 47308 evoking a scene of yesteryear as it stood alongside the platform with its three-coach train. The red signboard visible on the station roof advertised the fact that it was in use as the Stroud Depot of British Road Services. Bill Potter/KRM

Left: The other views in this spread all feature the tour that ran a fortnight later, on 21st July, with No. 82036 first seen on the branch approaching Bridge No. 8. John Ryan

Below: Later, with its six-coach train taking up most of the platform, the 'Standard' Class '3' tank runs round to attach itself at the far end. Again the light was poor but this was a result of time having been lost, with the booked arrival of around 5.15pm having slipped by at least 90 minutes by the train reached here. Bill Potter/KRM

With the locomotive and the first two coaches of the train actually standing on the viaduct, the crew get ready for departure as the last stragglers make their way back to the train. It is this end of the viaduct that has been demolished to make way for the new town centre by-pass, Dr Newton's Way, in the mid 1980s. The run round loop extended to the western end of the viaduct. Bill Potter/KRM

With the evening sunlight glinting off the carriage windows, the tour departs over the viaduct. Surprisingly, none of the published books and articles about the branch give any indication as to the structure's size or the number of arches. Fortunately, the aforementioned *Bridge Register* came to the rescue: Stroud Viaduct, No. 10, had eleven spans, comprising ten blue brick arches and a wrought iron girder span on a skew over the approach road to the station, with a total length of 332 feet. Demolition of spans at both ends has left a free standing centre section of six spans, which survived mainly because the interior of the arches had long been converted for commercial use. The old station approach road has been truncated following the removal of the span carrying it over the canal and most of the old Wallbridge houses and properties in the foreground here have also gone. NPC

The goods yard at Stroud being shunted on 16th March 1962. Roy Denison's colour views are almost all full of interest and from unusual viewpoints, and my only complaint with them is that he did not take anywhere near enough! The locomotive in charge here will be Class '4F' No. 44264, which he was to photograph a later that day taking water at Nailsworth (page 202). The road entrance to the yard is hidden by the two box vans which had just been dropped off. The creosoted timber shack on the left is not annotated on plans of the station but was probably a platelayers hut. Creeping in to the picture on the right is the magnificent main building of Williamson Tratt & Co. Ltd's clothing factory, built in 1898 and a distinctive feature of the centre of the town, gazing down on the ex-GWR station on the far side. A handsome mix of red and yellow brick, following closure of the factory in 1989 and with development plans having not progressed, it became unsafe and was in imminent danger of demolition. A determined campaign by local people, including barricading the building to stop contractors starting work, coupled with the formation of a regeneration group, happily saw it saved at the eleventh hour and restored as luxury housing apartments. We shall see more of it when we travel the Stroud Valley in Volume 5. Roy Denison

ABOVE: The goods yard was spaciously laid out and the accommodation provided commodious, as this view of 3rd May 1964 shows. The timber-built goods shed had four covered loading bays for road vehicles, three smaller ones at this end and a much longer one at the far end, the building being around 150 feet in length, with office extensions at both ends. A line of rails ran right through, with the unusual arrangement of a double crossover at the far end allowing use of it as a loop in both directions. In thge yard, the two centre sidings were used mostly for coal traffic, certainly in the later years, and the creosoted timber storage sheds on the left, with curved corrugated iron roofs, seem to have been a war-time provision, as they do not appear on the mid-1930s 25 inch OS. Note the inlaid stone setts for road vehicles to cross the line in the foreground. It is likely that, hidden beneath the tarmac, the whole yard was still laid with these. JOHN RYAN

BELOW: A similar view but with No. 78004 shunting sidings now almost completely hidden by grass and weeds on 12th May 1965. BILL POTTER/KRM

ABOVE: On his visit of 3rd May 1964, John Ryan also took this view of the passenger station. The corrugated iron building on the right was another later addition, again probably dating from the Second World War period and built on the loading platform which already held the livestock pens. JOHN RYAN

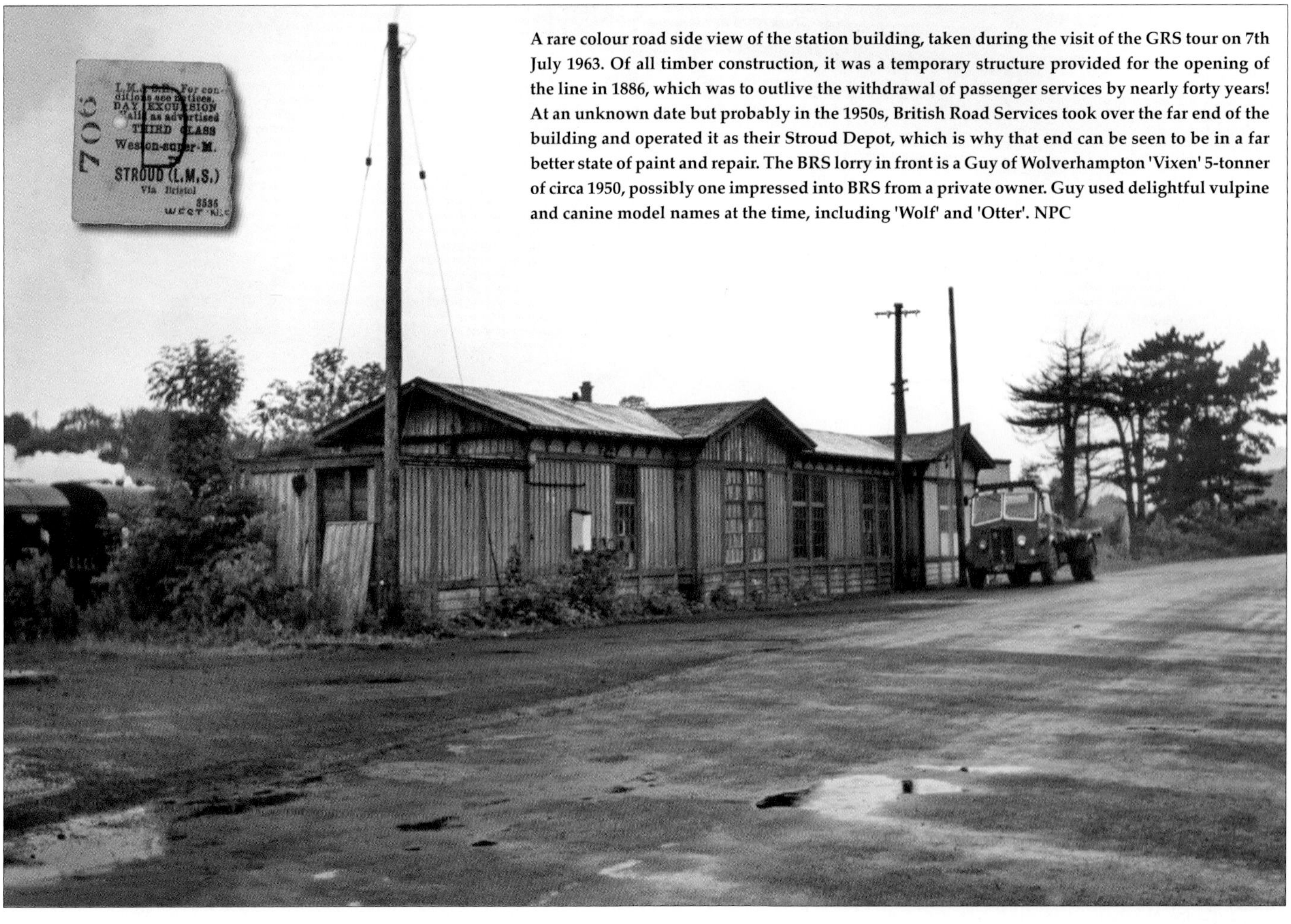

A rare colour road side view of the station building, taken during the visit of the GRS tour on 7th July 1963. Of all timber construction, it was a temporary structure provided for the opening of the line in 1886, which was to outlive the withdrawal of passenger services by nearly forty years! At an unknown date but probably in the 1950s, British Road Services took over the far end of the building and operated it as their Stroud Depot, which is why that end can be seen to be in a far better state of paint and repair. The BRS lorry in front is a Guy of Wolverhampton 'Vixen' 5-tonner of circa 1950, possibly one impressed into BRS from a private owner. Guy used delightful vulpine and canine model names at the time, including 'Wolf' and 'Otter'. NPC

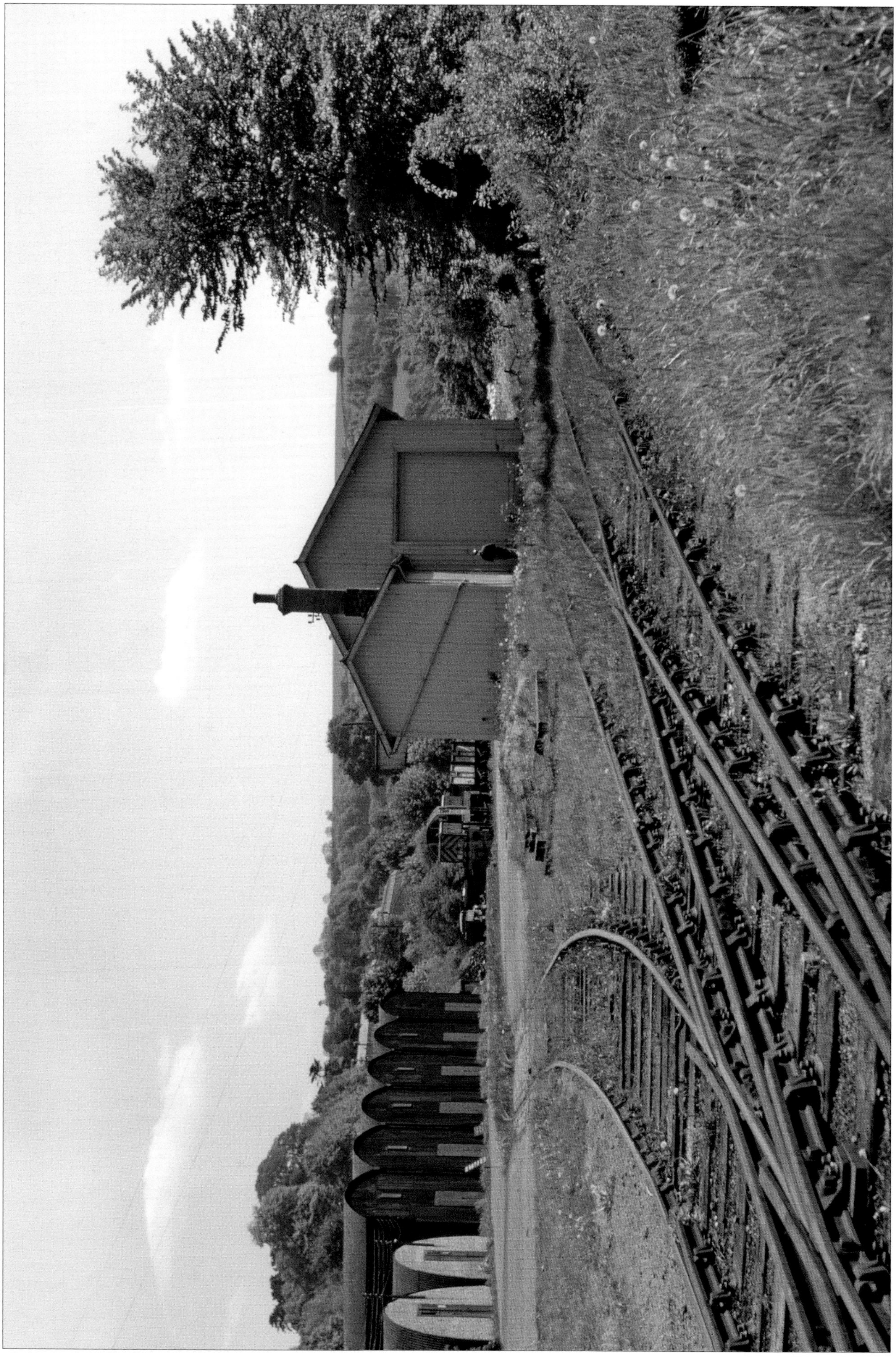

The Oxford University Railway Society made a largely unheralded visit to the station on 16th May 1966, when No. D9553 was the motive power for the day. A small OURS headboard was placed over the left buffer to mark the occasion, with the fortunate few having a brake van ride along both branches. By this date the goods shed had been out of use for at least a year, with the sidings rusty and overgrown. The double scissors crossover between these two lines was at the far end but despite being an extremely unusual feature in a goods yard, I have yet to see a photograph of it. The nissen huts on the left were undoubtedly a Second World War addition. The whole site found alternative commercial use after closure of the railway, surviving intact apart from the rails until the mid 1980s, when it was obliterated during construction of Dr Newton's Way. Bill Potter/KRM

Another unusual feature of the track layout at Stroud were the back to back three-way points, the nearer one leading in to the goods yard, whilst the other provided access to the loop and the old livestock bay. The brick building on the right was certainly there by the turn of the century and may date from opening but its purpose is unknown. The stacks of bricks probably belong to a local builders merchant operating from the yard at this date. BILL POTTER/KRM

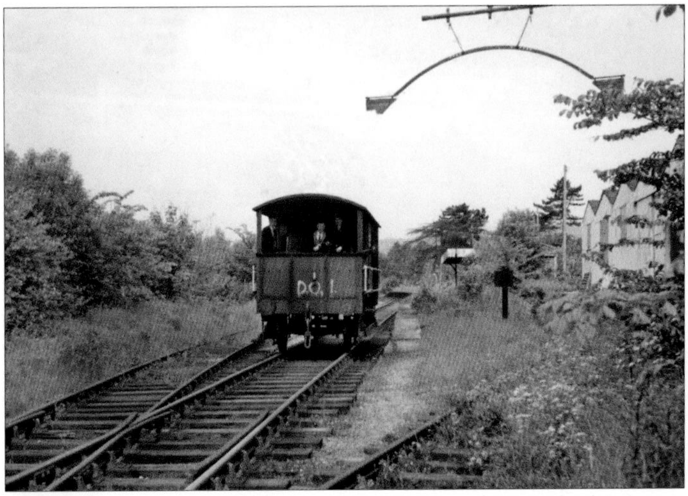

LEFT: Some of the few fortunate beneficiaries of the OURS trip pose on the verandah of the ex- GWR 'Toad' brake van. BILL POTTER/KRM

BELOW LEFT: Probably taken on the same occasion, this is the front of the MR cast iron notice at the entrance to the old livestock bay. JOHN STRANGE/NPC

BELOW: Looking across the three-way point along the line of the bay siding, showing the buildings that had been erected on the old livestock platform. JOHN STRANGE/NPC

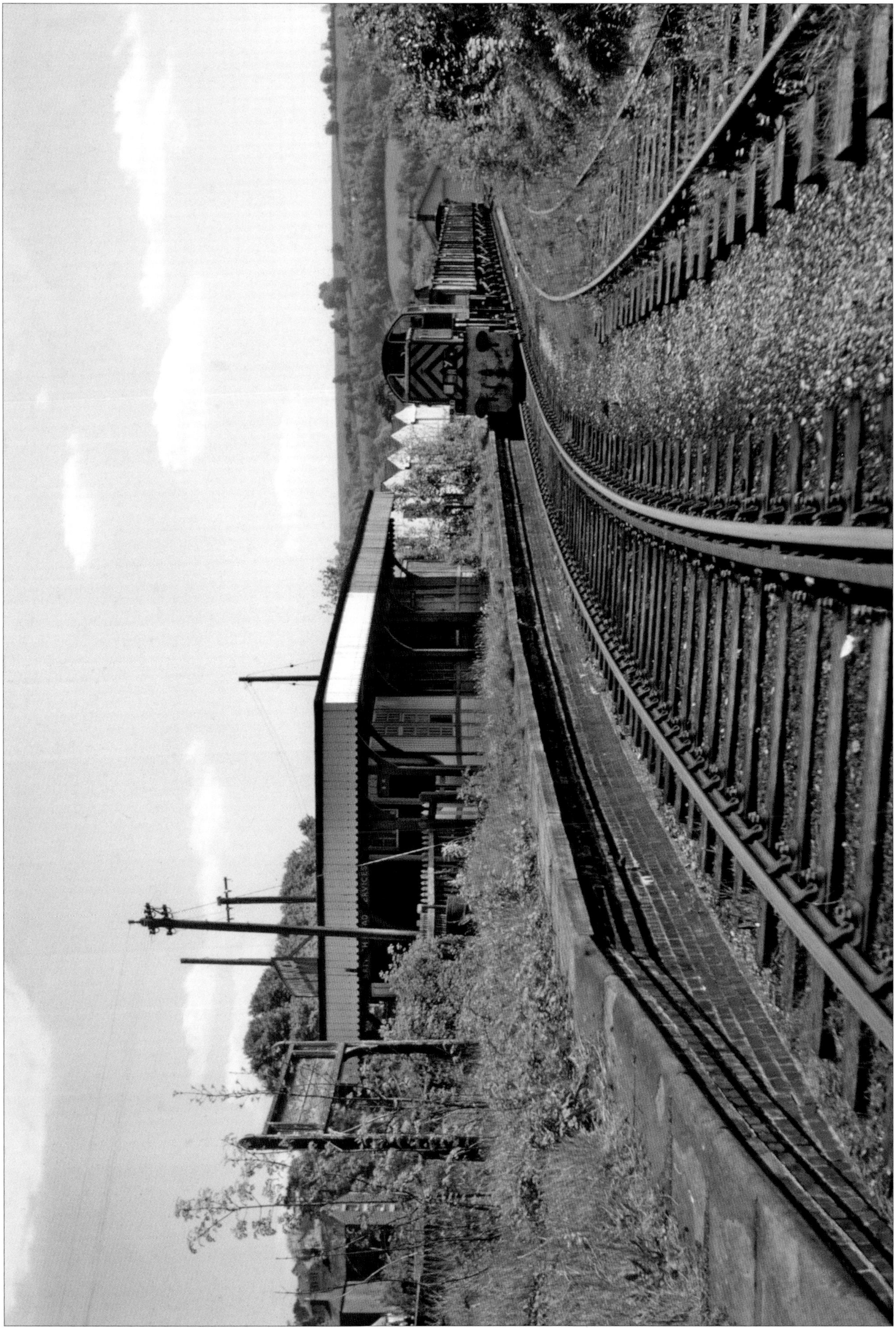

The well-maintained paintwork at this end of the station building stands out clearly, as does the BRS signeage, as No. D9553 waits to depart. The OURS headboard over the left buffer is more discernible in this view. This part of the station was built on the partly in-filled mill pond serving Wallbridge woollen mill, the buildings of which suddenly found themselves hard up against the viaduct. The station was simply named Stroud, although was apparently referred to in *Bradshaw's Time Tables* as 'Stroud Cheapside'; there is no evidence that it was ever officially known as 'Stroud Wallbridge', although it is often referred to by that name. BILL POTTER/KRM

ABOVE AND BELOW: Clearly both John Strange and Bill Potter were amongst the few who enjoyed the OURS trip. These last two views on that day, shortly before the line shut completely, show the platform frontage of the rather attractive little wooden station building in more detail. The view below, looking back towards Dudbridge Junction, reveals the Ladies Room sign still in place nineteen years after closure to passengers. ABOVE: JOHN STRANGE; BELOW: BILL POTTER/KRM

ABOVE AND RIGHT: No. 44045, which we have already seen a few times, heads southwards past Dudbridge Junction with the Nailsworth goods on 5th October 1962. This had originally been two tracks in both directions for a short distance, with a double junction between the two branches. The signal box was positioned in the 'V' between the two lines. The layout had been simplified in December 1957, which enabled the signal box to be closed and demolished, although the outdoor privy was left standing as can be seen. The single point remaining was controlled by the East Ground Frame – the lever just to the right of the tender. No. 44045's train includes three laden coal wagons and another containing probably empty barrels – given the way they are loaded – along with empties collected from Dudbridge yard. Dudbridge House, to the left of the high wall built of blue engineering bricks and no doubt provided by the railway when the line was constructed, still remains today. BOTH BILL POTTER/KRM

LEFT: BR 'Standard' Class '3' 2-6-2T No. 82036 of Bristol Barrow Road shed passes the junction for the Stroud Branch, which would be visited later, as it coasts through Dudbridge on the way to Nailsworth with the RCTS Gloucestershire Rail Tour of 21st July 1963. Note the check rail on the sharply curved Stroud line. Built at Swindon Works and new in to service on April Fool's Day 1955, No. 82036 was on its final posting, withdrawal from Barrow Road taking place in July 1965. In a varied career, it had also enjoyed allocations to both other Bristol sheds, Bath Road and St. Philip's Marsh. JOHN RYAN

Moments after the previous picture, Bill Potter photographed the tour heading south past the Lightpill Mills of Erinoid Ltd, the leading UK manufacturers of casein plastic, which was derived from milk curd by an Austrian chemist and developed by the company from 1913. Used particularly in the manufacture of buttons, the major advantage of casein over other early plastics such as bakelite was that it could be dyed in bright colours. In 1973, the business employed around 700 people but it closed in 1982 as the demand for casein collapsed following the introduction of oil based plastics. The mill site today houses numerous small businesses and the chimney remains a local landmark. The RCTS Tour had set out from Paddington behind No. 6841 *Marlas Grange* at 8.55am, travelling direct to the Port of Bristol Authority (PBA) passenger terminal at Avonmouth. A tour of the docks followed behind PBA 0-6-0ST No. S11 *Bristol*, with No. 82036 then taking over for the major part of the tour, which left Bristol via Mangotsfield and then visited the Sharpness, Dursley, Nailsworth and Stroud branches. Travelling then to Engine Shed Junction at Gloucester, No. 6993 *Arthog Hall* was attached to haul the carriages from there to Eastgate whilst the 2-6-2T ran round prior to returning south. At Westerleigh West Junction, No. 82036 then came off to head back home, with the run back to Paddington being behind No. 1020 *County of Monmouth*. The tour was, however, marred by late running, with many passengers forced to leave it early at Stroud to get back to London, a journey in itself further complicated by a replacement bus service being in operation between Kemble and Minety. Bill Potter/KRM

LEFT: A view from up on the hillside, looking south as the tour wound its way back up the Nailsworth Valley. Frigg's Mill, in existence since 1633, burnt down in 1914 but the 17th century mill house survived and is seen in the centre of the picture here. At the turn of the century, a siding to the right of the train had served a brick kiln. JOHN RYAN

BELOW: Bill did not follow the tour to Nailsworth, where water was taken when running round, preferring instead to wait in the same spot for it to return. He took two shots of it here heading bunker first back to Dudbridge and I have chosen the first of them, with the train slightly further away, in order to show the span of the bridge, which crosses a footpath near Friggs Mill and still remains. BILL POTTER/KRM

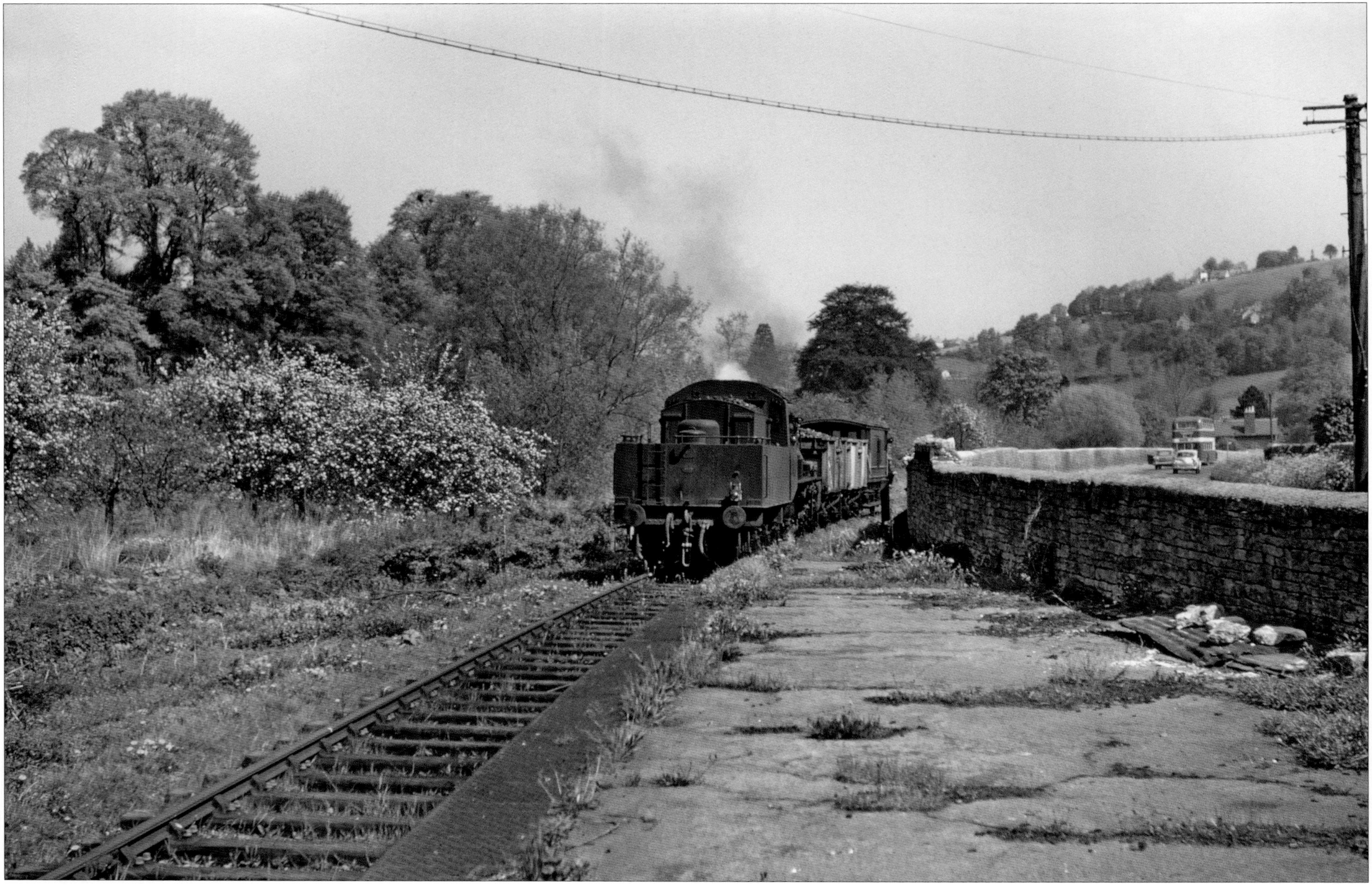

Whilst many photographers were sparing in their use of colour film, which was expensive not just to buy in comparison to black & white film but also in processing, the chemicals for which were beyond makeshift home laboratories, Bill often took two or three shots of a location and train which appealed. Consequently, I had three views of the Nailsworth goods arriving at Woodchester behind No. 78004 on 12th May 1965 from which to choose. Again, rather than go for a close-up of the rear of the locomotive, I have picked the first picture in the sequence, with the widest aspect that included the A46 Bath Road and the Bristol Omnibus Co. double-decker heading for Stroud on the far right. The stone wall still remains, whilst the trackbed is now a footpath and cycleway. The red brick house in the right distance has gone, however. BILL POTTER/KRM

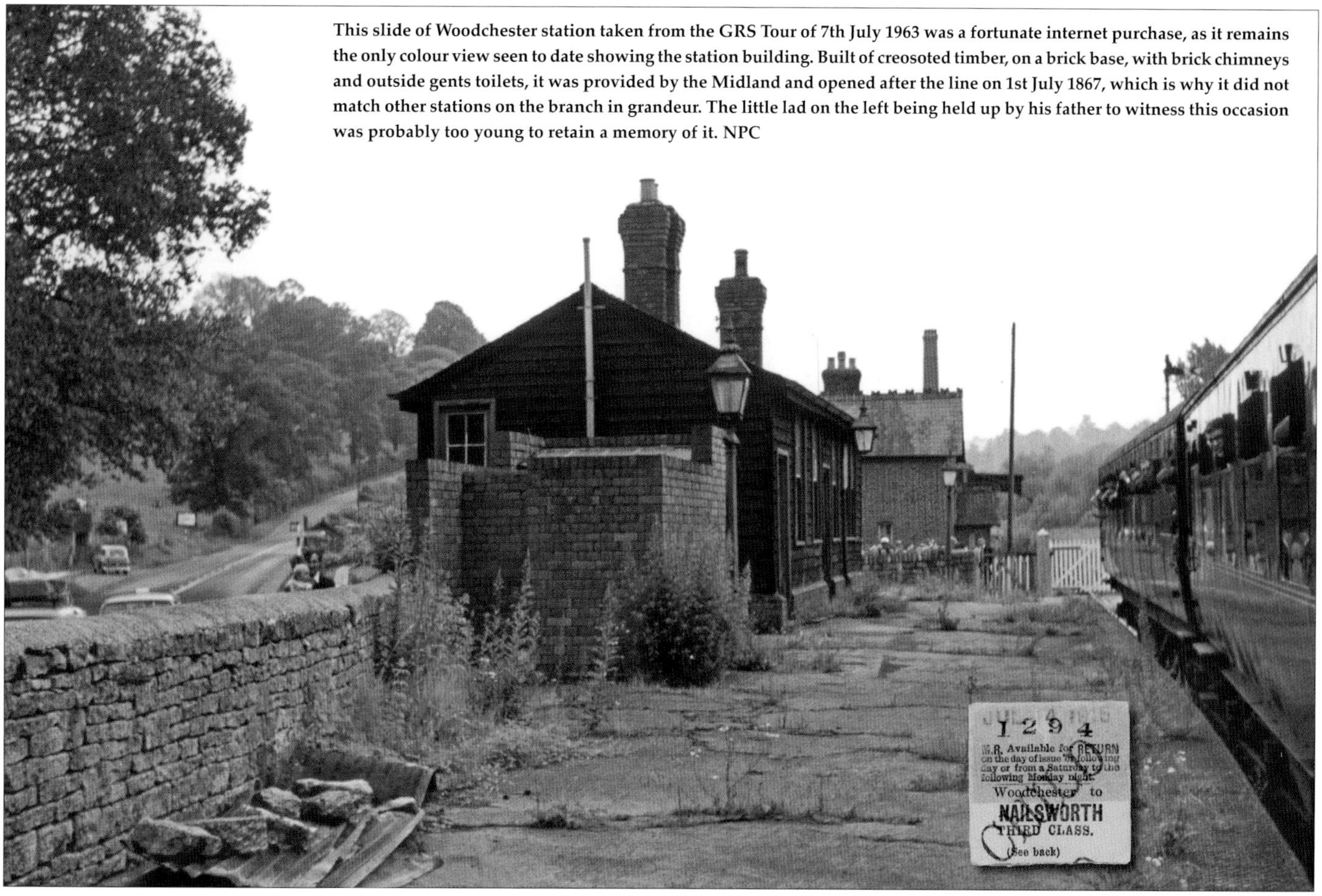

This slide of Woodchester station taken from the GRS Tour of 7th July 1963 was a fortunate internet purchase, as it remains the only colour view seen to date showing the station building. Built of creosoted timber, on a brick base, with brick chimneys and outside gents toilets, it was provided by the Midland and opened after the line on 1st July 1867, which is why it did not match other stations on the branch in grandeur. The little lad on the left being held up by his father to witness this occasion was probably too young to retain a memory of it. NPC

When No. 78004 passed through on its way back to Dudbridge on 12th May 1965, the station building had been demolished and piles of bricks, stacked seemingly ready for collection and re-use, were all that remained. The house in the background, provided originally for the station master but later, after that post had been abolished, lived in by the local porter, survives today. Bill Potter/KRM

With the gate key in his hand, the guard watches as No. 78004 eases carefully over Station Road level crossing. The demolition of the station building is likely to have been only a week or so prior to these pictures being taken, with the gents still awaiting the same treatment. Bill Potter/KRM

A few weeks later, on 12th July, Bill returned to capture more of the operations on the branch. Classmate No. 78001 was in charge on this occasion and is seen easing past the Midland goods shed, the siding in front of which had clearly not been used for some time; it had originally formed a loop but the northern connection had been removed in September 1958, with the Station ground frame taken out at the same time. Bill Potter/KRM

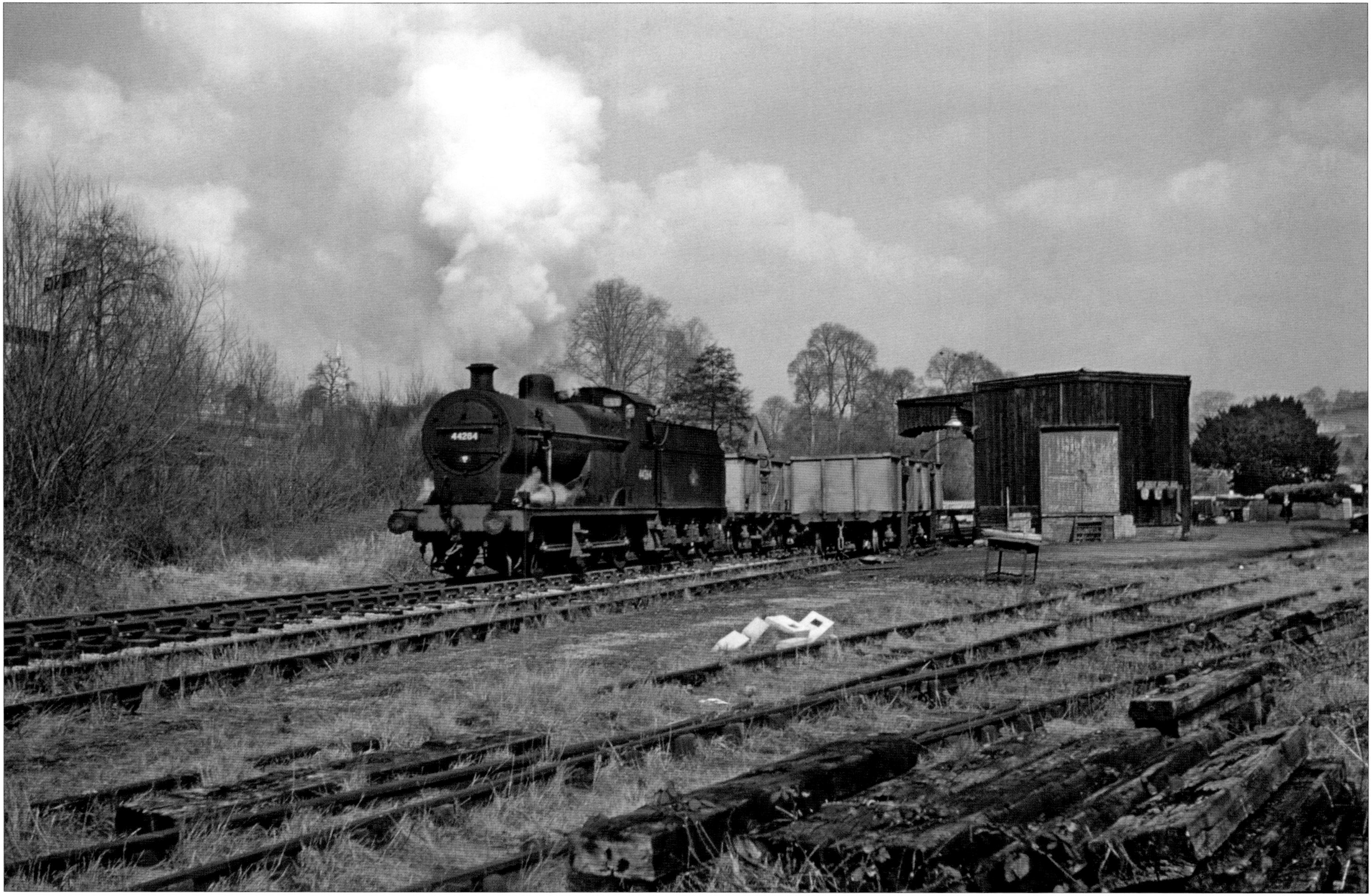

An invaluable view a few years earlier, on 18th March 1962, with the sidings still extant in the goods yard as Class '4F' No. 44264 headed past with the Nailsworth goods. The siding in the right foreground connected to private sidings which kicked back off it to serve Henry Workman's timber mills, a line from which also ran across the Bath Road at one time to a loading bank, presumably for logs for sawing. Shunting at the mills was carried out by a steam crane and special instructions for its working in to Woodchester yard were included in MR and LM&SR *Working Time Tables*. The PSA was terminated in 1964 but Workmans had ceased operations in 1957, hence had probably seen little use since then. The sidings were all removed in 1964, apart from the one in front of the typical MR timber-creosoted goods shed. As an incidental aside, Workmans used a Burrell traction engine (Works No. 4010 of 1925 and named *Empress*) for hauling log trailers to the mill and this does still survive today, restored to working condition in the company's livery. ROY DENISON

Bill Potter's similar view of 12th May 1965 shows the yard after the sidings had been lifted, with the one in front of the goods shed being all that remained. Official closure of Woodchester to goods was on 1st June 1964, with traffic latterly only the odd wagonload of coal for the local merchant, as the previous picture showed. No. 78004 would thus not be calling here on this day. In its heyday, however, surrounded by local industry, the goods yard here was the busiest on the branch and also had a very healthy parcels traffic. As well as sawn timber leaving Workman's mills, other traffics included coal, paper, sheepskins and timber incoming, with magazines and posters (from a local printing company, recipients of the paper), leather and incubators all being products despatched from here. The Second World War brought more traffic, with Woodchester NAAFI depot having food products coming in and going out, whilst a locally based US Army unit was also supplied by rail. Modern industrial units occupy the site today. Bill Potter/KRM

RIGHT: Although Woodchester no longer required a call, as this view shows an unofficial stop was made near the station on the way back, in order that the crew of No. 78004 could collect some beansticks! Such were the rigours of working a rural branch line on a fine spring day. It was a way of life which could not last and, indeed, for which the last rites were already being called. BILL POTTER/KRM

BELOW: Around half a mile south of Woodchester, a short private siding served the engineering firm Newman, Hender & Co. Ltd, where No. 78001 is seen on 30th July 1965. As the extract from the *Sectional Appendix to the Working Time Table, Gloucester Traffic District, October 1960*, BELOW RIGHT, shows, the siding was to be shunted from Down trains only, with the brake van left standing just to the north on the falling gradient towards Woodchester and thus great care had to be taken. Wagons were rolled out by gravity, under the responsibility of Newman, Hender workers, with the locomotive then gently shunting them back to couple up with the brake van. It is not possible to be certain from the pictures that Bill took on this day but it is likely that the wagon to be dropped off here was positioned two or three back in the train; the sharply curved siding was prone to derailments and it was preferable to have a couple of barrier wagons so that the locomotive did not have to venture on to it. BILL POTTER/KRM

BETWEEN WOODCHESTER AND NAILSWORTH

Newman, Hender and Co.'s Siding

Up trains must not attach or detach traffic at this siding.

Vehicles must not be placed in or removed from the siding until the Guard or Shunter has obtained permission from the firm's foreman for this to be done.

Wagons in the shed will be coupled together and made ready for drawing out by the firm's staff, and B.R. staff must not enter the shed.

B.R. staff working at the siding must, as far as possible, do so from the main line side.

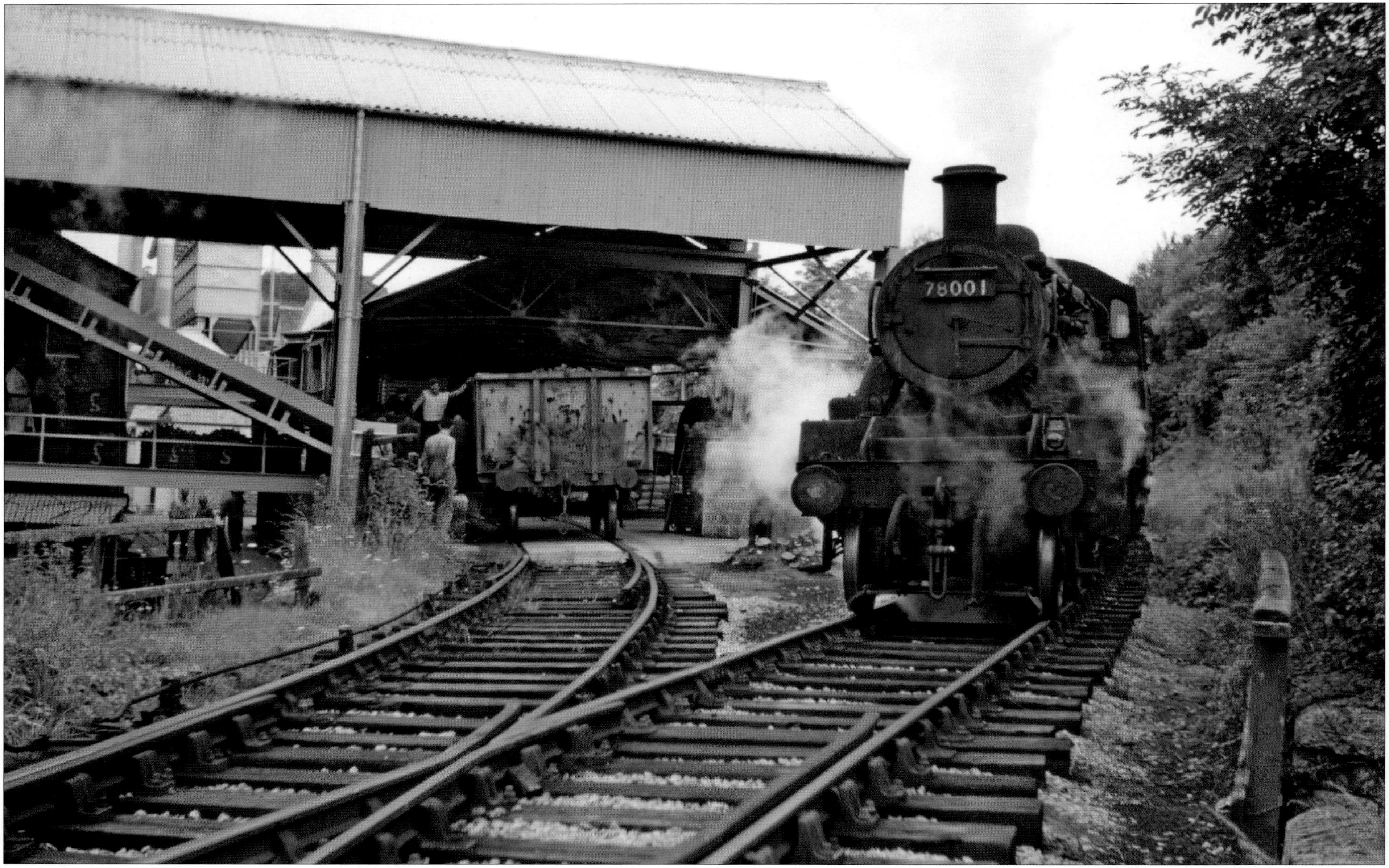

Having shunted the loaded wagon – probably containing coke – in to Newman, Hender's siding, No. 78001 couples back up the rest of the train to complete its journey to Nailsworth. Newman, Hender & Co. Ltd were brassfounders and manufacturers of valves, cocks, steam and water fittings, operating from various sites in the UK, of which the Woodchester factory was the largest, employing 900 people. The firm could trace their origins back to 1879, becoming a public company in 1948; they had also been engaged on significant war work during both world conflicts. As well as coal, the siding received regular deliveries of coke, sand and pig iron, all required in the casting process. The covered bay seen here, complete with conveyors and an electro-magnetic crane for unloading the pig iron, had only recently been erected, to handle the wagonload of coke and three of pig iron that were being delivered here weekly, so closure of the branch must have been something of a surprise. After a decade of expansion through the 1960s, in 1969 the company became the subject of a hostile takeover bid but eventually merged with another competitor. It was to be the beginning of the end for Newman, Hender, years of political upheaval within the business leading to the run down and eventual closure of the Woodchester plant in 1985. Now named Inchbrook Trading Estate, for which the site of this unloading facility is now a car park, many of the original factory buildings remain in commercial use. BILL POTTER/KRM

LEFT: After the withdrawal of the passenger service in 1947, Nailsworth station was left to slumber in peaceful isolation, interrupted only by the occasional rail tour visit. The first was the GRS 'Gloucestershire Area Rail Tour' on 17th May 1952. There was then a hiatus until 1956, when there were two: the Railway Enthusiasts Club's 'The Severn Venturer' on 15th April and then the train seen here, the 'Dursley Branch Centenary Rail Tour' run by the Stephenson Locomotive Society (SLS) on 25th August. For the Nailsworth and Stroud leg, the train of three crimson and cream coaches were 'top and tailed' by immaculate Ivatt Class '2' 2-6-2T No. 41208 of Bristol Barrow Road shed and ex-MR Class '1F' 0-6-0T No. 41748 from Barnwood. With no record of any excursions having been run from either terminus, the next and final calls were to be made in 1963. C. BANKS COLLECTION/COLOUR-RAIL

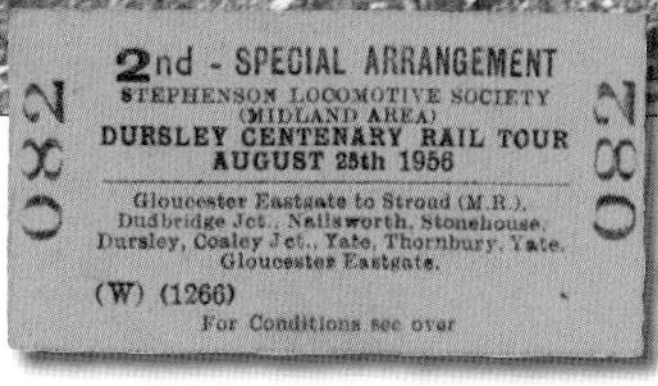

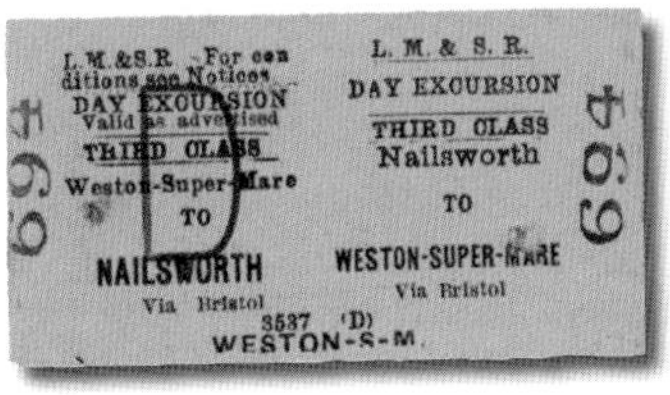

RIGHT AND RIGHT BELOW: The arrangement at Nailsworth was unusual in that the goods yard was separate from the passenger station, a result of the original intention being that the railway would extend southwards. In anticipation of the line being carried on, the station was situated on a ledge on the lower slopes of the valley side raising it away from the town. Various schemes were mooted, with one, the Wiltshire & Gloucestershire Railway, which proposed an extension to join the GWR main line at Christian Malford, a few miles north-east of Chippenham, making it as far as a ceremonial cutting of the first sod in July 1865. Thwarted, however, by a ruling preventing the Midland from extending in to GWR territory, which would thus preclude them from operating the new line, no further progress was made and Nailsworth was forever to remain a terminus, facing down on to the goods yard around 15 feet below and from which it was largely hidden by trees in later years. These two views show the GRS Tour of 7th July 1963, hauled by No. 47308, standing at the platform. The lower view shows the end of the station master's house that is not normally seen, which was still lived in and with washing on the line, the incumbent housewife clearly not having anticpated the special's arrival! A short siding to a loading dock had abutted the end of the garden, accessed from a double slip and kicking back from the headshunt and a line which had originally run to the turntable. The turntable had been taken out in 1920 and the sidings were lifted in December 1957. BOTH NPC

RIGHT, BELOW AND BOTTOM LEFT: Three views of No. 47308 running round its train on 7th July 1963. The picture below, from Ben Ashworth's usual vantage point up a tree, provides a fine view of the main building and station master's house, which has been Grade II listed since 1975 and is now a private residence. The style of the building reflected the Stonehouse & Nailsworth company's grand ambitions and also housed their offices. JOHN RYAN; B.J. ASHWORTH; BILL POTTER/KRM

(7556)
2nd - SPECIAL ARRANGEMENT
The Gloucestershire Railway Society
TOUR TO NAILSWORTH & STROUD
SUNDAY, 7th JULY, 1963
Gloucester (Eastgate), Standish Junction
Stonehouse (Midland), Nailsworth and
Stroud (Midland), Hempsted and High
Orchard Lines and Return to
Gloucester (Eastgate)
(W) For conditions see over

BOTTOM RIGHT: Two weeks later, on 21st July, the RCTS Gloucestershire Rail Tour became the last passenger train to visit the terminus. Far less pictures seem to have been taken on that occasion but here we see No. 82036 replenishing its tanks. In those pre-Health & Safety conscious days, no-one blinked an eye at the young lads who climbed up on the water tank positioned at the entrance to the goods yard to lend a hand. NPC

ABOVE AND BELOW: The station building from the entrance road on 12th May 1965, with the fine colonnaded entrance portico to the right. Although the branch remained open to the goods yard, the tracks to the station were removed a year after the last two tours had called, in July 1964 and the view below shows the scene a few months later, on 1st November 1964. Everything seen here remains today, including the brick-built gents toilets on the right. BILL POTTER/KRM; R. PATTERSON/COLOUR-RAIL

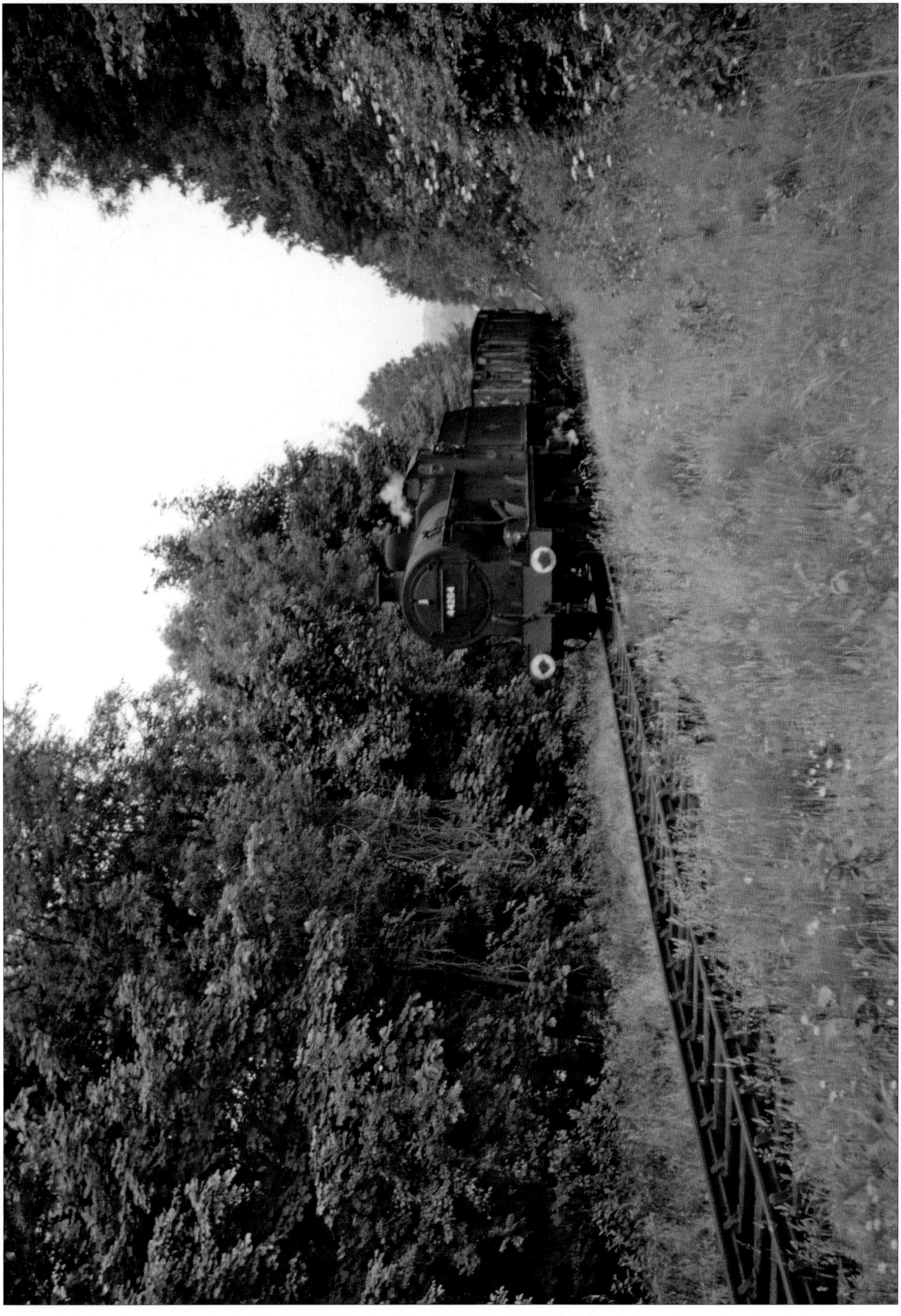

On a line that abounded in rural locations, despite the various routes and communities that were crowded along the Stroud and Nailsworth valleys, the half mile approach to Nailsworth goods yard was perhaps the most sylvan of them all. No. 44264 threads its way down between the trees and bushes on 30th June 1965, with a couple of wagon loads of coal for the local merchant. BILL POTTER/KRM

Before the goods yard was reached, a short siding branched off to the south-west to serve a loading platform and livestock pens. After closure in 1895 of the wooden engine shed situated alongside the goods yard, the attendant coaling stage and water tower were moved to a new position near the head of this short siding. As this view of No. 44264 inching towards it shows, the tank remained in use until the end of steam and it seems most trips along the branch included topping up with water here. The coaling stage was rebuilt just to the left of the water tower but a photograph of 1936 shows it derelict and out of use. Note the point lever almost hidden in the grass by the pile of sleepers. The point it controlled led to the siding that ran the other side of the loading platform and also then continued on to run through the goods shed and serve C.W. Jones & Co. Ltd's store; however, the coating of rust on the rails would suggest that it had seen little or no traffic for a year or so prior to this picture. Bill Potter/KRM

Nearly three and a half years previously, on 16th March 1962, the same locomotive was photographed taking water here. The gas lamp at the northern end of the loading platform was a notable survivor at this date – it does not feature in the 1965 views. There was no facility for an engine to run round in the goods yard and there are no special instructions given for working the yard at Nailsworth in the *Sectional Appendix to the Working Time Table, Gloucester Traffic District, October 1960*. Maggs mentions fly shunting by means of uncoupling the wagons, with the locomotive then sprinting ahead in to one siding, as the guard then threw the point lever over for the wagons to run in to their intended siding. This seems a little fraught to me and I'm wondering if the wagons were not just gently run down the slope whilst water was being taken, with the guard then applying the brake once past the point so the engine could reverse out and then attach itself to the rear of the train. Shunting in to the yard would then be much more controlled. Roy Denison

A '4F' 0-6-0 that we have otherwise not seen in these pages to date, No. 44167, a long term resident of Gloucester Barnwood shed, shunts the yard on 13th June 1962. Whilst the seemingly unchecked grass growth is perhaps not a surprise at this rural backwater, later views show that it was periodically treated with weedkiller. The engine has just dropped a couple of loaded coal wagons at the end of the siding, with the local coal merchant standing alongside his lorry, waiting to start unloading them. As the selection of wagons shows, there was more than just coal traffic still on offer at this date and the next port of call will probably be the goods shed, partially in view on the right. Built by the LM&SR at Crewe Works in March 1926, No. 44167's stay at Barnwood was to end six months after the picture was taken, when it transferred to Templecombe S&D shed. Note the Railway Hotel still open for business in the background. Built by 1820 and originally a private residence named *Corunna House* (after the Peninsula War battle), it became the Railway Hotel probably not long after the Nailsworth Branch opened and traded until the 1970s. Grade II listed in 1980, the building is now converted as luxury holiday apartments and retains the painted name on the frontage. COLIN MAGGS/COLOUR-RAIL

ABOVE: An unidentified Class '4F' drops some box vans in to the goods shed in August 1962. Two more gas lamps can be seen, one by the crane and another at the southern end of the livestock platform. Note the station building just glimpsed through the trees up on the right. The wooden engine shed, which had been closed in 1895, stood at the end of a third siding beyond the pair on the right. Remaining in use as a siding afterwards, Cooke notes that it was '*lifted by 1964*' but there is little sign of it in these 1962 pictures. NPC

K51

TIME ALLOWANCES FOR FREIGHT TRAINS—continued.

STONEHOUSE (BRISTOL ROAD), STROUD AND NAILSWORTH

DOWN	Point-to-Point Times	UP	Point-to-Point Times
	Mins.		Mins.
Stonehouse (Bristol Road)	—	Nailsworth	—
Dudbridge	10	Woodchester	—
Stroud	8	Stroud	—
		Dudbridge	5
Woodchester	7	Dudbridge	5
Nailsworth	7	Stonehouse (Bristol Road)	8

ABOVE: This extract from the *Working Time Table of Freight Trains, Gloucester District, 17th June to 8th September 1963,* gives the time allowances for working the Nailsworth & Stroud Branch. As we have seen, given that crews were largely 'out of sight', these allowances were only loosely adhered to and in fact probably mostly ignored all together; a prompt return to Stonehouse may well have then been followed by a wait for a path to Gloucester, so the Stonehouse signalman probably expected a branch train to be gone for two or three hours.

LEFT: With the roofs and chimneys of the station buildings peeping over the treeline behind, No. 44264 poses whilst shunting the yard on 30th June 1965. Note the track is now relatively weed free. BILL POTTER/KRM

THIS PAGE: Three views of No. 78004 when shunting the yard in late August 1964. The view from the footplate, ABOVE RIGHT, is useful in that it shows a wagon being propelled in to the yard, rather than being fly-shunted. The guard, holding a shunter's pole, can be seen by the points in the centre distance. The picture showing No. 78004 framed by the loading gauge, RIGHT, also includes a glimpse of the brick-built, whitewashed platelayers hut that stood at the entrance to the yard. These sturdy 2-6-0s were good workhorses but the pictures show that this particular engine clearly spent its last couple of years in service in a fairly unloved state. ALL CHRIS WALKER/NPC

Left: Partially hidden by weeds and undergrowth, heavily work-stained Class '2MT' 2-6-0 No. 78001 takes water at Nailsworth on 30th July 1965. G. Parry collection/Colour-Rail

Below: Classmate No. 78004 in the same place but from a different angle on 12th May 1965. The locomotive is a little further down the siding than was necessary – at the request of the photographer perhaps? As the pictures in this section show, a trip along the branch on a fine day was undoubtedly a treat and something of a 'grand day out' for footplate crews and guards, locked on the line on their own on the 'one engine in steam' principle, on a relaxed schedule and largely out of the way of official scrutiny, so a helpful pose for a friendly photographer would not have been a problem. Note the gas lamp has gone in this view. Bill Potter/KRM

Below: A short while later, No. 78004 gets ready to leave the yard and head back to Stonehouse and then on to Gloucester. It is unlikely that the goods shed saw much use – if any – in the last two years or so of goods services to Nailsworth, house coal deliveries to the yard being the final mainstay. The shed, built of red brick with yellow brick decorative string courses and wooden doors at either end, was recognisably Midland Railway in design. The siding ran right through the building and terminated the other side, in front of the C.W. Jones & Co. Ltd warehouse which it also served; there is just a glimpse of this building behind the goods shed and it survives today complete with its owner's lettering. The goods shed, however, unlike many of its bretheren around the country which have found other commercial uses, was demolished some years ago, although nothing has been built on its site. Bill Potter/KRM

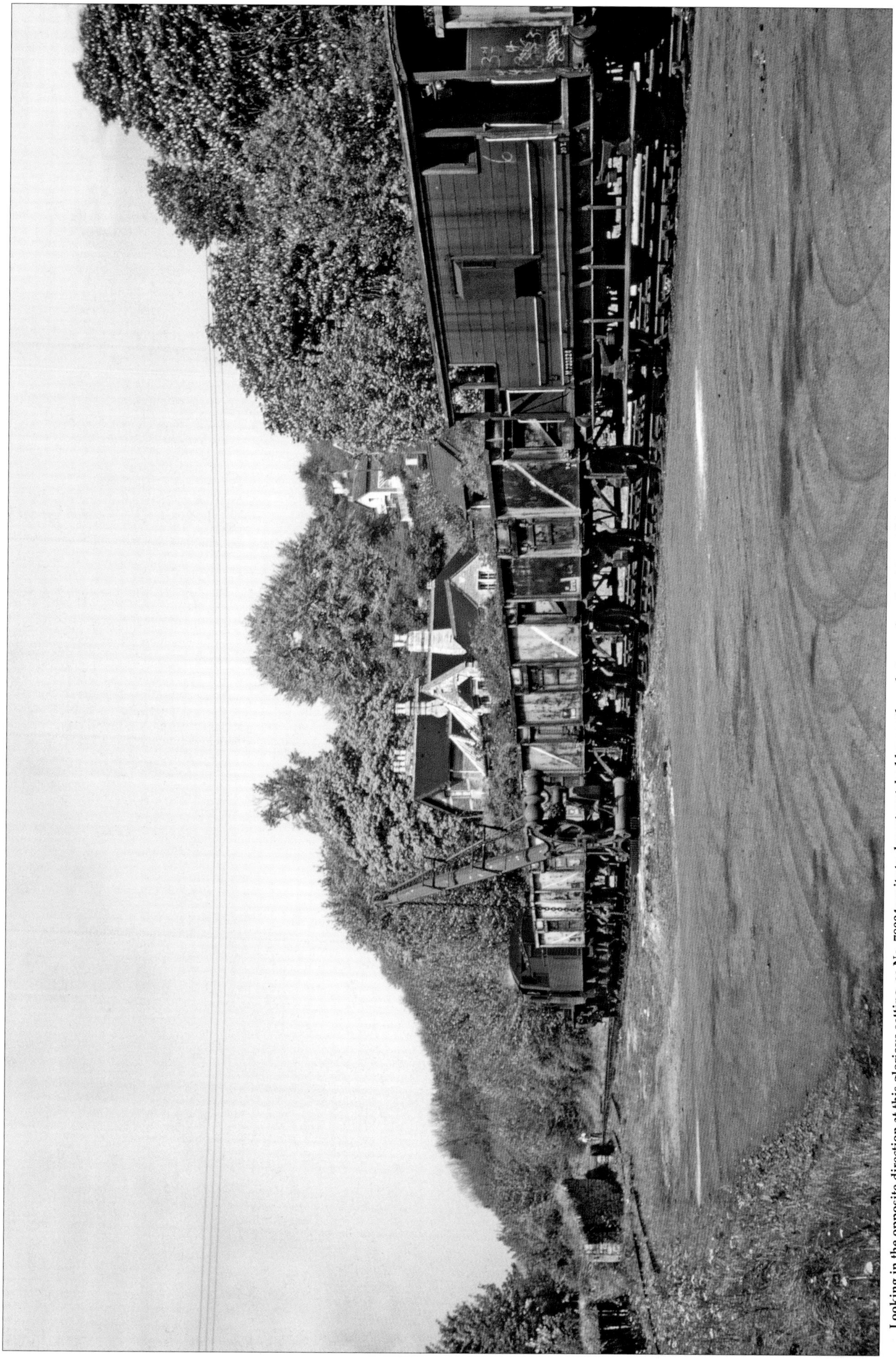

Looking in the opposite direction at this glorioys setting, as No. 78004 waits to depart watched by another photographer about to get his shot from the entrance to the yard. The top half of the station buildings can be seen peering over the hedgerow and the overgrown livestock loading platform can be seen on the left. This had clearly not been used for many years, probably since the early 1950s, with road transport having taken over the traffic. This had included weekly deliveries of pigs from Gloucester Market for slaughter by the local butchers, whilst cattle were despatched from here after the monthly Nailsworth Market. The 5-ton hand crane was erected in 1914, a cast plate on it indicating that it had been fabricated at the Midland's Derby Works in that year. It provided greater lifting power than the 1½-ton crane in the goods shed. The heavy coating of rust on the goods shed line in the left foreground gives a clear indication that nothing had run along these rails for at least a year. BILL POTTER/KRM

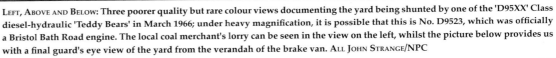

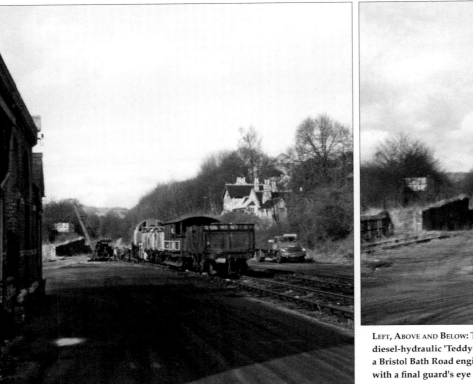

LEFT, ABOVE AND BELOW: Three poorer quality but rare colour views documenting the yard being shunted by one of the 'D95XX' Class diesel-hydraulic 'Teddy Bears' in March 1966; under heavy magnification, it is possible that this is No. D9523, which was officially a Bristol Bath Road engine. The local coal merchant's lorry can be seen in the view on the left, whilst the picture below provides us with a final guard's eye view of the yard from the verandah of the brake van. ALL JOHN STRANGE/NPC

K40 WEEKDAYS

STONEHOUSE, STROUD AND NAILSWORTH

DOWN		K 8.28 a.m. Gloucester		K 8.28 a.m. Gloucester	
		9F45		9F47	
		MW FO am		MW FO am	
STONEHOUSE (Bristol Rd.)	dep	9 23			
Ryeford	arr	9 37			
	dep	9 49			
Dudbridge	arr	9 56			
	dep	10 6		11 18	
STROUD (Wallbridge)	arr	10 15			
Woodchester	arr			11 25	
	dep			11 38	
Newman Henders' Sidings	arr			11 45	
	dep			12 0	
NAILSWORTH	arr			12 7 PM	

UP		8.28 a.m. Gloucester		K To Gloucester	
		9F44		9F14	
		MW FO PM		MW FO PM	
NAILSWORTH	dep			12 50	
Newman Henders' Siding	arr				
	dep				
Woodchester	arr				
	dep				
STROUD (Wallbridge)	dep	10 50			
Dudbridge	arr	10 58		1 5	
	dep			1 20	
Ryeford	arr				
	dep				
STONEHOUSE (Bristol Rd.)	arr			1 35	

ABOVE: The goods service for the branch in its final years, as given in the *Working Time Table of Freight Trains, Gloucester Traffic District, 17th June to 8th September 1963*. By this date the daily service of the late 1950s was down to trips on Mondays, Wednesdays and Fridays only.